Art, Design, and Topi

8-13

Also from Unwin Hyman

Teaching Art to Young Children 4–9
Rob Barnes

Understanding Educational Aims
Colin Wringe

Feeling and Reason in the Arts
David Best

Teaching Art in Primary School
Geoff Roswell

Art in the Making
Bruce Ridell

Art, Design and Topic Work 8–13

ROB BARNES
University of East Anglia
Norwich

London
UNWIN HYMAN
Boston Sydney Wellington

Published by the Academic Division of
Unwin Hyman Ltd
15/17 Broadwick Street, London W1V 1FP, UK

Unwin Hyman Inc.,
8 Winchester Place, Winchester, Mass. 01890, USA

Allen & Unwin (Australia) Ltd,
8 Napier Street, North Sydney, NSW 2060, Australia

Allen & Unwin (New Zealand) Ltd in association with the Port Nicholson Press Ltd,
60 Cambridge Terrace, Wellington, New Zealand

First published in 1989

British Library Cataloguing in Publication Data

Barnes, Rob, *1944-*
Art, design and topic work 8–13.
1. Primary schools. Curriculum subjects:
Arts. Teaching
I. Title
372.5'044
ISBN 0-04-445179-2
ISBN 0-04-445178-4 Pbk

Library of Congress Cataloging in Publication Data

Barnes, Rob, 1944-
Art, design, and topic work 8–13 / Rob Barnes.
p. cm.
Bibliography: p.
Includes index.
ISBN 0-04-445179-2 (alk.paper). ISBN 0-04-445178-4 (pbk. : alk. paper)
1. Art—Study and teaching (Elementary)—United States. 2. Art–-Study and teaching (Secondary)—United States. 3. Design—Study and teaching (Elementary)—United States. 4. Design—Study and teaching (Secondary)—United States. I. Title.
N353.B37 1989
707'. 1273—dc19

88-20824
CIP

Typeset in 10 on 12 point Bembo
Printed and bound in Great Britain by
Butler & Tanner Ltd, Frome and London

To C.

Contents

List of Illustrations

Colour Plates

Monochrome Illustrations

Photographic themes by Thomas Plowman (following page 84)

Photographs of natural forms by the author (following page 100)

Charts

Foreword

The middle years of childhood are by common consent regarded as the most problematic for art and design education. The terms 'latency period' and 'representational crisis' have been used to describe this period when the direct and appealing responses of very young children seem to go underground and when their image-making abilities often fall short of their intentions. It has been observed that further artistic development may be irretrievably impaired unless certain milestones are reached by the onset of puberty.

Rob Barnes stresses that the years from 8 to 13 are not a time of stagnation; rather this is a crucial period when the young artist or designer is particularly susceptible to sensitive teaching. Children in this age group have an increasing capacity to work with some thoroughness and accuracy; technical skills and aesthetic considerations become subject to greater control. There is a developing ability to solve a range of conceptual problems - particularly those of an emotional nature or those that have immediate personal relevance.

Good teaching often comes from those committed individuals who are not afraid continually to reappraise and reassess their ideas and approaches. This book is not intended to absolve teachers from the need to think for themselves but it will provide valuable insights and a variety of suggestions to help construct a balanced, broad and relevant curriculum in art and design for 8–13 year-olds.

John Steers
General Secretary
National Society for Education
in Art and Design

Acknowledgements

Particular thanks are expressed to all those teachers and students who over the years have helped form the ideas contained in this book. Special thanks are extended to Maxine Anderson, Gill Coathup, Connie Forsyth, Chris Gamble, Peter Gibley, Jane Harcombe, Chris Hemmings, Maggie Howard, Margaret Jackson, Sue King-Davies, Norman Manners, Amanda Parker, Polly Plowman, Nicky Roberts, Hugh Robinson, Tim Wilson, Jackie Worsley, Aylsham High School, Beccles Middle School, Brundall Middle School, Dereham Church Middle School, Dickleburgh Primary School, Dulwich Prep School, Merrywood School, Monmouth School, Moorfield School, Nonesuch High School for Girls, Sir Hugh Owen Lower School, Woodford County High School.

Five children have helped in various ways. They are Peter Barnes, Nathan Flanders, Madeleine Handsley, Joseph Murray and Amy Roe.

I am grateful to Richard Dunne of the University of Exeter and Dr Derek Haylock of the University of East Anglia for their mathematical advice. Two professional artists have allowed me to use examples of their work. They are Thomas Plowman, whose photographic themes are included, and Paul Jackson, who made the porcelain figure.

I should like to thank Cathy Whalen for her tireless constructive help and support during the writing of this book.

Rob Barnes, 1989

1

The shrinking artist

> The crucial factor in developing creative work is not so much whether the teacher has artistic skills or knows a Rembrandt painting from a Van Gogh. What matters most is their attitude towards its value as a useful way of learning about the world.
>
> (*Primary headteacher*)

ONE OF the attractions of using a computer seems to be the way in which it deals with information rapidly and does not linger in apparently vague or grey areas of reasoning. Art by contrast appeals to many people precisely because it deals with less accessible areas such as human feeling, visual response and the way in which we identify with what we see. Often these aspects reach us as only half-realized truths about our existence as we understand it and we may struggle to make sense of our perceptions of the art we see around us. Experience of art, whether through seeing or producing it, touches part of us which cannot easily be expressed through words. That part of our make-up is more intuitive and as devoid of reason as the art form which tries to express it.

Much as we might like the world to be logical, clear cut and straightforward it turns out to be rather different. Yesterday's truth is superseded by today's new realities and by its very nature art reflects the endless change which takes place in human values. Rules, logic, reason, right or wrong ways to do things, measurement, factual information, or fixed established procedures are not the stock in trade of most art processes. Even when the computer has performed its logic we are still left to make some meaningful sense of the experience we have had and in that respect there is a significant similarity with art.

For children, art can not only be a means of reinforcing the other classroom learning they do, but it can prove to be a catalyst to their understanding as they attempt to explore their world and reconstruct their experience. Even if we took the naive view that art was there as some glorious visual aid to children's memory it could still make their experience more meaningful. Yet for many teachers art is much more. The marks children make and the shapes they draw involve them in a unique language of expression and discovery, a language which is remarkable in its power to engage our attention. The shape of a twisted tree, patterns seen through a microscope or the movement of clouds across the sky can be expressively interpreted by means of colour, line and all manner of materials. Such artistic expression can encapsulate far more experience than a split second's camera shot might do. If anything is true of art it is that we expect it has something special to tell us about the experience of living and the language it uses cannot be substituted by commonplace words.

At the age of 8 years, many children have found their experience of using art materials exhilarating and developed considerable skill and control over what they can do. Others have generated a flair for using words or numbers in much the same way as their teachers have developed different strengths and skills. Yet any child who has had the slightest contact with art and design touches on concepts, perceptions and emotions which have the potential to affect fundamentally the way they feel about what they see. If art experience has not merely been frustrating the majority of children retain their enthusiasm and are sufficiently encouraged to try out new materials, draw, paint, produce collage and make a variety of lively artefacts.

Yet unless art persists as a major means of expression, their concerns and those of their teachers will change. Dissatisfaction with drawing skill can set in and children may find they are discouraged by parents keen to see them engrossed in reading and writing. Their growing ability to use words and a capacity to absorb information begins to shift the balance of the school day and far less do they use art as a way of communicating ideas, a necessary alternative to words. The potential within children of this age to be creative is by no means diminished. But constraints of the school timetable, curricular demands and the desire in teachers to develop other abilities often displace what once seemed an indispensable part of their education.

'How do I fit everything in?' is a familiar question raised by teachers as pressures on the curriculum grow increasingly restrictive. There are new fields of learning for an 8 or 9 year-old to include, information to

Figure 1 Newspaper Portrait – collage. Age 12.

gather from books and life skills to develop to the full. How can they be expected to give time to art?

Maybe it is not so much a question of cramming more and more into an overcrowded curriculum as one of developing existing activities and examining their aesthetic, creative or artistic content. Only when we fail to see a relationship between art and the rest of the curriculum does there seem to be a serious problem regarding the allocation of time for art. As one headteacher puts it,

> There's always pressure on the curriculum but what gets in the way of art is that many teachers see the mechanics of reading, writing and dealing with the practicalities of life as separate and this makes art look something of a luxury. We don't, in society, take our artists very seriously at all . . . a colleague of mine says he feels guilty every time he sees children painting and wonders how they might better use their time.

This book is about teaching art and design. Inevitably in the 8–13 age range there is also considerable enthusiasm for topic work, projects or working from themes. For some teachers this seems the only way to fit art into the curriculum and an important part of the book's emphasis lies in making the art content of topics relevant, interesting and above all an artistic learning process. Though the constraints of the curriculum are always there, the view taken here is that teachers and children are far more inventive than they suppose and have a considerable capacity to be creative given the opportunity. The importance of art activities need not diminish as young children grow older and the book tries to discuss ways in which art, design and topic work can prove to be a powerful framework for learning. Although creativity in any field cannot necessarily be taught, it can certainly be developed and unlocked in children by sensitive teaching.

Almost everything which can be said about art can be challenged and there is not an argument that can be advanced which does not have an exception to it somewhere. A variety of approaches to teaching is offered in these chapters and nothing should be taken quite at face value if it is to be put to the best use. Experienced teachers will no doubt see ideas in a much wider context than that of art and design. The focus of art is a central concern here but that of the 'creative teacher' who makes the best use of topics and themes encapsulates the underlying principles of the book.

The mistake would be to think that from the age of 8 to 13 children are less creative than they were as infants, as if creativity could be a matter of age. There are, after all, creative adults who are capable of bringing invention and freshness to their work. Creativity, particularly in connection with artistic ability, does not suddenly shrink as children grow their second set of teeth. It takes different forms. Naturally, if all we find children of this age range doing is absorbing facts, learning rules and copying information from books then they will inevitably seem to be less creative. If their artwork consists of tracing or copying from history books we need not be surprised if it lacks imagination. Fortunately there are enough teachers who want more for their children than this and are prepared to organize children's learning in a variety of adventurous and worthwhile ways.

Superficially, some of a 10 year-old's artwork can still look rather unimaginative as a quest for detail and realism in drawing pushes aside the uninhibited and attractive work we see done by the very young. For many children there is a crisis of 'realism' as they find that their drawings no longer satisfy them and they search for more adult skills. A concern for 'getting it right' in terms of proportion and detail can mask the child's capacity for invention, fantasy, expression of feelings and creativity in solving problems. Much of this desire to draw like an adult is undoubtedly reinforced by seeing and copying illustrations from books. After all, the final results of copying can be quite impressive to children's eyes even if they are not at all original. No wonder the work can look so dull if the aim has been to copy the imagery of an adult illustrator.

Curiously, the more sure children are of what they are trying to achieve in their artwork the more likely many of them are to fall short of their expectations and be disappointed. Much more creative work seems to take place when they are not 100 per cent certain what the outcome will be. It cannot be denied this approach is often time-consuming and involves an element of risk for both teachers and children. The whole endeavour can end in disaster. But if uncertainty may seem an uncomfortable ethos for creativity it can also prove to be the pathway to originality of thought.

> Creative work needs time. It needs space but it needs above all somebody to acknowledge that they don't know where they're going to get to when they start. A teacher has to be prepared to take risks knowing the children may not produce models or paintings . . . they may produce drama, for instance, which by no means decorates the walls or remains as evidence of what has been done.
>
> (*Primary headteacher*)

Figure 2 Bandsman – lino print. Age 12.

Children thrive creatively where their teacher is willing to allow them the psychological space in which to take risks. Uncertainty is surely an essential condition for this to happen and as with any risk-taking there is plenty to lose as well as gain. Dismal failure can just as likely be the outcome as resounding success. Uncertainty and failure are part of what makes us human and the teacher who does not sometimes feel uncertain or experience failure is yet to be born. Could it be that the most successful teachers are ultimately those for whom to accept failure and uncertainty is part of the normal pattern of learning, and playing safe invites educational stagnation? After all, though certainty may be reassuring it can also lead to dull repetitive work, complacency, boredom and exclusion of the rewards which might come from discovering something new.

Not all learning involves risk or uncertainty and it would be quite wrong to suppose that it did. Parts of the curriculum using mathematical rules or spellings, for example, cannot be learned without being certain they are correct in the first place. This aspect of learning is referred to at various points in subsequent chapters, especially as it is often cited as a constraint on creativity. Pretending it does not form a crucial part of how we learn is to ignore its importance in this age range. Areas of any curriculum will involve some factual information even if the acquisition of such knowledge is gained through highly inventive methods.

Art, design and topic work are areas where a lively approach to learning is possible and it does not take anything like genius to begin working creatively with 8–13 year-olds. The shift of emphasis towards realism in drawing and information gathering in topic work can generate an illusion that children's stature as young artists has shrunk to a third of its size. Yet if we believe that they can be creative when we enable them to be so the battle is half won. We do not need particularly artistic skills because we ourselves are not the ones making models or painting pictures. Children, in their innocent originality, will show us far more about the excitement of artistic learning than we can ever imagine, provided, that is, they are given the chance.

Figure 3 Dustbins – lino print. Age 13.

2

How we have creative ideas

IF WE describe something as 'creative' it usually means that we approve of it. In practice, very few people would apply the word to anything which they strongly disliked. Such a popular and over-used term has become commonplace currency in arguments about the different ways we develop our mental powers or how we balance the contents of a curriculum. Leslie Perry (1987) points out that all meanings of 'creativity' are in fact correct. He also goes on to suggest how it is that one word can have so many varied meanings.

> Whenever a word is frequently used in arguments to persuade people to believe some opinion or other, our mental twists and turns to make the opinion plausible involve shifting from meaning to meaning without realizing it. This has happened to 'creativity' on a grand scale. All of its meanings are loaded with attitudes to approval or disapproval depending on whether people are for or against it.

Such shifts from meaning to meaning prevent us from formulating neat definitions of what creativity or for that matter creative thinking are. If we choose to define them we will consequently ignore most of what they might be. Both R. K. Elliott (1971) and Harold Osborne (1984) have commented on the difficulties of laying down rules as to how the words 'creative' or 'creativity' should be used and the matter seems to be one of choice. We can no more accurately define 'creativity' and have it to put in our pockets than we can capture dreams and nightmares. To be a creative thinker involves us in a never ending stream of thoughts, images and half-realized feelings. There is nothing to grasp, only a complex process which sometimes provides the tangible evidence that something we call 'creative' has been going on. We may choose definitions to our heart's content but we are still left wondering how the process of creativity works.

So much has been written about creativity in the past thirty years that examining the process involves a minefield of choices. In the 1950s and 1960s, especially in the United States, 'creativity' experienced a boom as a subject for enquiry. What can be attempted here is to gather together useful and important strands and state a point of view which informs the more practical content of subsequent chapters. It is not that knowing about how we think creatively will reveal some magic which has eluded us. The aim here is to deal with many of the experiences we already have and to encourage some of the more consciously creative paths of thought that are possible.

There are two main ways in which we have ideas. These are easily recognized and are common to all of us. They have been extensively written about, notably by Sinnott (1970) and Koestler (1964), and reflect the fact that our minds operate creatively at both conscious and subconscious levels. The first way consists of surrounding ourselves with the widest possible array of images, sketches, fragments of images, facts, information, feelings, words and existing ideas. We then search for unusual and previously unrecognized relationships between them. Sinnott cites Einstein as an example of someone who worked this way in the development of his theoretical ideas. Quite unrelated fragments proved to be the foundations of theory once the connections between them had been recognized. As we will see, there are implications for the ways in which teachers gather together a wide array of resource material for any project or topic they are keen to begin. The importance of making connections between unrelated ideas is crucial to creativity.

The second way in which we have ideas is when they arise spontaneously in the mind, usually unexpectedly and almost always when we are thinking about something entirely different. We may be washing the dishes or having a bath (the Eureka effect) when an idea involuntarily demands our attention. There seems to be no conscious effort to think of anything. Alternatively we may be reminded of something while we are in the middle of doing something else such as listening to another person. Being reminded is not necessarily the same thing as having an idea but the experience of involuntary thought impinging on the mind is quite similar. Again, a thought or idea arises from the unconscious and we have no control over the process which has led to its arrival.

Mozart in his letters describes how musical ideas would suddenly flow into his mind and he would store those he felt might be useful later in composing his music. He had no idea where they came from nor could he force them into his conscious mind. Tchaikovsky, Picasso and countless artists recount that ideas just came to them unbidden and there seemed to be no particular way of knowing how or when this would happen.

Now it might be thought that we cannot do much about encouraging inspired ideas to come spontaneously into the mind. Yet, as many artists will recognize, we do not simply sit around waiting in the hope that inspiration will eventually arrive. We actually have to work with the ideas we have, however impoverished they are, or we cease to be immersed in our subject. We no longer habitually explore it. By contrast, when we are absorbed in ideas, surrounded with resources or wrestling to solve a scientific problem, connections are already being made. When there is a flash of inspiration it is as if we have set our mind the task of finding solutions and it has continued working when we turned our attention elsewhere. Searching for relationships and making connections became a process which we were not able to switch off.

Inspiration takes us by surprise yet it is obviously linked to the first and more conscious way we have ideas. We cannot have spontaneous ideas about a particular problem or topic without spending some of our time sifting through the resources and aspects which are attached to it. Selecting, rejecting and making connections between a wide variety of materials can be going on at a subconscious level but it is doubtful that this takes place as if in a vacuum. The resulting inspiration, spontaneous as it may seem, can still be a product of previous efforts to organize ideas intentionally. In other words, the second spontaneous variety of thinking is highly likely to be a result of the first kind.

This is no doubt one of the reasons why artists continually juxtapose and compare what they see. They deliberately collect material in the form of sketches, drawings and photographs and try to find unusual relationships and connections between the various fragments. The hope is that learning to search for interesting connections at a conscious level permits the subconscious to join in. Conscious involvement in gathering ingredients and making connections encourages the conditions in which creative ideas are born.

Two factors in this are critical. One is to make unusual connections frequently enough for the process to become a habit. The other is to

Figure 4 Cauldrons. Age 8.

gather sufficiently varied resources for there to be fewer limitations on the outcome.

> Creativity is the ability to make connections . . . and some children are going to make all the connections they need for there to be a creative response. It is not that you have to make connections for them . . . they are already there. But you do have to build a few bridges for some children and teach them to practise making connections for themselves. If they are used to making connections they begin to make their own . . . inside the heads of other children there are connections made which never get out. For connections to get out teachers have to be open-ended . . . creativity is shut down if they already know the responses they're going to get.
>
> (*Primary headteacher*)

It cannot remain unsaid that the quantity, variety and quality of resources have a direct bearing on the connections we make. Most teachers will recognize that if children's interest is to be captured they need to find sufficiently varied resources from which to choose and about which to think. As teachers are already a resource this is just as likely to comprise varied and stimulating ideas as do books or art media. Children are entitled to good quality material but this does not necessarily mean requisitioning a truck full of expensive work-packs or paints. It is not up to teachers to provide creative responses for their pupils but creativity can be found in questions, presentation, evaluation and intriguing development of ideas. Their responsibility lies there. Additionally, if we want the making of connections to become a habit in children then examining the bric-à-brac of everything attached to the subject should take them long enough for it to be thoroughly engrossing. Otherwise, connections are obviously difficult to make and spontaneity is less likely.

Our minds like to run in well worn paths (see Buzan, 1974) and habitually making connections has some similarity with what is known about the function of memory. Most memorizing techniques are based on making connections or associations between words and images. To remember a name like Mrs Barr we are enjoined to imagine her pulling pints of beer in a public bar, or standing before us trying to bend an iron bar. Such evidence as there is (Buzan, 1974) shows that not long after this name-remembering technique is practised it changes. We become better at remembering names anyway, without recourse to memorizing techniques and if we do need to make associations in order to remember, we become quicker and better at doing it. A consciously learned technique has become more automatic as the brain has learned to work for us with spontaneity.

Of course, it is still tempting to assume that new ideas which arise as a result of connections come from nowhere. Yet in both art and science it is practically impossible to find anything which is absolutely new because every idea or discovery is built on a thousand related ideas which already exist. Discoveries like that of the structure of the DNA chain and cures for cancers do not suddenly appear as if nothing has gone before. Famous painters such as Braque and Picasso borrowed ideas back and forth from each other. They combined them with their own to express something new within the artistic culture of their time. Like building new rooms on a house, or changing the position of walls within it, the development of a creative idea largely depends on previously established structures.

Just as we cannot abandon the house in order to build on rooms, we cannot entirely abandon the concepts we already have in order to adopt completely new ones. Where our thoughts go depends very much on where they are now and there is a point of reference from which we start and to which we periodically refer. In other words, creative thinking takes place in a context of existing ideas. We cannot say it comes from nowhere.

Even when there are flashes of inspiration they usually have to be refined, revised and made to work. Creative ideas do not always rise to the surface of our minds in the form we want them to and many ideas are not worth pursuing as they stand. Yet within the deliberate revisions we make, our subconscious mind still seems quite able to work away on our behalf. When we least expect, it is disposed to snap into consciousness like a tightly sprung jaw as an appetizing morsel passes by.

We can speculate that parts of the brain have been talking to each other or that the right side of the brain is continually making connections with the left. Such speculations need not detain us long, however. What is clear is that we are capable of piecing together ideas at more than one level of consciousness but we cannot control what happens. Nevertheless, if we cannot do much about the second spontaneous way of having ideas we can certainly do something about the first. If it is true that our mind continues to work when our attention is elsewhere we need to find appropriate morsels for it to chew over.

Connections or collisions?

How might this work? It is one thing to surround ourselves with excellent resources but quite another to make connections. At its simplest we consciously concentrate on two things and see if we can make a discernible connection between them. If, over a period of time, we develop the habit of doing this we are actually extending the way our mind already works. As far back as the nineteenth century it was claimed that thinking was entirely the association or connection of ideas. Since then, both Koestler (1964) and Cropley (1967) have joined the long line of philosophers and psychologists who have recognized that we associate or connect dimensions of experience both consciously and subconsciously. The critical factor in this is that however rapidly the connections are made they generally involve two ideas, two meanings, two concepts, two images, two words, or *two* of anything at a time. Koestler called this making of connections 'bisociation' and Cropley 'association'. Meanwhile Newton had already demonstrated that he saw an unusual connection between an apple and a planet.

Writers contributing to an analysis of creativity have their own favourite (and imperfect) explanations. For Koestler, 'bisociation' meant that creative thinking was *'any mental occurrence simultaneously associated, with two habitually incompatible contexts'*. A further explanation is that two ideas or contexts are so different (and incompatible for Koestler) that they actually collide. In the collision is found sufficient useful overlap between them, however strange and fantastic that might happen to be. Fundamentally the two ideas do not really fit together or have much in common but they create a third and new idea as a result of colliding. The resulting dramatic connection between them proves to be useful enough to generate a new concept or meaning.

Cartoonists and humorists deal with these collisions daily. They are disposed to look for the unusual and present us with a resulting bizarre logic of their own. More often than not, from Buster Keaton to Woody Allen, we are presented with colliding concepts of reality as if they were perfectly normal. When (in the film *Take the Money and Run*) Allen holds up a bank, a discussion ensues in the bank about the spelling of his hold-up note. Bank officials studiously compare views about the legibility of the handwriting and our concept of a bank raid is therefore challenged. The collision occurs between the expected drama of a bank raid, which is portrayed by the bank officials as uneventful, giving little cause for concern, and the spelling of the hold-up note, which has assumed unnecessary importance.

In humour it is possible that collisions also include a change or reversal of expectations and the tension created is released through laughter. In effect the ideas have remained in collision. A well-known cartoon about art by James Thurber reverses our expectations when one gallery visitor says to another, 'He knows all about art but he doesn't know what he likes.' Where we can establish connections between apparently unrelated ideas and this leads to further ideas there is no longer collision. We have resolved any tension by making connections more compatible and consequently left behind their original estrangement.

Douglas Hofstadter (1985) goes much further and suggests that part of one concept or idea has elements already predisposed to slipping across and overlapping part of another concept. A simple example in art is that of 'shape' and 'pattern' where visual ideas can be triggered by the overlap of both concepts. And if (as Hofstadter claims) two things can be seen as instances of the same phenomenon, or share the same principle, the effect is even more striking. Ideas can be borrowed back and forth between the two in a highly productive way. Shape and pattern are typically compatible concepts in that 'shape' can be found in 'pattern' and 'pattern' within 'shape'.

In some cases not only will collision produce a connection but concepts can also redefine themselves in the process. Connections which result from collisions between concepts such as 'femininity' and 'masculinity', 'extremism' and 'convention', or 'tradition' and 'innovation' can evoke other ideas which in turn invite new perspectives on the original concept. Where they appeared to be fixed they become fluid as ideas which were well established are disturbed, overlap and invite comparison. It is interesting to note how concepts such as 'femininity' and 'masculinity' have continually been redefined as expectations of each have changed through collision between the traditional roles of men and women.

It is not that we have to force concepts to connect, associate, collide or overlap. In the same way as the colours yellow and blue could potentially become green, so there are areas of productive overlap which already exist but have not yet been brought together. But a key point here is that to be inspired 'creatively' is actually to recognize the value of an idea. Recognition is crucial to its ever being called 'creative'. A wild idea, the product of connections resulting in unconventional thought or divergent thinking, is not necessarily a creative one. It has to be recognized in the context of previous ideas and events for us to test how effective and appropriate it promises to be. A new idea can actually be blindingly obvious but if it takes us by surprise we may still refer to it as 'creative'. It appears to be just right for the situation to hand.

Recognition of the value of an idea can excite, intrigue and motivate us to put ideas to use. Usually we experience recognition of the value of something as being accompanied by the feeling that we are able to solve some problem or explore a new dimension. Naturally, such recognition is dependent on insight but we are unlikely to have any of that unless we already are predisposed to looking for useful connections. Seeing the application of an idea and recognizing its value may well need as much practice as does formulating it in the first place.

Creative thinking, variation and flexibility

A related factor in creative thinking concerns connections which are actually variations on a theme. To explore ideas in a creative way is to try to exhaust all possible variations of those ideas. This is particularly true where there is a more deliberate attempt, as in the arts, to engage specifically in creative activity. Artists like Henry Moore with his theme of 'reclining figures', Cézanne and his 'still lifes', or Monet and his 'lily ponds' explored variations on a theme for most of their lives, yet could hardly be described as lacking in creative ideas or being in a rut. Composers such as Mozart and Beethoven used variations over and over again yet their music is by no means boring or repetitive.

Variations are inevitably explored as we hang on to one idea while exploring others. We try out alternatives by adapting ideas, changing them, looking at information in a variety of ways, finding ways to break away from the commonplace, combining and rearranging as the mind chews over as many variations as it can. But the existence of a theme, or continued thread of ideas on one topic, holds together and makes sense of widely differing thoughts.

A very good reason why the mind explores variations is that the alternatives it finds are prone to imperfection and only work as possible solutions for a period of time. Many creative ideas arise because of dissatisfaction with an existing solution, model, or concept we have constructed. We search for new structures because the old ones do not fit the present context or are just not good enough.

There are also happy accidents which spark original connections. Mistakes of speech and idea can create new meanings as our minds try to order the chaos created. Recently a teacher who was talking to children about 'speckled frogs' occasioned a slip of the tongue and called them 'freckled spogs', a mistake which led to considerably imaginative class discussion of what a 'freckled spog' might look like. The discussion temporarily lost sight of factual information but developed useful ideas about how creatures like the 'spog' would live. Visualizing the freckles was not a problem but 'spogs' invited much more open-ended and imaginative ideas. The fantasy was in contrast to what had gone before but enlivened the level of discussion and informed subsequent learning. It also had potential for further imaginative work in art, drama and writing.

Such flexibility of approach throws into sharper focus the way in which different definitions can still be valuable even where they conflict with facts. A key element in creativity is for us to put dissimilar ideas into the same category. This is not quite an 'anything goes' principle but means that apparently unrelated ideas are found to have some tenuous similarity. In the case of Henry Moore's sculpture both human figure and landscape are evident within the same piece of work. The category for 'reclining figure' includes rock structure as well as human form. In other sculptures, Moore makes associations between broken bone and huge monumental human figures and throws our categorization of human form into question.

The idea is not a new one (see Bruner and Oliver, 1963) and A. J. Cropley (1967) described it in the following way.

> Clearly, the more a person treats data which look to have nothing to do with each other as though they are related, the more likely he is to make data combinations which are unusual (i.e. to think creatively). The kind of person who codes in this broad way is referred to as a wide categorizer, while the opposite kind of person is called a narrow categorizer.

If we value flexibility then we must also be willing to live, at least temporarily, with strange and conflicting ideas. They may be totally unrealistic yet ultimately prove to be a stepping stone to something else more credible. The differences are frequently examples of the same widely found phenomenon (such as natural forms in the case of Henry Moore's sculpture) and the more similarities we can find, the wider the categories can become. Flexibility in art must also include making use of fantasy in conjunction with fact, imagined as well as real images.

For example, it might be possible to see a link between a piano keyboard and a zebra, or between the bark of a silver birch tree and hospital bandages. To an artist, the category which both examples fit is fairly obviously one of pattern. But the examples would still work in wider and more unusual categories, though to widen them is possibly to threaten and disturb our sense of reality. We might imagine a piano-playing zebra (wide categorization of musician) or the work of a tree surgeon who dressed in full face mask and used a scalpel and bandages (wide categorization of conventional medical surgery).

For narrow categorizers there need to be high levels of similarity before ideas seem to fit the category they have defined. Connections then become rather conventional and may be unproductive since they do not offer much potential for flexibility or compromise between the credible and the incredible.

If we are to make the best of the creativity we already have, we may need to learn not to be afraid of living with ambiguity. When we put anything in a wide category we are quite likely to say that something is the case when others will say it is not. As Hofstadter (1985) points out, we often use analogies which considerably stretch the truth to make a point. We do this every day. He goes on to say that in fact analogies will always eventually break down but we need them because they guide our thought patterns. For him 'being attuned to vague resemblances is the hallmark of intelligence, for better or for worse'.

Subjects, such as art or mathematics, seem well established as being in different categories. Yet the fact that we name them in this way is really only a convention and even within subject areas we use categories which are not really arbitrary and fixed. A glaring example is the way in which we might fix periods of history by date alone. A Victorian photograph of a room interior and its furnishings, for example, has elements of style which are also predisposed to being Edwardian. In the same way, an Edwardian photograph is bound to have elements which can be traced back to Victorian times. The categories are already wider than we might describe. Of course, to say that Edwardian is the same as Victorian is a nonsense, but temporarily to try out the idea that they *are* the same can often help us to sharpen the main differences between the two periods. If we live with an idea which does not ring true we have performed a leap of the imagination which can nevertheless later lead to a relevant point of view.

Maybe incredible ideas are best thought of as the jumbled parts of unformulated ideas. Think of how the human race hoards pieces of miscellaneous junk in boxes, jars and attics, in the hope that one day they might prove useful. They lie unused until they are attached as appropriate missing parts. Connections within wide categories act similarly like unassembled parts. They do not necessarily have to be diverse to be ingenious but enough of them must fit any category we have devised. Besides this, we can argue that to stay with apparently useless thoughts and crazy ideas increases the capacity we have to think in a creative way. There are simply more spare parts to call on at any one time.

Being flexible will entail allowing our mind to go off at a tangent to our first thoughts. Exploring for the sake of exploring, looking for the unexpected and daydreaming all manner of random thoughts is almost a way of life to creative thinkers. Thoughts do not always fit the immediate situation and an idea may be taken as a point of departure rather than a controlled focus of attention. The irritation is that further problems are often encountered as a result of wandering off in new directions. The original problem grows extra limbs and several heads.

Consequently, it is important to defer judgement on any of the

Figure 5 Freckled Spog. Age 8.

ideas we have. Premature judgement of artistic ideas merely hampers flexibility. We cease to think. We turn off the process of making further connections and developing the fantastic in the hope it might lead somewhere inspiring. True flexibility embraces change so that the most finalized of plans can still be developed, rearranged and adapted. Judgements are seen as necessary but not first considerations in the process. Options are kept open, nothing is rigidly fixed and we can still respond to the way ideas are actually working out. Only later, and perhaps according to the level of uncertainty we can cope with, do we make judgements and settle for irreversible decisions.

A major part of this chapter has been concerned with connections. To that have been added explanations and ideas such as 'variations on a theme', colliding concepts and the ability to be flexible and defer decisions. Later on (particularly in Chapter 5) the ability we have to make connections is channelled in a more practical way. Its importance as described so far may be masked by the fact that we tend to take connections rather for granted. Like going to sleep or eating a meal, we have lived with the process of thinking and grown with it. Even so, on making connections depends the flow of inventive and inspirational thought. On the quality and outcome of connections we make depends creativity.

Connecting thoughts and ideas, useful though the activity can be, is insufficient in itself and must lead to much more than this. In fact, to use the term 'creative' at all we must apply it to some endeavour or field of activity or it has little meaning. People are not just 'creative', they are creative in respect of something they have said or done. To make interesting connections and leave the matter there cannot be the same thing as sifting through the many ideas which have come to mind, then evaluating, developing and adapting them. Making connections is not just having an interior experience of dream-like thought.

We must also leave room for misunderstandings which are nevertheless creative. A professional artist tells the story of his failure at school in the art examinations.

> We had to draw this carrot as a test of drawing for what was then the GCE examination. I cut mine in half and drew dozens of little people coming out of it. I failed the exam. The following year I chose the carrot idea again amongst others, but this time I took a much more traditional approach and I drew it without the crowd. I got a grade A.

This well-known conflict between realism and fantasy haunts inquiry into art and design. Creative thinking in the above example conflicted with examination of the ability to demonstrate representational drawing skills. In the context of examinations there are many famous artists whose drawings would not pass such formal tests of skill. This does, however, point to a more problematic question for teachers concerned to be creative thinkers within their classrooms. Can creative thinking be applied across the whole curriculum, in equal measure and to equal effect? Topic work, which tends to involve a considerable spectrum of subject areas, is a case in point. The view that everything can be made creative should at least be questioned.

Are those in the 'creativity at all costs' camp to ignore that there are other vital kinds of learning? Some ways of learning will involve memorizing and checking to see if things are right or wrong according to known information. Writing down information and practising particular skills also have an important place in children's lives. As with any apparently conflicting concepts, such as knowledge as memorizing versus knowledge as understanding, fact versus fantasy, the sciences versus the arts or intuition versus reason, there is generally some degree of overlap. The line between fact and fantasy, for example, has always been drawn very thinly. The folly of finding ourselves firmly in either camp is well illuminated by Perry (1987) when he says:

> Those who teach knowledge as a matter of memorizing forget that it is the product of past creativity and should be presented as such. Those who teach creativity to the neglect of knowledge should remember that past creativity is preserved and brought into a continuity with present creativity by knowledge well learnt.

Creative thinking is not confined to the arts. Neither does it automatically take fright when facts and memorizing enter into the activity. Searching for ways to make learning more creative than it is should not destroy essential areas of endeavour but should enhance the way subjects are taught. It should encourage flexibility of thought and be an antidote to rigid thinking. There is still room for creativity in the most factual of subjects but the arts are obvious areas in which to develop it. Beyond connections, collisions and variations there are issues of originality, organization and skills. We need to find a balance between established knowledge and new ideas and that balance hinges on two factors. One is the educational climate of the times, which raises the question 'Do we need more creative thinking in schools than there evidently is?' The other is the capacity we have to cope with ideas which fundamentally change the way we already teach.

3

What does art do?

> There has to be part of *you* available to be able to teach. The development of yourself is important so you have something to give children when you are with them. Many of the things we do in life hinder this process of personal development and inhibit our ability to be ourselves.
>
> (*Headteacher*)

THERE ARE popular extremes of caricature about the status of artists and their art. For that matter, there are also extremes of view about the place of art and design in schools, views which range from the over-enthusiastic to the downright dismissive. On the one hand we have the artist as designer who can apply skills which literally can have a profitable outcome. The designer sounds respectable and has associations with function, skills and industry. On the other hand there is the fine artist, caricatured as a starving willowy figure, less concerned with the economy, oblivious to constraints of time, a dreamer who is more likely to promote cultural and personal development than apply art to industrial products. For the fine artist, idealism (which some would say was self-indulgence) may loom large with words such as expression, truth and freedom creeping into the vocabulary.

Declaring that art is concerned with truth is too vague a way to explain what it has to offer. After all, claims of truth and idealism have been made for other fields of endeavour including the most disastrous of political objectives. There are similarly arguments that art is a powerful language which does not distort the original truthful message of expression (Field and Newick, 1973). The view is that anything other than expression of an original idea through art is deemed less truthful and therefore less valuable than expression through words.

Such claims set us off down well-worn yet inconclusive threads of discussion and, like lists of artistic skills, can depend on sheer quantity of benefits or shortcomings for their ultimate persuasion. No wonder the scientist, who has evolved convincing models to explain the world, often regards artists as muddlers who have the arrogance to create without explaining what they are doing.

Scientists deal with shifting and changing explanations of the nature of their own subject just as artists do. Despite scientists' apparent ability to prove or disprove things, they are still concerned with making professional judgements in the light of newly formed concepts. Those judgements inform their next projects and redefine science in terms of what they have discovered.

When we teach art we make a variety of judgements which are based on our own artistic values. If these are well informed we can say they are 'professional' and children consequently can benefit from the values we reflect. If they are based on ignorance their damaging effect on children's creative work can be long lasting and inhibit creative thinking. What does it matter that we understand the values which inform art and design? We may well be entitled to the view that since any one of the arts is a bonus, to be deprived of it does no serious damage. There is, after all, no recognized system of job interviews which includes a check on the artistic values teachers hold. Yet from the appreciative or dismissive comments teachers make about art it is clear that these values affect the way it is taught. If we ourselves do not consider the important values of art, there is little reason to suppose that children will either.

Figure 6 Old Man and Fisherman – lino prints. Age 11.

What art *does* in respect of its function or value to society is known through a consensus of views none of which can actually be proved. All artistic values are continuously open to question. People will report being better off for this or that experience of the arts and their claims are permeated with common strands of shared insight. Yet the very nature of the arts is that they are surrounded by controversy and criticism. They do not seem to stand still long enough for us to know exactly how to define them or to give one clear statement of what they do. The arts survive by continually redefining what they are, and what they do can just as easily take public form as it does private anguish. There are also obvious differences between looking at a painting and producing one, playing a concerto and writing one or acting in a play and being in the audience. Anything which can be said about art and design will inevitably concern points of view which, on closer inspection, turn out to be many-sided as well as problematic.

To those who find visual art a total mystery, the benefits which are proclaimed can defy reason, logic and scientific measurement. Measurement and logic are poor substitutes for our imagination, feelings and senses. If we are to examine what art does then to use the arguments of science and reason is not appropriate. In arguing their case, however, art educators are often guilty of failing to understand the viewpoint of the scientist, whose perspective on the world is bound to be different and may necessarily exclude emotion, feelings and fantasy. In education, however, controversy does not so much surround whether or not art or science should be included in the school curriculum. That battle was won long ago. Subject value concerns how much emphasis each deserves and how much time should be allotted to them on the school timetable.

The designer can turn to 'function' as a means of defending the worth of art. But most artistic values are far less concerned with function and more associated with what they will do for us in a civilizing, learning and humanizing sense. In short, art gives a meaning to life which is particularly and uniquely 'visually aesthetic'. The qualities it embodies give significance to the way we perceive our world.

A commonly held view is that the main purpose of art is to enrich us in some way. This may be true but, on closer inspection, enrichment does not prove to be a central reason for artistic endeavour. Enrichment implies an additional ingredient, something rather like the extra 'icing on the cake'. The value of art lies elsewhere and the view taken here is that far from being one of life's enrichments, art is *essential* to our understanding the world we inhabit. Whatever else can be said of art, of one thing we can be certain. Unless it actually affects us in some way we are unlikely to conclude that it has value. Sometimes its impact is the antithesis of reason. The soul-stirring effects of the greatest works of art transcend anything we can accurately quantify, reason about, or analyse.

From cave painting to the present day we have needed to express ideas through art. Galleries and architecture across the globe are evidence of who and what we are and there is clearly part of us which needs to be surrounded by forms which have a particularly aesthetic visual refinement and power. Sensing the time in which we live, we have created down the centuries art forms which encapsulate and affect how we feel about the world and our relation to it. Art fulfils a need which is already there. It is as if we are incomplete without expressing ourselves through art and the need to do this arises as we discover that there are ideas and inspirations which will not easily fit other ways of explaining. As the intriguing graphic artist and mathematician Escher (1972) describes,

> Ideas came into my mind quite unrelated to graphic art, notions which so fascinated me that I longed to communicate them to other people. This could not be achieved through words, for these thoughts were not literary ones, but mental images of a kind that can only be made comprehensible to others by presenting them as visual images.

Escher pinpoints the uniqueness of art as a way of understanding and communicating certain specific ideas. Try, for instance, describing the qualities of an irregular shape to someone else using only words. However good the description it is unlikely to equal drawing in its power to communicate the nature of the shape. Once we take this example much further and move to an examination of the subtleties of three-dimensional shapes, such as sculpture, words are not a substitute for walking around a sculpture and letting our visual perception describe it to us. Even at the mundane level of being a visual aid to communication, art has unique qualities associated with it.

The uniqueness of art has long been recognized by art educators as being fundamental (Read, 1943; Eisner, 1972). Naturally, most subject areas would make similar claims to uniqueness of contribution and if our education is not to be narrow and restricted it must include them all. Yet there are many teachers who are keen to emphasize basic intellectual skills to the exclusion of artistic experiences, often because they lack the confidence to pursue learning through art. They see this subject as providing for the emotions and nothing else or they find their own experience of art has convinced them it is a mystery best left to the innately talented. Others are far more prepared to take a wider view of what it means to be educated. They recognize that art has value for children precisely because of its appropriateness as a visually aesthetic way of knowing the world. In that sense it is unique.

Looking as a legitimate way of thinking

We set great store by using words to communicate our ideas and most of our thoughts would take too long (for our convenient everyday use) to set down as a drawing or painting. The practical problems of rapidly turning speech into images are far too complex for looking and drawing ever to be a substitute for spoken words. Even so, whether words are spoken, written or read, they do not deal adequately with the complexity of visual qualities in the way art does. Though we may say a colour is 'red', the quality of 'redness' has to be experienced for us to know just how 'red' is the colour we are looking at. We also need to experience 'red' in relation to other colours which are next to it. How it appears in relationship with its surroundings affects how we perceive it as a particular quality of 'red'. 'Red' can also be experienced in a painting where we see how a particular artist has used it to express feelings and perceptions. The artist may, for instance, use red to interpret subject matter as different as blood or sunsets and the way the colour is organized on the canvas determines its power to communicate a particular 'redness' to us. Such aesthetic qualities of colour, shape, form, light and texture cannot be absolutely and accurately described. The development of visual sensitivity to them requires a thought process which puts words aside in favour of images.

So used are we to thinking in words that it is very difficult to imagine that any other way of thinking exists. A process of 'wordless' thought may, for example, include the subtleties of comparing one colour with another, one curve against another, or the balance of light and shade. Within this process *the actual comparisons made* cannot involve words, though we may of course think that they do if we verbalize to ourselves. Responding in words is in fact only an additional mental activity, not the comparison itself. At the point where we are discriminating, looking for a few seconds rather than taking our attention elsewhere, we can still be involved in wordless thought. Comparing colours and curves is still thinking and the thought process may well go on at subconscious as well as conscious levels. Developing artistically relies considerably on the use of looking as a legitimate way of thinking.

Visual thinking depends on such concepts as, for example, 'straightness', 'circularity' and the 'redness' already mentioned. When we say that we noticed how red something was, we mean we measured it against our previous experience of 'redness'. We would not expect a red apple to be exactly the same red as a London bus. Our concept for the 'redness' of an apple depends on having seen red apples and London buses. We regularly use concepts drawn from experience as benchmarks for making wordless judgements.

This is not to deny centuries of philosophical writing on the relationship between thought and word. Much of our thinking depends on this relationship. Yet, although information may be enshrined in many elaborate words, understanding of it is not necessarily confined to words at all. *Understanding something involves concepts, many of which we may never have to verbalize.* As Douglas Hofstadter (1985) describes,

> The vast majority of concepts are wordless although we can certainly make stabs at verbalizing them when we need to.

If we define thinking solely as the use of words in response to looking, we rule out a variety of other ways in which human beings have thoughts. Most musical or mathematical ideas, for example, do not depend on words. Naturally, we put a certain amount of trust in our use of words (which often become important to us as much by sheer volume as by their usefulness) and to develop visual discrimination we must also learn to trust the process of looking just as we trust words. We must treat looking and drawing as seriously as we do reading and writing, thinking in images as seriously as thinking in words. The prize visual thinking offers is to widen our concept of what it is to know and understand our world and ourselves other than through words. A natural inclination in any case is for us to think partly in images and partly in words and that particular process is not easy to separate. It appears to operate simultaneously even though it is more likely that image and word are switching back and forth with lightning speed. It is not unknown for people occasionally to claim that they never think in visual images, relying on words all the time. Yet if we probe further and ask them 'How many windows

Figure 7 Shoe Show. Age 11.

are there at the front of your house?' their response usually changes as they try to visualize their homes. Without visualizing windows it is virtually impossible to answer such a question. We regularly think using visual images even if we take them for granted and no doubt use this form of thought far more frequently than we suspect.

The ability to see visual qualities and make judgements based on our response is so far described as visual thinking. (Educators have used their favourite descriptions and alternatives include visual literacy, visual awareness, artistic literacy, aesthetic awareness and so on.) What artists do is to look, and develop the ability to think visually in response to what they perceive. Ordinarily we limit the term 'perception' to the means whereby we recognize everyday objects. In visual thinking the development of perception is actually only a step along the way. Art teachers are concerned with an aesthetic or artistic kind of perception, not merely the ability to perceive in order to recognize things. As Southworth (1982) says, 'we are not just dealing with perception we are trying to teach *visual aesthetic perception*'.

This special dimension of perception is a major pillar of art education and the fact that developing it can take place at subconscious levels should not blind us to its importance. Without this component of visual thinking we can remain in a state of rather generalized and indiscriminate awareness. The special qualities of form to be found in paintings, drawings and the natural world can be closed off to us. For artefacts and natural forms to have special meaning for us personally we must develop the ability to perceive them in ways which make aesthetic 'looking' a habit.

This process is much as a musician discriminates between sounds or a wine connoisseur develops a taste for good wines. Repeated experience refines awareness of the special qualities which are there to be discovered. What begins as a crude and primitive awareness gradually filters out into recognition and discrimination as similarities and differences are established. The obvious implication of this is that a significant amount of time must be devoted to developing aesthetic perception if any sensitivity is to be had.

Art media offer the chance to learn to manipulate qualities of colour, shape and design so as to become something of a connoisseur of these elements. The art materials give us a very immediate way of doing this. Paint, collage and drawing materials are flexible and afford opportunities to respond to them and make adjustments in qualities as we perceive them. Growth in the ability to discriminate between various qualities will obviously depend on the frequency and range of the experiences we have. But the fact that artists are able to influence designs and change colour qualities has an additional benefit. It closely involves them in discovering how visual art media behave when they deliberately manipulate them to judge the effect.

Left to their own devices children might by chance use a variety of media, but the sensitive art teacher can ensure that they find out about and make specific comparisons between the nature and qualities of different materials. This can be approached particularly through problem-solving and design activities (see Chapter 9) though it is just as important for teachers to talk about the particular qualities which materials have as it is for children to use them.

It is all very well to demonstrate how a particular material is used (and demonstration is usually necessary) but the expression of ideas can take on special characteristics as the constraints inherent in each material are discovered. How far can clay be bent? What is involved in sticking card or carving wood, using a colour wash or dyes? Such questions are catalysts to finding out about the best ways in which to use each material and understanding the characteristics which are typical of them.

At a superficial level, children might perceive what is around them but it is not the purpose of art to deal with mundane perceptions of a day-to-day sort. On the contrary, the purpose of art is to give meaning to their visual ideas at a deeper and more sophisticated level. Such attention to looking can grow from very simple beginnings. One teacher describes how she approached this in her class of 8 year-olds. She had spent some time encouraging her children to look at the changing sky and clouds.

> We had spent days talking about the appearance of the sky . . . at every opportunity we went out to look at the changes. Children came in each day and told me exactly what they had seen . . . it really affected the way they painted and drew. I was amazed at their observation and skill . . . they found subtle colours and shades, patterns and shapes. One day, though, two of them came in from the playground having noticed there were no clouds at all. They couldn't fully understand where they had gone so it led on quite well to discovering and teaching about how clouds are formed and disappear.

Looking at cloud formations had been important but so had translating these perceptions into paint. The two activities complemented and reinforced each other. Colour-mixing helped children to develop sensitivity to the subtlety of shades they saw when they were looking and, in turn, the experience of discovering what pigments could be mixed together reinforced their aesthetic perception.

It would be foolish to suggest that visual thinking cannot be developed outside of art sessions but there are facets of perception which will not automatically come children's way. An extreme example, and a difficult area, is that of perceiving areas of light and shade, usually called 'tone' or 'tonal values'. Particularly where lighting effects and shadows are involved children do not easily understand how these values exist. It is rare to find them very fully aware of tone before the age of 11 or 12. Judgements about light and shade, and their relationship to each other, have sustained the lives of painters for many centuries and the thinking involved in dealing with such qualities is as difficult as any other thinking we might do.

The boundaries between art and intellect, thought and feeling become rather blurred when 'qualitative' thinking is involved. As Eisner (1972) comments,

> The tendency to separate art from intellect and thought from feeling has been a source of difficulty for the field of art education. Such a conception does justice to neither art nor education. Artists are thoughtful people who feel deeply and who are able to transform their private thoughts, feelings, and images into public form. Because the ability to do this depends on the visualization and control of qualities, it may be conceived as an act of qualitative thought. As a process of using qualitative thought to solve qualitative problems, such a process can be conceived of as depending on the exercise of qualitative intelligence.

Consider the problem of producing a three-dimensional sculpture. The very process of dealing with spatial qualities (which are by no means fixed as we move around the sculpture) demands a high level of qualitative thinking. Though we live in a three-dimensional world, we also perceive it second by second as images from one viewpoint at a time. We also know there is more to encounter than a fixed 'snapshot' view. The art medium makes us think in a different way, demands a different part of our attention and exercises our sensitivity to its message. Even the snapshot photographic portrait differs remarkably from that depicted by an artist. A portrait painting captures a thousand snapshots at the same time and tries to express the character of the person rather than a fleeting image. The artist is searching for far more in terms of qualities than an instant photographic likeness of the sitter provides.

Eisner mentions that developing the ability to visualize is widely accepted to be one of the main concerns of art education. Of course, it can readily be pointed out that many children arrive at their first school able to visualize to a greater or lesser extent. Indeed, it could well be that those who have this ability in abundance are given a head start in developing artistic thinking. Some children by contrast have little ability to visualize how things will look and find difficulty creating a 'mind's eye' picture.

> I remember my father trying to teach me maths by using apples, oranges and bananas as examples. How frustrating it was. I was supposed to find this made maths easier but I could never carry the images in my head well enough to add them or take them away. In fact if you draw them it makes much more sense . . . that seems to help in visualizing.
>
> (*Teacher*)

Visualizing is thinking in images conjured up by memory and imagination and most of us have some ability to imagine the appearance of things. It is very difficult to look for our own front door key, shoes, or coat without already having some mental image of what they look like. Though we may not fully understand how we recognize these objects we tend to pick them out and classify them as one 'of a kind' (Sadler, 1974). Unless we had some expectation of what they looked like we could not sort them from the wealth of images before us. When we consider how as babies we learned to do this it seems an even greater mystery. In Sadler's words 'it is as if from the beginning we had a vague idea what it was all about and gradually fitted the pieces of the jigsaw together'. However, developing the capacity to visualize in order to produce artwork requires us to conjure up images of what things *might* look like, not just what they already *are*.

Art is an area where visualizing is severely put to the test and artwork is a very obvious outcome of this speculation. A claim made for art is that the process of producing artefacts assists and practises the ability to visualize. Moreover, our mind is so busy visualizing and manipulating images and media that when this process takes place there is simply no room for words. They are excess luggage and act only as a commentary on the process. They are certainly not the visualizing process itself.

If as adults we never so much as picked up a paintbrush again or drew a pencil line, the development of visual thinking would still be important. A long-term aim of developing a sharpened aesthetic perception is to go on looking and visualizing when we are grown up. David Hockney (1976) sums up the importance of sharpening the visual sense like this:

> Even if one isn't going to be an artist (of course, most people aren't going to be artists) art training sharpens the visual sense, and if people's visual sense is sharp you get beautiful things around you, whereas if it's not they don't care about their surroundings. It makes a vast difference to a city, to a country.

Although involvement in art can lead to more sensitive ways of organizing our environment so can politics and geography. The artist and designer, however, are concerned with responding aesthetically to their environment as they create their works. Within society, art provides far more than can be gained from organizing an environment according to function, power or finance. For many adults art stands for glimpses of realities beyond the human condition. It is a dimension of life which can have sufficient hold over us to make us want to comprehend it further.

One of the effects of looking is that children begin to make what can be called 'mental sets'. A mental set is not so much a concept as a specific focus of recognition, rather as we recognize vehicles which are the same design as our own. If we have just bought a Ford motor car we tend to notice the same model in among all the other makes on the road. We have formed a mental set for cars. So it is with other concerns of our attention such as comparing leaf shapes, colour schemes, circles, stripes, rectangles and so on. We build 'mental sets' of the essential nature of each object in our environment, sets which influence our next encounter with the same visual stimulus. Naturally, mental sets are found in the social sciences and mathematics as well as in art. But in art these are also 'aesthetically visual' mental sets. They carry with them more qualities than are necessary for recognition alone.

A further effect of developing a mental set, such as for leaf shapes or stripes, is that children will soon see examples of them almost everywhere. The shift in consciousness is from 'looking' to 'finding' and this generally increases the ability to find even more. 'Finding' comes not only consciously but also spontaneously from the subconscious (as has been described in more detail in Chapter 2). It could be said that the true artist is someone who develops the ability to find rather than just look, a well-known example being Picasso, who said this was exactly his own experience as an artist.

> We used to walk to the next school for swimming lessons once a week. I took it as a good opportunity to talk about the design of everything we passed . . . we looked at different shaped doors, windows, gardens and the plants we could see. That's how it started out, but before very long the children were finding all sorts of things for themselves . . . really without trying. They managed amazing descriptions and feats of memory when we got back to school.
>
> (*Teacher*)

It is difficult to believe that a sharpened sense of vision does not also enliven children in their writing and fire their imagination and curiosity in other subjects. There are topics in mathematics, for example, which concern shape, pattern and division of mathematical shapes into areas. Could it be that those children who are most visually aware are also the ones who progress academically in subjects which traditionally are unrelated to art?

This is not to suggest that the main purpose of art is to support other subject areas. Far from it. The view expressed here is that art can develop fluency of creative thought. Principles such as risk-taking and invention can be applied to other subjects as well as to art. Naturally, art provides one of the best platforms on which to try out the visually unusual and manipulate it for its own sake. Yet the connections with other subject areas cannot be ignored if we are to take advantage by enhancing, enriching and understanding to a greater depth than before.

Individuality, feeling and expression

Traditionally we think of art as being associated with individuality. When we are looking to art to provide for expression of personality it seems strange that in many schools there is such a conflict between individuality and conformity. The difficulty is that we want children to conform in some respects and be individuals in others. Teachers who ask children to write creatively often spend the next half hour emphasizing neat and tidy handwriting, thus valuing certain rules of conformity and technical mastery whilst at the same time trying to elicit individual, original and creative writing (Bennett *et al.*, 1984).

Despite the best of intentions there are times when we try to elicit the 'right' answer from children even in tasks such as art where there are theoretically no 'right' answers. There is also peer-group pressure for children to conform rather than be set apart from the rest of the group. It must be remembered, however, that in certain instances individuality can actually grow out of conformity. Without first being put in chains and perhaps even pressured to conform, some individuals might never break out to respond with true originality. A feature of individuality is often the consuming desire to reject what anyone else is doing.

Freedom denied other subject areas finds approval in art sessions where individuality can be expressed in a tangible form. It is here that children can discover that there is a variety of ways to do things and individual response is the expectation rather than the exception. Their efforts demonstrate that art can be a celebration of diversity, a celebration of individuality for its own sake. Here personality is often revealed and children take the risk to be themselves, a risk which consequently makes them vulnerable to highly personal criticism of their work by their teachers or peers.

All the more reason why we need to appreciate each piece of work a child does for the individual statement that it is. The process of creating anything is a very fragile one and the alternative to taking the risk of encouraging individuality is to over-direct. Wherever teachers take over the problem-solving and work from predetermined or stereotyped end-products there might appear to be less chance of failure but there is also less chance of success.

> What isn't valid is when art isn't from oneself. Eight children could have very similar responses but each could be individual even though they looked the same. On the other hand, seven of them could copy and only one of them would have a valid creative experience.
>
> (*Primary headteacher*)

Much poor art teaching is the result of underestimating children's ability to learn artistic skills and perceptions. Successful art teaching depends on discovering how far their ideas and skills can be pushed. We cannot value what art does for children unless we ourselves experience seeing just what remarkably individual work can come from them. Clearly, we cannot value what we have never given children the chance to produce. A more difficult undertaking still is to value the kind of artistic thinking which has taken effort and courage, even when it has not resulted in anything particularly spectacular.

Children become vulnerable as individuals because their artwork takes public form. Of all subjects in the school, art can stay on public view for us to see exactly what has been done. Great art is evidence of media translated into public form but all art reflects the culture and context in which it is made. Perhaps this is less easily understood in a gallery than it is in a school where very often we know what a child's painting is about. In a gallery the cultural context can be more difficult to know. Why for instance was there so much Dutch still-life painting in the seventeenth century? Why were Dutch interiors so basic yet the picture frames of the time so elaborate?

Each period of art is also 'art as culture' and individual expression is part of that culture whether it takes place in a school, an art studio, or a gallery. Children's art will reflect the culture in which they live even though they interpret it in a very individual way. As the artist David Hockney has often said, it is impossible not to create art which is of the present day even if the style seems to come from the past.

One of the additional strengths of art produced by children is that it can take them into the visual culture of times past yet still reflect this in terms of the present day.

We do not have to look very far to discover that art is closely associated with feeling and expression. 'Expression' is at the very core of art. We can argue that everything we do is an expression of ourselves, from the choice of our clothes to our own handwriting, and artistic expression (like expression in music or drama) involves interpretation of our world in as powerful a 'feeling' form as we can create. The expressive interpretation is in response to qualities which may have moved as well as interested us. When we respond to what we see, hear, touch, smell and inwardly feel, cold analytical descriptions are not enough. In art as in life, there are occasional 'moments of poignancy', which take us by complete surprise and motivate us to pursue our exploration of the visually aesthetic.

Like the experience felt in response to the greatest musical performances, paintings and dramas, or the shimmering light to be found in nature, such moments can reassure us that life is given particular and personal significance. Although art may act as a signpost to what is already there, expression of its essence must be felt rather than intellectually understood. Once we rationalize our feeling response and try to put it into words we can destroy the very thing it is. We move further and further away from our real feelings and are left with what was once deeply felt frozen into a description.

If we were beings who had no capacity to respond and be moved emotionally, we would hardly need to create anything artistic. As it is, we *do* respond by feeling and giving meaning to our existence. Art is a response to that feeling and can make us identify with aspects of our world which were possibly hidden to us before. Inevitably, each of us creates our own reality, a reality which is the sum of our experience and the sum of our response. Art can help to expand the dimension of that reality and occasionally give us glimpses beyond it.

There is a view taken in some schools that the sole purpose of art is to release children's emotions. Traditionally the idea is that children have become pent up through doing academic work and art is the therapeutic antidote. Of course, children can easily become just as pent up doing art as they can doing anything else. The view that art is necessary as a release may have grown from a timetable habit (continental timetabled day apart) dictating that creative activities are for the afternoons. Small wonder that in some schools, concentration in the mornings is still reserved for subjects like mathematics and topics become difficult to organize in terms of their artistic content. By the afternoon many children are often less able to concentrate whatever the work might be. That, coupled with an atmosphere of enjoyment and expression of feeling, marks out art as a strong candidate for being misread as merely therapeutic. No wonder its status is so frequently questioned. Are we then to treat art as some kind of mass therapy or psychiatry? If we do, we will ultimately rob it of its especially aesthetic dimension.

Art as a vehicle for *expressing* feelings is quite different. We are not looking to purge pupils of their pent-up feelings but to encourage them to express them and respond to other artists' expression. Children are not simply unloading but translating feelings into a visual expression of themselves. When we look at what art does, feeling or emotional response is essentially what makes it live and communicate its message. For some children, feelings are profound and the very practice of doing art in schools allows them to use part of themselves which can never quite be articulated any other way.

Emphasis and quality

At the end of what can be a very formative period of their lives children will pick up the emphasis we gave to their art education. During their time with us, decisions about what we should emphasize will be based on our own values which, in turn, condition the outcome of their work. There are important decisions we can take to ensure children actually learn rather than dabble in art.

Suppose we decided that art was mainly for wall displays or to decorate the entrance to a school. Would this really be the best reason for doing it? There are always good reasons for putting up a lively display of work and to be proud of what children produce is obviously one of them. A lively display of work is to be welcomed and has impact and influence on the school. Yet to be obsessed by this and become like a 'tinsel merchant' is quite another matter. If our main reason for doing art is to display it, we can be driven towards the cul-de-sac of thought which has only 'end-products' as a foundation for planning work (Chapter 4). This is not to decry display. Far from it. What must not happen is that display becomes the instigator of art, rather than good artwork being worthy of display.

> As a headteacher I'm aware that I actually do want the school to look interesting. I want good displays . . . I might be against window dressing but I would find it very difficult to cope with an empty school. Educationally, to dress the walls might be dreadful but I know I want something there. The trouble is that for every parent who would like to see a child's original work on the wall, there's also a parent who is happy to see the teacher's drawing, coloured in by the children.
>
> (*Primary headteacher*)

An experienced teacher will recognize to what extent art is valued by looking at what is displayed on the school walls. Some of it may be over-directed, preconceived and even tidied up by the teacher into a series of adult stereotypes. By contrast, well-displayed work can be a record of lively visual thinking and expression. Yet teaching art mainly for the contribution it makes to display is not the best of reasons and can undermine its more central ideals.

Earlier it was mentioned that art fulfilled a need which was already there. A central ideal of art is that it involves qualitative thinking of a visually aesthetic kind not experienced in any other subject. Without experience of qualitative thinking those needs are unfulfilled and the liveliness which might be brought to other subjects can be diminished. The unique qualitative nature of visual thinking makes it indispensable to the growth of children's mental powers and way of understanding the world. Put another way, when we ask 'What does art do?' the answer is that *art makes us think qualitatively and as a consequence it develops our visually aesthetic perception to a more refined level of sensitivity.*

Qualitative thinking has been described as excluding words and it could therefore be argued that it is a less contaminated form of thought. Visually aesthetic 'qualitative' thought is, after all, international and not bound by constraints such as foreign languages. We do not necessarily have to speak French to experience the colour and light of French Impressionism or German to enjoy Bauhaus designs. Describing our experience and discussing artistic judgements with children are secondary to this wordless visual thinking. Using words is essential to teaching art but not always necessary for producing or looking at it.

When children are thinking visually their task is as difficult as anything else they might do. It is therefore hard to imagine how art which is presented merely as a leisure activity or a recreation has any place in schools. Art can be enjoyable but we should not ignore the fact that it involves difficult decisions and highly complex thought.

Schools are equipped with televisions and video recorders, all of which could be used for leisure activity. We expect the content of schools television programmes to be educational, however, and the same must be said of art sessions. If teachers see art only as a leisure activity, then they should seriously look at the content to find out what is missing. Visual thinking is by no means a recreation.

Qualitative thinking, which Eisner (1972) regards as depending on the exercise of qualitative intelligence, is unlikely to be valued by children unless we seek to promote it through the practice of art and design. It encompasses a whole range of experiences. Not least of these is an emotional, affective level of responding to what we see. Within any school curriculum we will learn a variety of things. Later on in life, when examinations and attainment tests have faded into the distance, we are left with memories of those experiences which had special significance and meaning for us. What art does for us now may well hinge on the extent to which it meant anything when we were at school. If that is true we have a responsibility to consider the experiences we provide for children each time they do something as deceptively simple as look and think.

4

Making art original

VERY FEW artists can be original at the drop of a hat and those who can are probably unaware of how original their work appears to other people. Originality is elusive partly because it is the mark of someone who has not 'tried' to be original. Frantic striving to be original rarely leads to originality and a popular misconception is that if we try hard enough we will succeed in being dramatically different. As described in Chapter 2, the brain prefers to make connections which are not necessarily the result of conscious effort. Besides which, truly original artists cannot but help make their work look different from anyone else's, any more than they can change their own handwriting. The last thing we should do is to encourage children to 'try to be original'. Their originality must appear without our deliberately forcing it.

If trying is not the way forward what is? How is it that one teacher's children can produce different and original work whilst another class produces pieces of artwork which are almost identical to one another? Answers to these questions will almost certainly involve individuality and decision-making on the part of children and an absence of solutions decided in advance by the teacher. It is difficult to conceive of an entire class of children having an original idea, or a creative idea being the product of a large committee. Individuals have original ideas even if they are part of a much larger group of people.

One view of originality is that it comes from people who are so out of step with life that their actions and ideas are bound to appear original in the eyes of others. Mainstream thinking and conventions of society are not for them and they have their own rather isolated perceptions of life. A close parallel to this can be found with very young children. They have not had a great deal of time learning to see their world in any conventional way. Consequently they are able to bring to it a fresh viewpoint which has its own originality.

Another view of originality is that we generate ideas and put on one side those that are least interesting or strike us as unpromising. We mentally try idea after idea picking out the most original ones discovered along the way. It is not that we have to try. We allow as many ideas as possible to flow uncensored and only later begin to discriminate and discard the least original. In drawing and painting, looking for originality has often followed the pattern of selecting from several ideas. Van Gogh was known to work by producing several drawings for a painting. He would draw the same subject over and over again and pick out the most unusual drawing. This would be the drawing he would choose to use as a basis for his painting.

Originality is a component of creative thinking but it is perfectly possible to think creatively without chancing on a particularly original idea. We can also have original ideas which do not seem original at the time but later turn out to be eccentric, unusual yet still appropriate for our work. Just as common is to find that what we thought was an original idea has, to our frustration, already been well tried by someone else and often with greater success.

The nearest we can come to producing original ideas, original artwork and original solutions to problems is to create the climate in which they can evolve. This means understanding how to avoid producing identical artwork from children, how to encourage them to develop their thinking independently and how to work individually. The concerns of what follows here are therefore in answer to the questions 'What prevents children from producing original artwork?' and 'What clues are there to being original instead of producing stereotypes or teacher-directed artwork?'

There are well-known examples of doubtful art teaching to be found in many schools but we should not assume these are always the outcomes of a poor teacher. They arise mainly in the absence of having enough confidence to try anything better. If children are to work in more original ways teachers need to know not only how good practice can be developed but also what impedes artistic development.

Direct copying, colouring books, outlines drawn by the teacher, tracings of adult drawings, even templates or ready-cut shapes have long been recognized to have little to do with originality. They have even less to do with visual thinking, expression and individuality. Tracing may be necessary for producing a map or a diagram but it is surely not personal enough to be called art. Unfortunately for many teachers there is a strong peer-group culture in this age range and copying gains considerable approval. Children are quite happy to demonstrate their skills in copying and tracing images from advertising, the popular music scene, tattoos and cartoon characters such as Superman or Mickey Mouse. Mass-produced cult images, especially in the form of posters, bombard children in department stores and specialist shops. It is not that cult images have no artistic merit in themselves but regularly tracing and copying them can quickly become a substitute for creativity.

Copying gives the illusion of skill and many children find that reproducing a design someone else has worked out is actually very rewarding. They are not particularly concerned about its being their own work. Copied images have a peculiar fascination as can be seen by the response to the efforts of a pavement artist, doyen of the copied image. Pavement art, despite its clichés and trite content, still arrests public attention as the visual equivalent of a street busker.

A further influence is book illustration and magazines. Of course, the quality and source of these second-hand images is highly questionable compared with gallery art. If children were copying from a work of art in a gallery they would be doing what artists have done for centuries. One way to develop a concept of what artists do is to try to copy their work and discover some of its qualities. Aspiring art students have often found copying from original artefacts valuable as a way of going through a process similar to that of the artists who created them. Copying original works of art has a long tradition in art education.

The aim in copying of this kind is to find out about particular *qualities* and be put in touch with the artistic culture of the period, not just to show off how skilful we can be at copying. Usually, children are not to be found in a gallery copying works of art. Their copying comes from each other, the teacher and the popular culture so far mentioned. Copying is frowned on, along with such practices as drawing with a ruler, because it appears to exclude qualities which are characteristic of the person producing the work. One ruled line looks very much like another.

There are shades of opinion as to what constitutes copying (so readily associated with 'cheating') and what is a legitimate use of other people's images. A distinction can be made between direct copying of illustrations or photographs, and creative use of these as reference material. The ultimate in copying is to produce a forgery.

Here the result is as exactly similar to the original as it is possible to be. Nothing is added, changed, or taken away. Children who regularly trace from books are closely involved in this kind of forgery especially if they try to pass the results off as being their own art. There are also forgeries which are 'in the style of ', such as those done by Tom Keating in the style of Samuel Palmer. Paintings of that kind are regarded as forgeries for a different reason, however, and our concern here is to examine the use of images which are already to hand. As any art student will testify, painting 'in the style of ' another artist is practically unavoidable at art school.

Where direct copying in artwork is rife, children are enslaved by the solution someone else has already found instead of making decisions and solving their own artistic problems. Though this might seem obvious, whether or not to use images such as photographs and illustrations is not nearly so straightforward an issue as it at first appears. It cannot be denied that using reference material for art, such as drawings by other artists, photographs and illustrations, does not necessarily close the door on originality. Creative thinking and originality lie in the way the source of reference is being used.

Reference material which is regarded only as a starting point for creative work can be a very useful learning tool. All artists need reference of some kind but there are matters of quality and application at stake in what they choose. Photographs, drawings and paintings are useful so long as there are enough of them to give more than one idea of shape and structure. Lack of originality tends to arise when only one fixed image provides the source of information.

By contrast, changes of all kinds can be made to any copied image by enlarging it, adapting it, or perhaps making it part of a far more ambitious piece of work. Where *interpretation* is involved there is some scope for originality. But it must be added that it is difficult to understand why children should copy or interpret a drawing of a building if there is the real thing to be seen only a short distance from the school. There is nothing quite like direct experience of the world either by going out and looking or handling things which have been brought into the classroom. Occasionally, however, it might be necessary to include an elephant in a painting when the nearest live source is miles away in a zoo. Not every resource is going to be found in the high street.

Originality is further constrained by the fact that most copied images are invariably from adult art rather than the work of a child. Whose interpretation of the world do we want? The point is that children and adults perceive things so differently that adult images are incompatible with the way children respond. This is precisely why ready-made craft kits, colouring books and templates are so suspect. Not only can we make the mistake of providing children with an adult standard as their goal, but we can inhibit their originality by allowing them to think they should imitate adults. Once an adult image is held up as the standard to be achieved, we are really saying to children, 'Your work is not good enough – stop being yourselves and do it like this.'

The worth of children's imagery is seriously undervalued if we see it as poor adult art. We would hardly give a child a violin and say 'Don't come back until you can play the Mendelssohn Violin Concerto.' Our expectations are that many primitive sounds will be made before a tune can so much as be recognized. In visual art the aim is to develop children's ability to respond in their own terms, not to work towards producing shaky examples of adult drawing and painting. Listening to Mendelssohn's violin concerto could teach us something about musical structure or a violinist's vibrato. Looking at a Van Gogh painting such as *Café by Night* might highlight qualities of complementary colours when juxtaposed. But we would not expect either work to be held up as the desired standard of performance to be achieved by children.

It cannot be over emphasized that by setting adult standards for children we will diminish their originality and undervalue their creative thinking. Classrooms which could have displayed lively and vigorous artwork will be full of the stumbling examples of their attempts to be something they are not yet old enough to be.

A major problem in this 8–13 age range can be that very many children actually *want* to draw like adults. As was mentioned in Chapter 1, the desire to be artistically more 'grown up' is fairly common and frequently leads children to feel frustrated with their lack of drawing ability. As Ross (1984) points out, children at this age become interested in the conventions of artistic representation. They have an increasing concern for the adult world and their art begins to show it.

What an excellent opportunity this is to develop originality if we handle it well. What can be harnessed is children's ability to learn to draw and paint from their own developing perceptions. Their sources will be primary ones taken from their own vision rather than any adult imagery. Suppose we had a group of children who were under pressure from each other to work independently and to despise copying and tracing. The common aim would be to produce something different from anyone else. Copying each other's behaviour would actually be to make original images because everyone in the class did. Peer-group pressure could go hand in hand with originality.

Most teachers have heard the criticism that some artwork is 'teacher-directed' or 'over-directed'. Generally this means that the finished work is very similar (and sometimes identical) in its appearance and demonstrates rigidly controlled direction bordering on interference. There are stereotypes used such as identical zigzagged fir trees or faces drawn with a perfect oval. Teacher-directed art is any art which is controlled by a teacher in such a way that the end-product is for the most part predetermined in its style or content. It is the antithesis of artwork which has genuinely come from children.

The effect of over-directing artwork is ultimately to undermine children's confidence to risk being original. Instead of making their own decisions they become quite dependent on their teacher. Such children may be very rewarding to teach but they are doing without really thinking, being mechanical and learning that art is not about working independently but is characterized by 'right' and 'wrong' ways to do things. These 'rights' and 'wrongs' are almost entirely transmitted to them by adults.

The antidote to teacher-directed artwork is by no means to leave children to do as they please. To do so can be as stifling of originality as is over-direction. Thankfully the idea that art is far too spontaneous an activity to need teaching has found little recent support in schools. Sometimes misnamed 'Free Expression', the general idea was to send children into an available space, supply materials and stand well clear. Many teachers were adamant that the child's art was sacrosanct and an end in itself. What children produced did not really seem to matter because it was meant to be free of any contamination by their teacher. In practice the random artwork which was done was neither free nor particularly expressive.

How attractive this was for the teacher who believed in it. Quite mindless artwork could be produced and the teacher was never responsible for it. Evaluation was unnecessary and the children's development could be left to chance or simply assumed to be taking place.

Versions of this way of working can still be found when we give children a one-line instruction which they must carry out unaided. 'Paint me a picture of a tree', 'Do a picture of your own house', or

'Draw me some flowers' are familiar examples. The approach assumes ability is already there, as if the experience of painting or drawing will in itself be enough to sustain their interest. There are no aims, no specific problems set and no exciting stimulus which might capture the children's imagination. Yet to go a stage further and give children a completely free choice of what they do is curiously to leave them little choice whatever.

There is logically no such thing as 'free choice' because choice implies that there must be certain possibilities from which to choose. Under a 'free choice' philosophy, children are consequently thrown back on remembered and stale art images rather than those that break new ground. No wonder some pupils quickly become bored and are greatly relieved to stop working. Having lost faith in their repetitive images they are bewildered by the teacher's praise and begin to associate this freedom with dissatisfaction rather than enjoyment (see Field, 1970). Privately they may also be angry about their lack of ability and frustrated that they have not been able to think of anything better to do.

It does seem that the teacher who allows this to happen displays a serious lack of responsibility. Could there not at the very least be some extension of the children's experience? In other areas of the curriculum, such as mathematics, we would hardly expect them to learn by providing practical equipment and leaving them to it. In art sessions it is often thought that the materials themselves will be sufficient to bring about sustained creative activity. An analogy in music is to give children musical instruments and expect they will be fascinated enough to produce music.

What are the alternatives? Many teachers who have suffered the organizational consequences of promoting an approach of 'free expression' have turned to rigid and directive ways of teaching art in order to survive. No doubt this is in some frustration at having seen an art session fall apart. Bored children and art materials are not a good combination. Consequently an obvious antidote has been to plan work by defining very clearly in advance what the end-product will be. Everyone has a clear idea of what is to be produced and the process whereby this is to be achieved is subsequently devised by the teacher.

The problem with this approach is that identical work is the usual outcome. Yet it seems a perfectly straightforward strategy to decide what we will draw or paint and go ahead. Ideally we would like to think we can be very clear about the end-product and still avoid the

Magical Jungle. Age 11.

Spirals. Age 9/11.

Going Home. Age 13.

Still Life. Age 10.

Musician. Age 13.

Open Drawer - lino. Age 13.

Triangular Pattern - inspired by the artist Hundertwasser. Age 11.

Symphony in Green. Age 10.

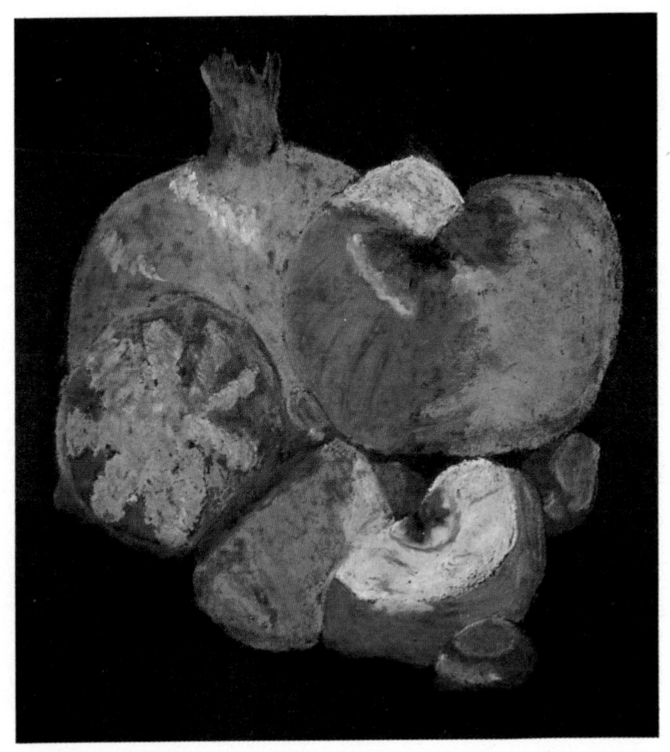

Fruits. Age 10.

Lace Pattern. Age 9.

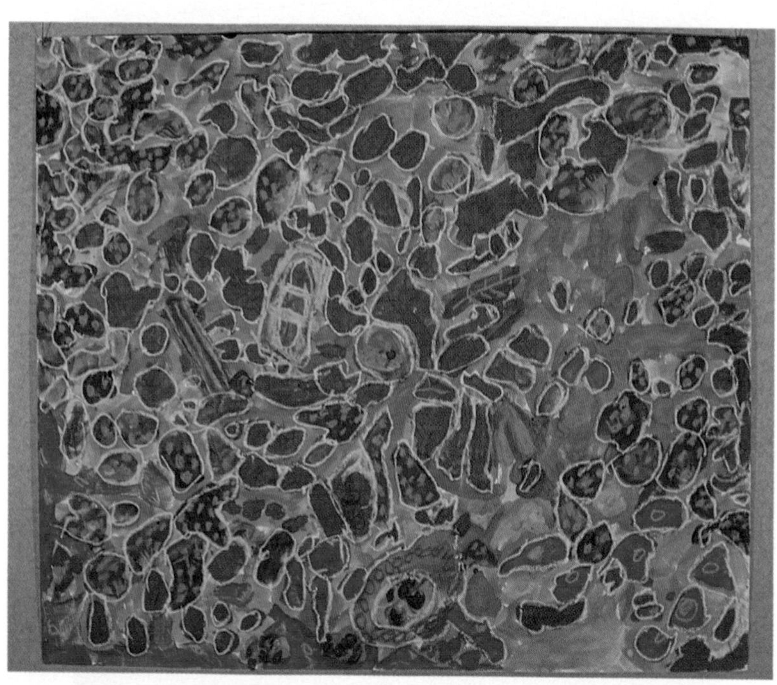

Design from Lace. Age 8.

Aborigine Topic. Age 10.

Painting inspired by Van Gogh's 'Starry Night'. Age 10.

I'm a Lady of Leisure. Age 13.

Allsorts - clay, paint, varnish. Age 13.

Fruit Collage. Age 8.

Ourselves Topic. Age 12/13.

The World's Greatest Hats. Age 12.

By Jove! Don't Dragon-Powered Machines Work Well? Age 12.

Shoe-Laces. Age 12.

Shoes. Age 12.

Portrait. Age 13.

Clowns and Pirate. Age 10/11.

Butchers, Chefs and a Waiter. Age 10/11.

Self-Portrait Heads. Age 11.

Painting based on Delaunay's Work. Age 10.

Mathematical Abstract. Age 13.

Hexagons. Age 12.

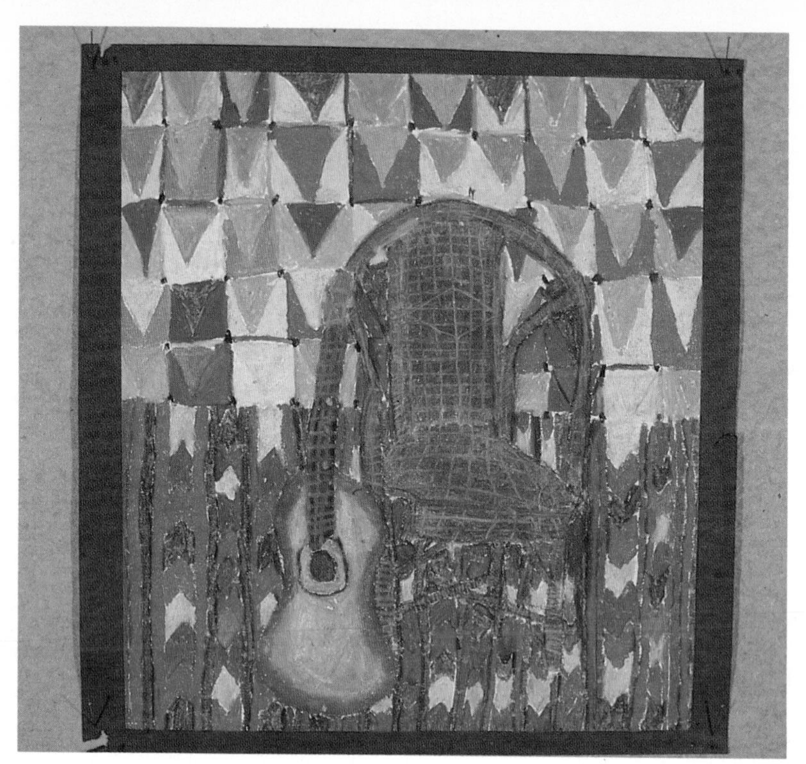

Still Life with Guitar. Age 10.

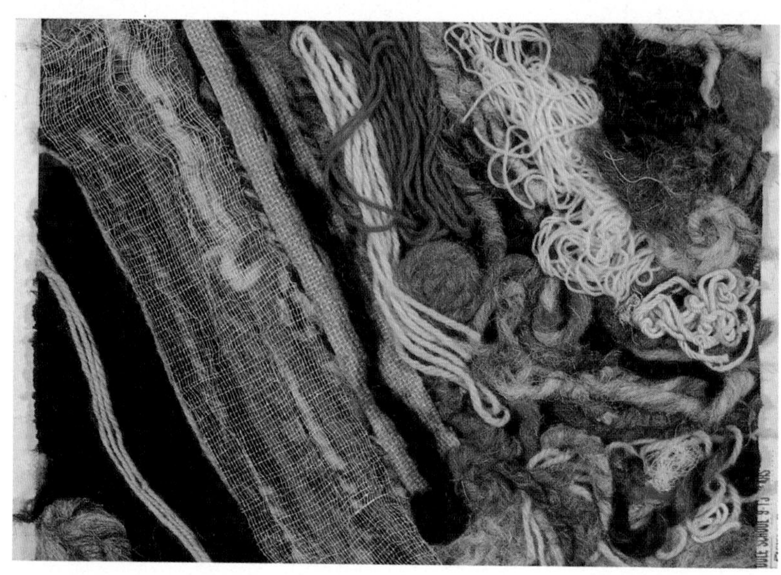

Wood Section - collage. Age 10.

dangers of being rigid or over-directive. In complete contrast, art educators will encourage us temporarily to forget the end-product and work with no fixed idea of the eventual result. They will urge us to concentrate on the process and whatever finally emerges is regarded as a record of what has happened. The trouble with this is that it is very difficult for most of us to work with absolutely no idea of what we want to produce.

Generally we feel we have to have something in mind before we start. If we decide to draw a pair of shoes we know well in advance we are aiming to produce a drawing of a pair of shoes. Producing a painting of a dream or nightmare will also involve a clear idea which is visualized well in advance. Whatever arguments are advanced for concentrating on the 'process' rather than the 'product' we ultimately need the assistance of both. They are complementary but how we actually handle them determines originality, creativity and the integrity of our art teaching.

Why art educators tend to applaud the process over the product is not particularly difficult to understand. Originality is most likely to be evident where the product has been changed, modified, reassessed and continuously developed by the children. Consequently the process which leads to this happening inevitably becomes a crucial concern of art education. Concentrating on the fixed and predetermined product leaves too little room for flexibility and decision-making whereas the emerging and changing end-product allows for considerable experiment. In experimental or adventurous thinking, children are not working towards something which is already 'there'. They are in the position of developing an idea which is not yet finished and adapting their first thoughts.

A fixed end-product, especially when it is predetermined by the teacher, is actually a form of copying. An example might be a puppet, made by the teacher and copied by the children. It acts as a very clear model. Slight variations to the design are allowed and there may even be some minor opportunity for children to produce differently finished puppets from each other. But they usually discover that their puppet is not quite so good as their neighbours' and not nearly so good as the example provided by their teacher. Disappointment reigns supreme.

A more flexible product would be a puppet devised by children who were involved in the process of taking decisions about design and construction. They had no more than a rough idea of how things would turn out and, most important of all, one model was not held up as an example or arrived at in stages prescribed by their teacher. They would, however, have built up some skills in order to make the puppet in the first place, practised looking for variations of approach and become used to changing the product as it grew.

Seeing creative artwork produced is rather like being at a play. We have a rough idea of what the play is about but we are taken into new experiences as it unfolds. Children usually know when something is not really their own work and copying examples holds few surprises. The more creative pieces of work are usually those which are not bound by rigid rules about how to achieve results and are rarely exactly as they were first conceived. As one teacher describes,

> The best advice I ever had when I was at art school came as a result of frustration that my painting was not as I imagined it would be. 'It never is', I was told. 'If a painting turns out as you expect it to be it ceases to live and you're not responding to what is happening on the canvas. Anyway, if it did turn out as you expected there wouldn't be much point in doing it would there?'
>
> (*Art teacher*)

Children need to have the psychological 'space' in which to generate ideas rather than follow set rules. The creative process (and the learning experience) lies between the glimmer of a child's idea and the final tangible product. Creativity, it could be said, lies in the gap between intention and outcome, means and not just ends.

One of the best ways of reinforcing this is to say that *the more clearly fixed is the end-product* in our minds before we start, *the less creative it is likely to be in the end.*

Of course, this does nothing to support the view that we ought to know what to do before we start. Are we therefore to be vague and indecisive in our planning? After all, teachers need to be very clear about their ideas and also take account of such things as materials, organization and time. Being vague is no way to capture the interest of children and in practice it is extremely difficult to think of organizing art without knowing what the session is all about. There are, however, ways in which we can be very clear and they involve action to be taken by ourselves and our pupils.

Rather than asking what end-product we want to produce, the questions we might ask instead are 'What do we want children to think about, what do we want them to encounter, what do we want them to choose, what do we want them to consider changing, how do we want them to use materials and what skills do we want them to develop?' We may, for example, want them to look carefully for shapes, change a shape or use it as a repeating pattern. We might want children to choose the materials most appropriate for an idea they have worked out roughly on scrap paper. Other parts of the process might be to generate images from imagination and fantasy, encourage children to arrange them in a drawing, adapt and change the design until it was as interesting as they could possibly make it. We might want children to try three versions of the same drawing or produce a collage from a drawing they have already made. Trying out different shades of colour, combining two sketches and enlarging a small section of a drawing are all tasks which have no fixed end-product. But they are nevertheless specific and clear and they encounter qualities of line, shape, colour, texture, paint and so on. The aim is to work towards refining the artwork in hand. Eventually it can be declared finished.

Of course it cannot be denied that seeing finished work in a children's art exhibition or on a visit to another school can be inspiring. The work strikes us as worthy of emulation and we want to try to produce similar work with our own children. For their part children are also often inspired by seeing each other's work. The way we might avoid directly copying is to speculate what skills can be developed and what concepts are involved in this example we have found. Instead of trying to work backwards to discover how the work was produced we can use the idea as a starting point and extend experience by allowing as many options and as much variation as we would in any other artwork. A further and more obvious solution is to encourage children to take the idea but look and draw from real life, and explore their own imagery. We still have a product in mind but have left open the option of exploring, changing, adapting and developing it.

In the previous chapter qualities and visualization were mentioned as being important. Even in the field of industrial design, products are designed according to what qualities we expect them to have. We may not know what a new design of supersonic jet plane will look like, but we do know what we expect it to do. Qualities such as speed, manoeuvrability and endurance determine the design of a jet. These qualities are not to be found in the component parts of the plane but are associated with how it will function. The analogy is not directly applicable to art because its concerns are more functional than aesthetic. But *qualities* as such would still be involved if children were trying to produce a drawing of a bird. If they were attempting to communicate smooth, soft fluffiness, or if their interpretation of a bird was that it was hard, mean and aggressive they could be dealing with qualities which were perfectly bird-like. There are additional artistic qualities such as brushwork, contrast, atmosphere and scale which might also be involved.

If we know what qualities we would like children to encounter we can be much clearer about what they are going to *do* rather than what they will *make*.

Choosing and deciding are processes in themselves and we need to ask ourselves:

What activities will allow children to use their imagination in their work?
How can they become more aware of colour qualities in their surroundings?
How can I develop their confidence to experiment with ideas and materials?
How can they use their feelings in what they do?
How can I get them thinking carefully about shape and pattern?
How can I develop their skills in colour-mixing?
How can I organize things so I allow choice in materials?
How can I develop their drawing ability?
How can I introduce them to design?

It could be that the way to develop expression through art is actually to begin with drama, build up strong mental images of dramatic action and move on to art. Alternatively, awareness of pattern and shape could develop through making rubbings from surfaces or through using a microscope and subsequently making drawings. On the other hand it may be important to bring specific examples of man-made or natural forms to children's notice. But the catalyst for planning these activities is usually a question, the most obvious of which is 'What do I want them to look at, imagine or recall?', a strategy which is far more satisfactory than asking 'What can we illustrate using art materials?'

It goes without saying that it will not be enough simply to bring things to children's notice and hope they will automatically produce art. What we ask them to do, how we encourage them to look and question, are equally if not more important. Children need to be pushed towards making comparisons and analysing what they see before they try to draw or paint. Much will also depend on what areas of learning are already under way and how well we understand what they can learn across the curriculum.

Originality in topic work

No particular mystery surrounds working through the focus of a topic, though in some approaches to be found in current practice originality is a low priority and creativity almost absent. A plausible reason for this is that it is not just art which is being encountered in topics and, as has been pointed out elsewhere, much of the material can be in the form of factual information. An advantage of topic work is that it offers teachers the chance to develop a variety of educationally worthwhile activities and can give coherence to an otherwise disparate content. Yet if we examine the content there are also particular ways in which *artistic* learning can take place. This is quite different from all the other things we expect children to do, such as measuring and recording, analysing and writing about their topic.

Every topic has visual content somewhere within it and offers opportunities for art and design. Each historical era, for example, is characterized by style in art, architecture, furnishings, weapons, costume, jewellery and adornment (as will be explored more fully in Chapter 6). The curves of one period of architecture are quite different from those of another. Decorative styles also offer the chance to explore and invent by using shapes, lines, curves and colours typical of the period. Topic work can, in this example, be a fusion of history and imagination. A more holistic approach to learning can be evident as art permeates history and history permeates art.

Recent years have seen a trend towards teaching history by encouraging children to imagine themselves living in the period of the time. A welcome feature of this approach is that children study the art and music of the period as well as political events. The material they encounter is not entirely confined to facts and information.

A severe handicap for the creative artist, however, is that because many topics tend to generate such a wealth of fixed information it is quite possible for this to displace creative thinking and originality. Who, after all, wants a new shape for a Viking ship or some creative spellings? Tudor beams which are at sharp right angles or star-shaped maps of Great Britain might be inventive but they are too far removed from fact to be valid. Suppose we are studying the life cycle of the frog or trying to draw details of a Roman villa. There are illustrative conventions to be observed. The shape of the villa must be as accurate as possible and the frog ought to look something like a frog. Yet in observing these conventions we should recognize that art is frequently forced into a role which is actually subservient to the facts of the topic. This role is none the less an important one but it is not necessarily creative or artistic.

Consider a class which is purposefully engaged in topic work. Children can be seen absorbed in activities like model-making, drawing ancient buildings and illustrating events. To all intents and purposes there appears to be art activity taking place and it may seem very unfair to be critical of art content for the way it happens to support factual information. Yet if it becomes solely (and the important word here is 'solely') a companion to facts, art is robbed of its unique and creative dimension.

We can see how easily the trap is laid. As one teacher puts it,

> I believe that art is valuable in that it gives a visual representation of the written work children do. It gives more meaning to the factual work and provides added interest to the topic.

So it does and there are occasionally times when we would want art to do exactly that. But must creativity in this age range become swamped by facts? Should art be only a glorious visual aid? The missing elements here are fantasy, imagination, expression and invention. Would we, for example, say that we believed language was important because it made the facts in the topic work clearer? Would we say that the reason for doing maths was to measure things in topic work? Or would we more honestly say that language, mathematics and art could all grow out of work on the topic?

Although children may have reached a stage where they are attracted by trying to draw realistically this is no reason why topic work should deprive them of the chance to use their imagination. Their concern for realism and detail does not mean that their creativity is dimmed or that they are for ever locked into a 'fact-gathering' strategy. Redfern (1986) points this out when she refers to the DES survey *Primary Education in England* (1978) which discusses painting and drawing less as arts than as a means of recording information and illustrating historical events. Redfern asks,

> Can aesthetic education, or more precisely, arts education, seriously be in hand when the main concern is something else – especially something involving matters of truth to fact?

Doubtless there are a number of well-established skills children use at this age which lend themselves to the recording of information and historical events. Tracing, writing and copying things is much easier to do than when they were younger. There are also so many tempting ready-drawn images to be found which provide examples for children to absorb and make use of. Yet imagine the consequences of allowing them to employ these skills almost exclusively as their art activity. Is an overdose of tracing and copying really such a good idea? The issue of product versus a more dynamic process looms large in the misuse of these skills.

A question which cannot be ignored is whether or not to develop artistic ability through topics at all. There may be many more worthwhile ways of stimulating interest in visual qualities and art-related problems. Perhaps confusion arises as we equate topics with themes (Chapter 5) where the focus can be more specifically an artistic one. Clearly, a theme such as 'colours' or 'liquids' is not so bound by historical or factual constraints as are topics like 'The Elizabethan Age' or 'The First World War'.

Not all topic work lends itself to art in the same way or to exactly the same extent. We have no right to expect that it ever will. At stake, however, is the significance of topic-work experiences we give children. Sometimes our emphasis will be on the aesthetic qualities of art, at other times on information and facts. If children find topics suddenly come alive because of the artwork associated with them, or art is meaningful because of a topic-related input, that can hardly be a bad thing. Teaching children through topics and including creative ideas, imagination and invention as well as facts may prove to be an original approach in itself.

5

Ideas in the melting pot

> We know from experience that the needs of the teacher who is actually going to do something are different from the needs of a teacher who is just going to talk about doing something.
>
> (*De Bono, 1976*)

CREATIVE thinking, idea manipulation, or 'putting ideas into the melting pot' are some of the ways we describe attempts to encourage the mind to make vital connections. Elsewhere the point has been made that forcing the mind to think creatively is a difficult if not impossible task. A more practical approach is to engage our mind in ideas and let it work as it will. In short, we play with whatever ideas emerge. The process is by no means a passive one, however, neither is it one which simply invades an idle mind (see Roe, 1975). The romantic view of the artist waiting to be inspired bears very little relation to the way most artists work and if we want to develop creative ideas we have to set aside time to give them specific attention. We must give our mind to ideas.

How might we do this without resorting to contrived techniques? Many teachers are already familiar with a random flow chart, word-spill, or web chart which results from a 'brainstorming' approach to problems. It must be said that these charts can look frightening to anyone not used to drawing them and they also tend to be very personal in style. As has been shown through countless study-skills courses, however, they provide a very useful way of thinking creatively about teaching and learning. Their purpose is also to avoid narrow thinking as well as generate a flow of unusual associated ideas.

Typical of these are Charts 1 and 2 (the process of making charts like these is discussed further in a previous book, Barnes, 1987). The guiding principle for making flow charts is that no idea is considered too ridiculous to be explored and thoughts must flow freely without the application of 'cold water' to them. A flow chart is not necessarily anything more than a catalyst to ideas and what matters is what we do with the final list of words, not the list itself. Connections between words are there to set off 'sparks in the brain' rather than sit proudly on the paper as a record of thinking already done. Stimulus is all important and the more ways we can find to fire ideas the better. Since the intention in Charts 1 and 2 is to produce relatively random collections of ideas, they can include activities as well as descriptive words associated with the theme.

Figure 8 shows a simple device for generating connections which could further stimulate ideas and images. Two circular pieces of card are pinned to a backing sheet so that they will spin or turn to connect any two words. Children can make their own collection of words or the word generator can be used as a resource for ongoing work. Options include fixing one disc and turning the other wheel, spinning both or chalking a new word on the blackboard and using both wheels alternately.

A development of this idea is shown in Figure 9 which works like a 'one arm bandit' by using different combinations of words or colours.

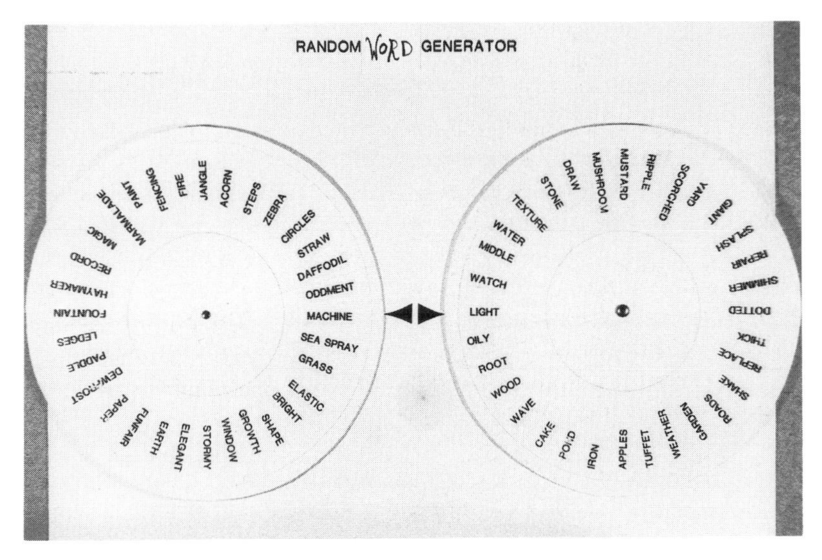

Figure 8 Simple Random Word Generator.

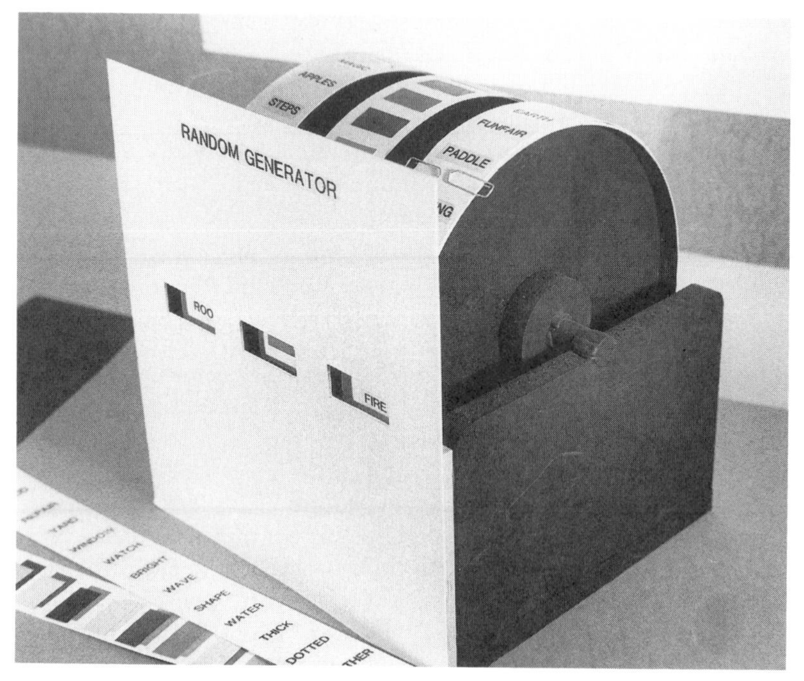

Figure 9 One Arm Bandit Generator.

From flow charts to useful outcomes

Charts 1,2 and 3 included here, are intended as stimulus for teachers, but there is actually no reason why children should not try to draw their own. (The relevance of these charts is discussed in more detail in the next chapter.) Further activities could include the following.

EXAMPLE 1.
Children take any two words from the flow chart and try to find examples of them in the environment, or alternatively from library resources. The emphasis is on looking and responding rather than remembering and imagining.

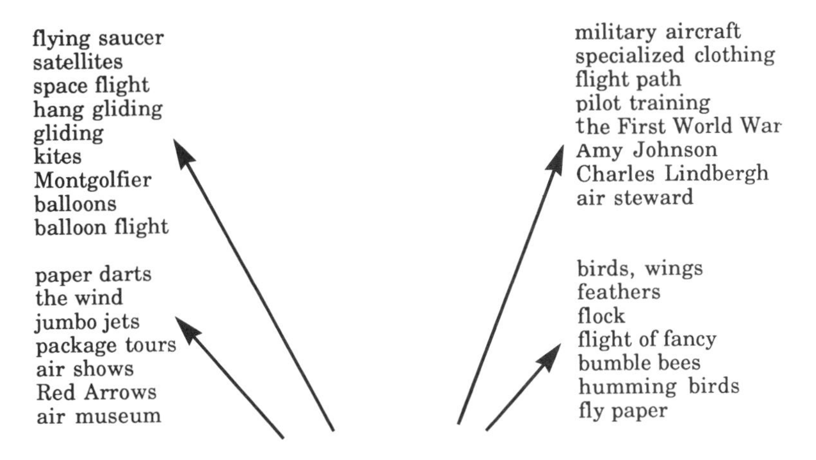

TOPICS WITHIN TOPICS

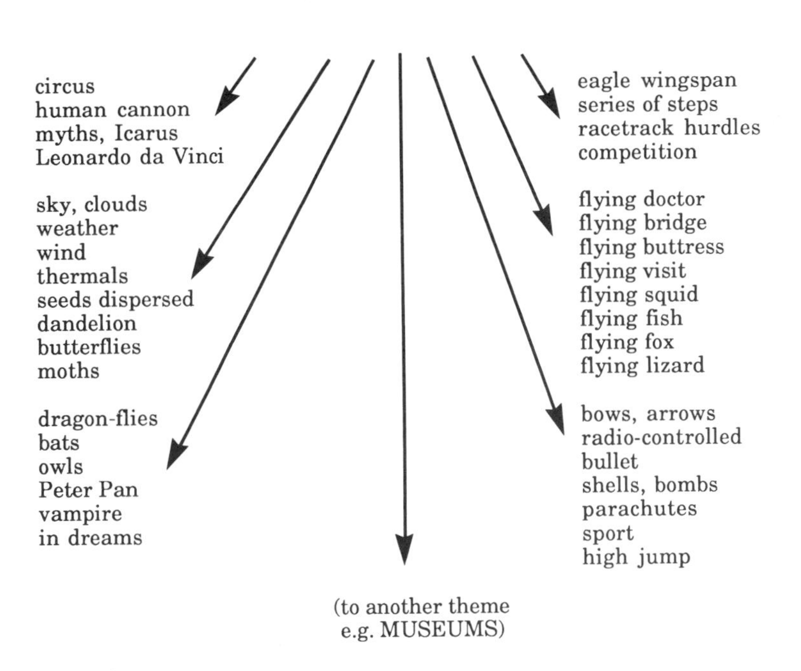

Chart 1

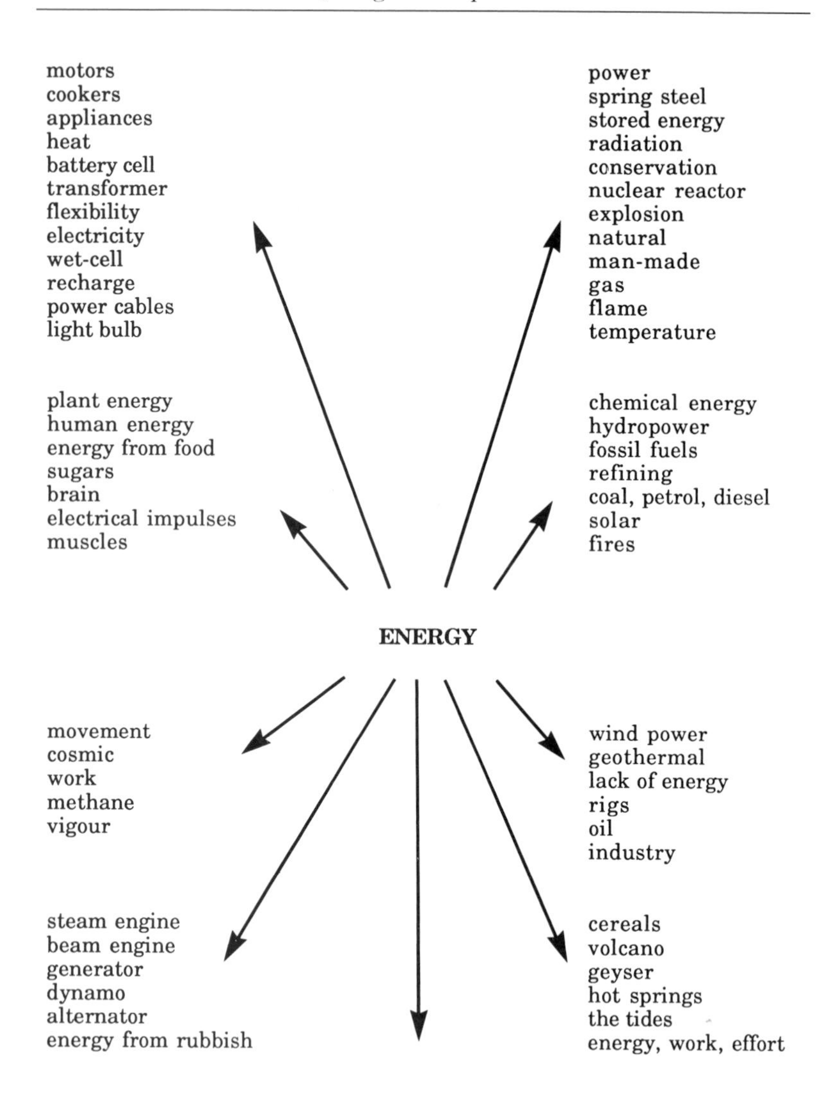
motors
cookers
appliances
heat
battery cell
transformer
flexibility
electricity
wet-cell
recharge
power cables
light bulb
power
spring steel
stored energy
radiation
conservation
nuclear reactor
explosion
natural
man-made
gas
flame
temperature
plant energy
human energy
energy from food
sugars
brain
electrical impulses
muscles
chemical energy
hydropower
fossil fuels
refining
coal, petrol, diesel
solar
fires
ENERGY
movement
cosmic
work
methane
vigour
wind power
geothermal
lack of energy
rigs
oil
industry
steam engine
beam engine
generator
dynamo
alternator
energy from rubbish
cereals
volcano
geyser
hot springs
the tides
energy, work, effort
(to another theme
e.g. CONSERVATION)

Chart 2

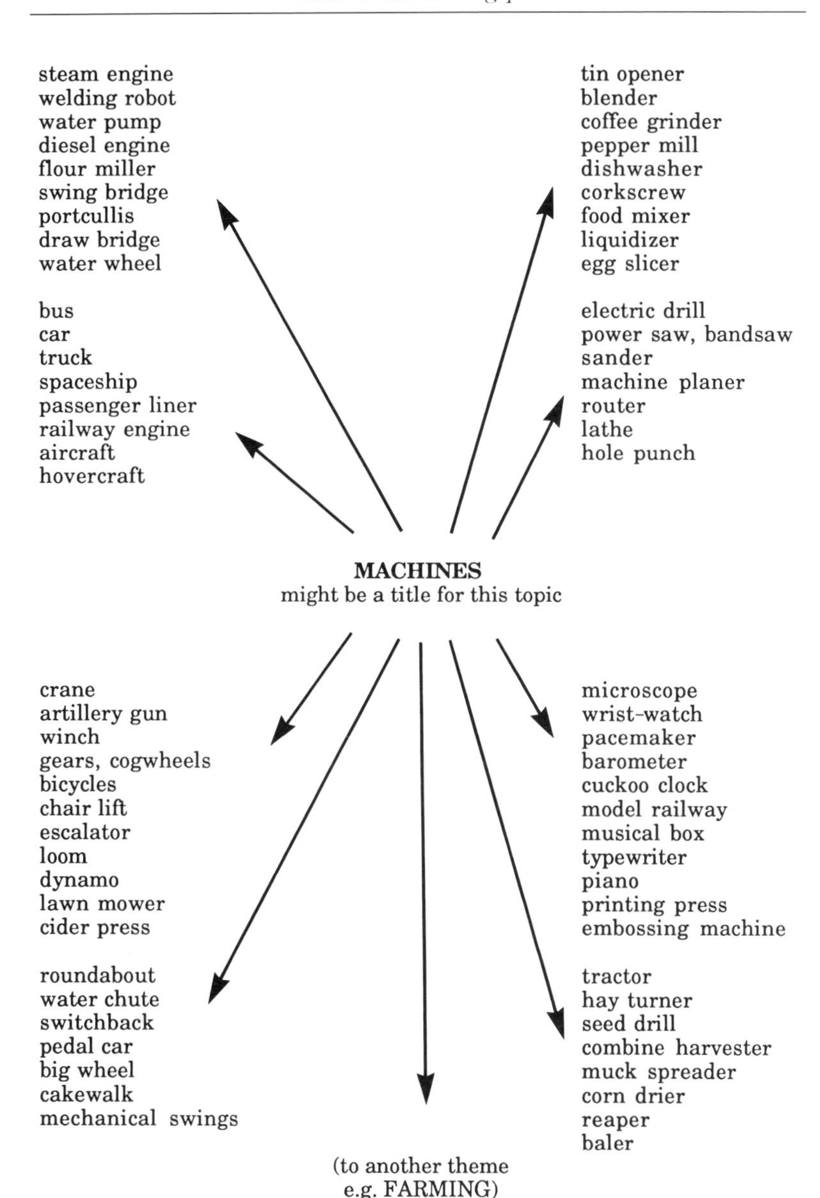
steam engine
welding robot
water pump
diesel engine
flour miller
swing bridge
portcullis
draw bridge
water wheel
bus
car
truck
spaceship
passenger liner
railway engine
aircraft
hovercraft
tin opener
blender
coffee grinder
pepper mill
dishwasher
corkscrew
food mixer
liquidizer
egg slicer
electric drill
power saw, bandsaw
sander
machine planer
router
lathe
hole punch
MACHINES
might be a title for this topic
crane
artillery gun
winch
gears, cogwheels
bicycles
chair lift
escalator
loom
dynamo
lawn mower
cider press
roundabout
water chute
switchback
pedal car
big wheel
cakewalk
mechanical swings
microscope
wrist-watch
pacemaker
barometer
cuckoo clock
model railway
musical box
typewriter
piano
printing press
embossing machine
tractor
hay turner
seed drill
combine harvester
muck spreader
corn drier
reaper
baler
(to another theme
e.g. FARMING)

Chart 3

EXAMPLE 2.
Children are given two slips of paper. They write one word on each slip. They then exchange one piece of paper with a classmate and see if they can formulate an idea, image or activity from the two words they now have. A further development is for the class to put together a flow chart using words from groups of children.

EXAMPLE 3.
Choose a medium such as drama, story, crayon, paint, collage, or pencil. Look at words on the flow chart and try to develop an activity in the chosen medium by making a connection between words.

The third example moves us nearer to taking decisions which fundamentally affect the outcome of what appear to be free or random ideas. In fact, 'freedom' or 'randomness' are not always the best ingredients for developing ideas. Constraints such as the inclusion of a particular medium like paint or pencil can be extremely useful and focus the mind in new directions. A constraint causes us to puzzle more consciously over the word pattern which is evolving.

The magic apple tree

Chart 4 shows a 'Magic Apple Tree' pattern of flow chart in which the constraint is that the word SHAPE, at the base of the tree, must breed two others which in turn breed two more. If a particular line of thought is not proving worthwhile or there is not enough space, then the flow of associated words ends with an apple. Unlike the random chart, there are decisions to be made continuously about the value of outcomes, slots to be filled and specifically two words to be found. The process is not quite like solving a crossword puzzle because crosswords have solutions which are fixed in advance. Yet there are similarities in that words have to fit the available space and we need to think of two associated words for every one we discover.

There are several ways in which the 'Magic Apple Tree' chart can be used. Each branch may suggest a line of inquiry, or alternatively could become the centre of a new flow chart. Words may refer back to the original word, SHAPE, or associations can be made between words from any part of the chart.

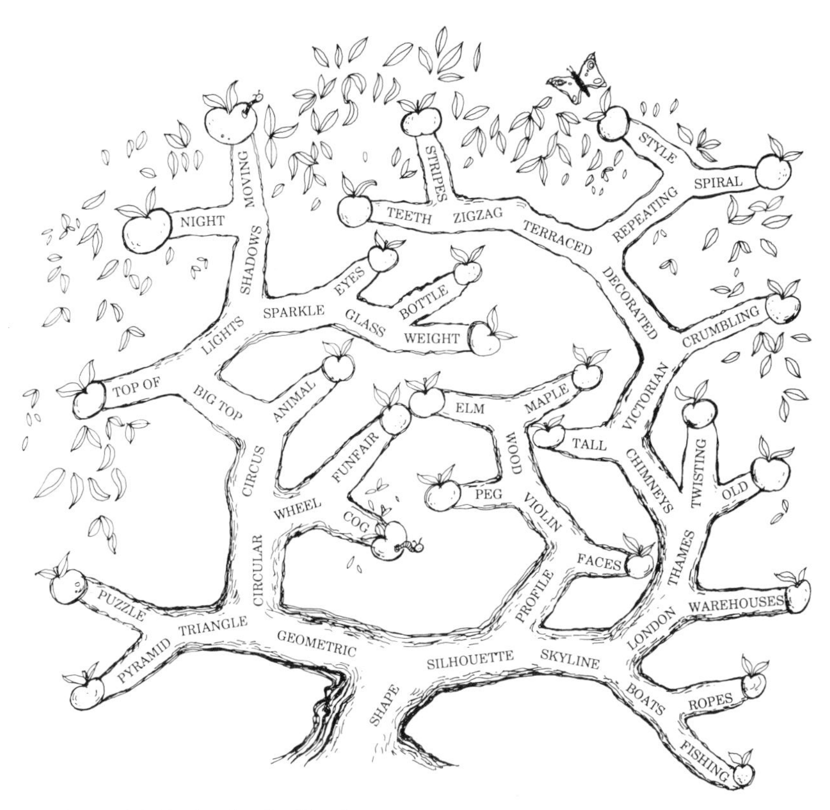

Chart 4 'Magic Apple Tree'

EXAMPLE 4.

A practical example of this would be to take combinations of words such as

SHAPE/DECORATED
SHAPE/SKYLINE
SHAPE/IRON

and work with children in groups. If the intention is to begin in art or drama, the outcomes can be left fairly open. However, we may want to introduce children to specific concepts in history, environmental studies, maths, or science, in which case it is not enough to use the flow chart in an all-embracing way. For the present we will keep this example a wide-ranging one but later on move towards concepts, skills and activities.

Working first in pairs, and later in small groups, children can take any two words as a starting point for developing their imagery. SHAPE and IRON may suggest iron railings, steam engines, spiral staircases and so on, evoking images which children might discover or research in their own environment. The shape of buildings and trees against the skyline can stimulate interest in comparisons of chimney shapes, branches and roof-tops. These comparisons might lead to discovering more about local history, producing collages of roof shapes, painting the silhouettes of trees or cutting out chimney shapes from black paper. The skyline silhouettes might be used in a symmetrical pattern or as a starting point for learning about the effect of contrasts between light and dark shapes. These could become three-dimensional cut-outs where silhouettes in black card or strong paper are arranged and stuck together so they are free-standing. They could then be arranged to form movable sculpture. Such sculptures could also lead to written work which had an historical slant or one which is set in fantasy, using imaginative story-writing as a means of expression.

EXAMPLE 5.
Children can try their own variations of the 'Magic Apple Tree' and three of these are to draw the tree first (before choosing words), increase the size of the tree so it fits a whole classroom wall, or develop mathematical sequences such as those in Charts 5 and 6 involving factors of 48 and 84. The concept of 'space' can be involved where the angles and lengths of line become important. Logic trees can also be a way of teaching multiplication, addition and subtraction.

Flow charts, skills, concepts and activities

One of the most difficult tasks is making use of a flow chart for thinking about skills, concepts and activities. Generating word associations presents less of a problem than does formulating a practical programme of work for children to do. The needs of the teacher who is actually going to do something are such that words must be transformed into action. A variation of flow chart which goes some way towards solving this problem is seen by comparing Charts 7 and 8. The first of these is in itself a variation of the random flow chart but divides the flow of thoughts into three separate segments.

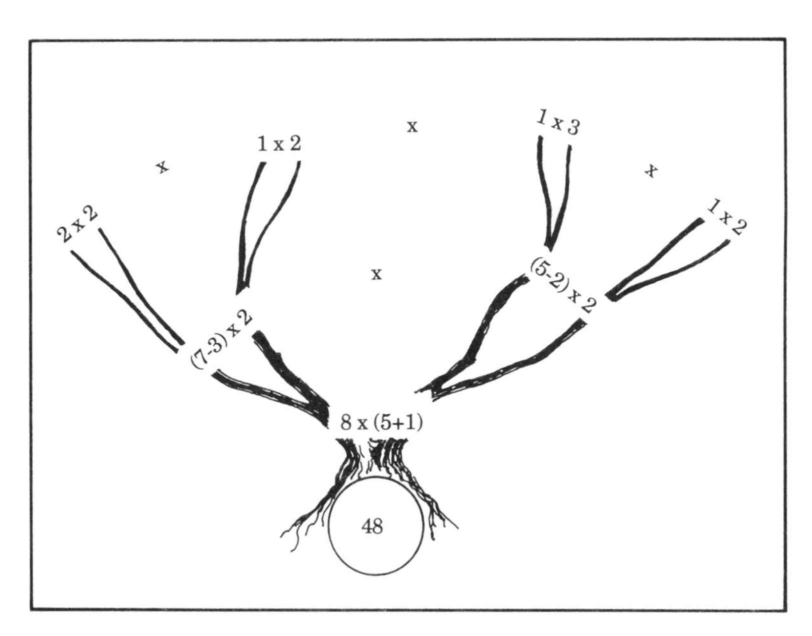

Chart 5 Logic Tree

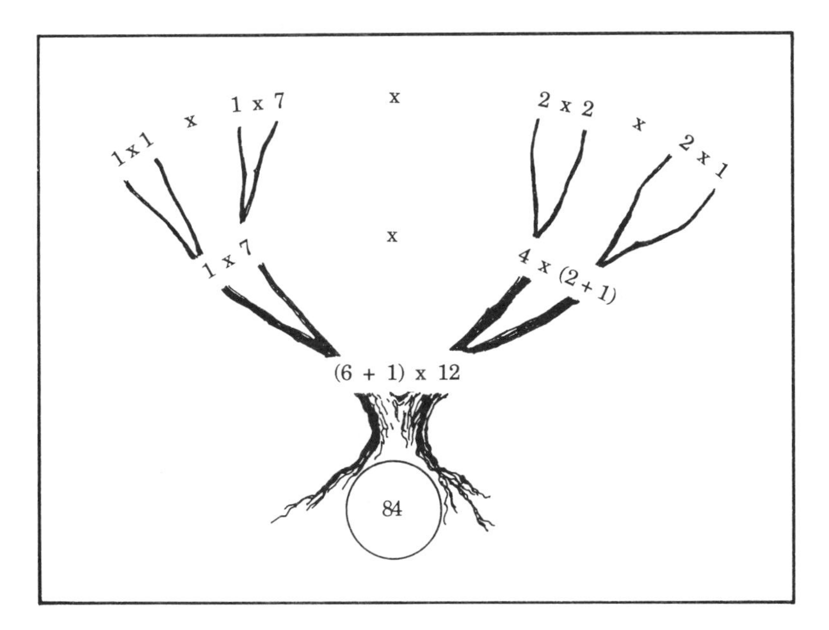

Chart 6 Logic Tree

An advantage of this technique is to channel the mind in more than one direction and encourage us to think more widely.

In Chart 8 there is a more conscious attempt to think about skills, concepts and activities. The list of skills and concepts is not unlimited and repeating them is somewhat inevitable. But the inclusion of them in each flow chart can still help us to arrive at worthwhile learning tasks and experiences because they match up with activities in uniquely different ways. The example given here is of IMAGES, ACTIVITIES, SKILLS/CONCEPTS. There are yet

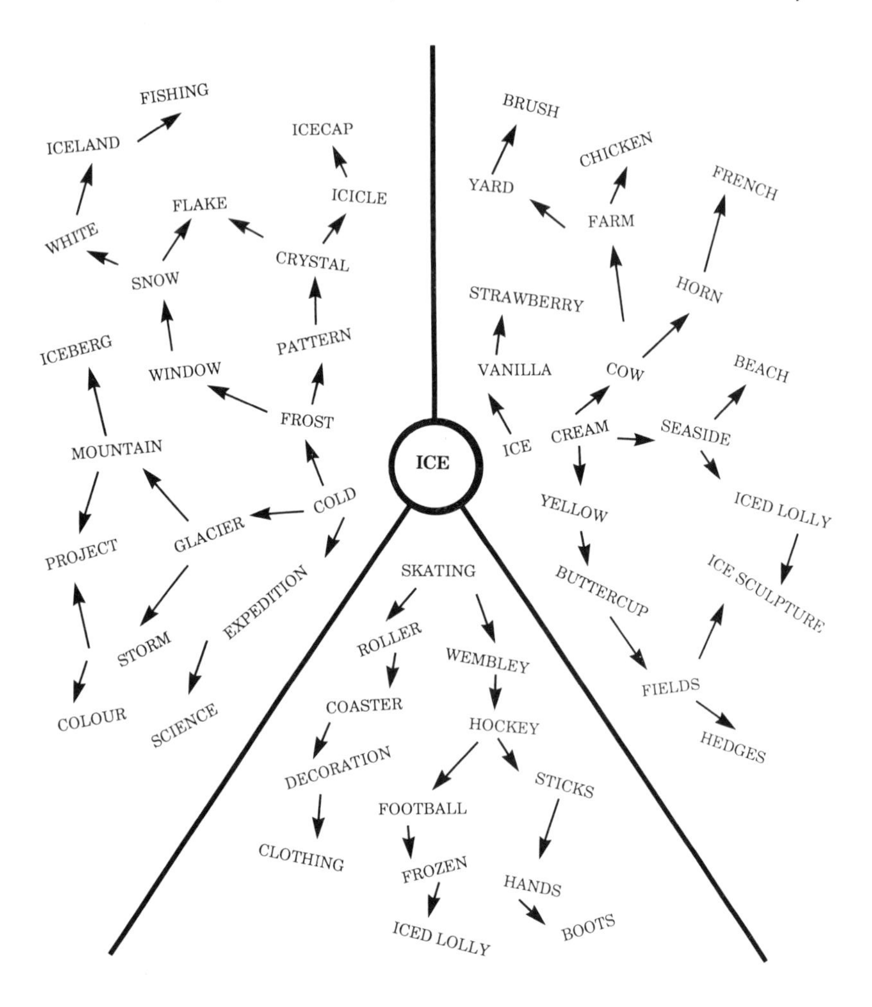

Chart 7 Ice Segment

further variations of the segment chart possible such as changing the headings of segments; for example:

PRACTICE TASKS
NEW LEARNING
DEVELOPMENT
AIMS
SUBJECT
CONCEPTS

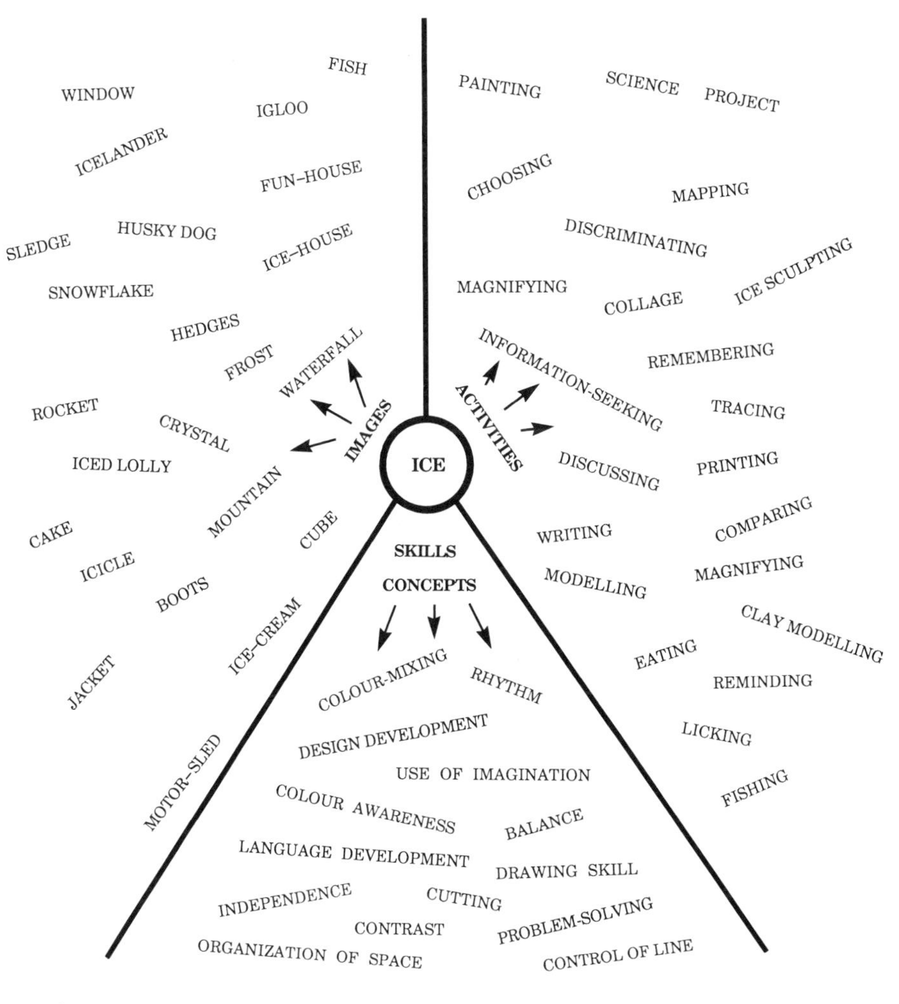

Chart 8 Ice Segment

Three segments seem to work better than do two or four (two are not enough and four confusing) but there need not be any limit on the space given to each segment. A sheet of A3 paper is a useful size, but teachers may well want to use much larger areas such as a classroom display board.

Logic boxes and role play

An intriguing way to develop creative ideas is through a 'Logic Box' like those pictured in Charts 9–14. The logic is constrained by the fact that only certain combinations of categories for boxes will actually work successfully. We cannot, for instance, have the arrangement shown in Chart 9

	ICE	WATER
MAN MADE		
NATURAL		

Chart 9 Logic Box

without seriously limiting the number of ideas which is possible. The logic does not work well enough.

A more productive and open-ended box would be that shown in Chart 10.

EXAMPLE 6.
An example of a logic box which has been filled in is shown in Chart 11.

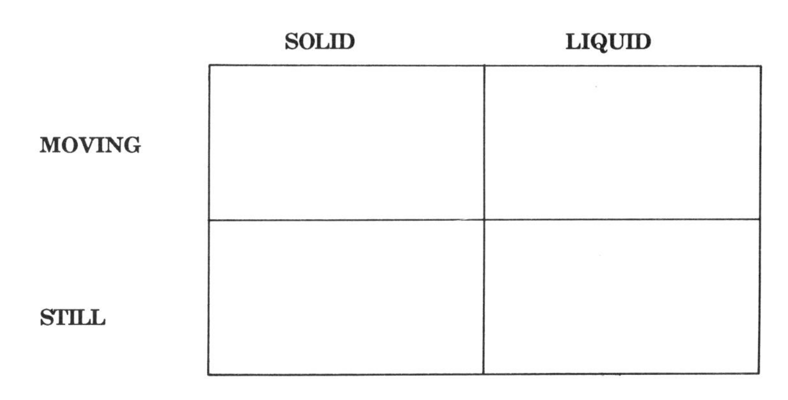

Chart 10 Logic Box

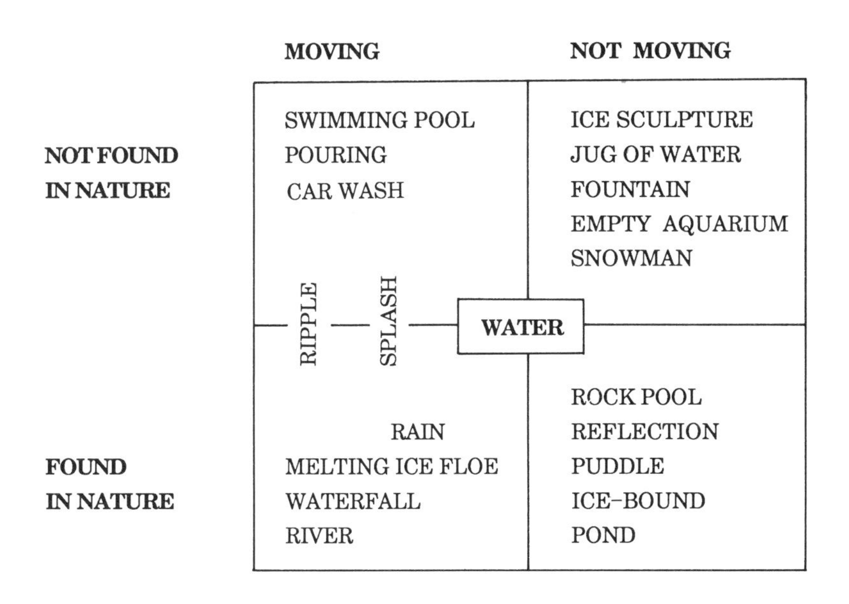

Chart 11 Logic Box 'Water'

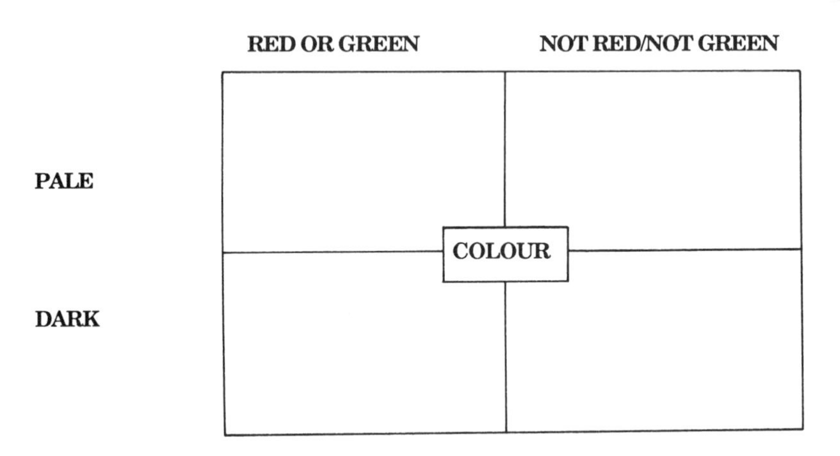

Chart 12 Logic Box 'Colour'

<table>
<tr><th>STRIPES</th><th>MAN MADE</th><th>ORGANIC</th></tr>
<tr><td>INSIDE</td><td>WALLPAPER
FURNITURE
PRISON BARS
BLINDS
FIRE GRILLE</td><td>STALACTITES
SKELETON RIBS
SECTION, SLICE
RED CABBAGE
SEEDS</td></tr>
<tr><td rowspan="3">OUTSIDE</td><td>RAILINGS
RAILWAY LINES
CABLES</td><td>SHELLS
LEAVES
SAND PATTERNS</td></tr>
<tr><td colspan="2">FURROWS</td></tr>
<tr><td>BIG TOP
DECK CHAIR</td><td>BLOOM
WAVES</td></tr>
</table>

Chart 13 Logic Box 'Stripes'

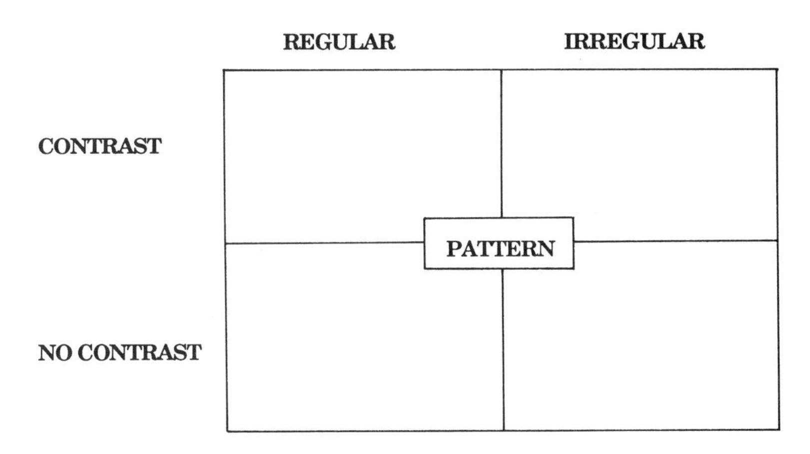

Chart 14 Logic Box 'Pattern'

EXAMPLE 7.
The logic box can be taken into the area of visual art by concentrating, for example, on colour, stripes, or pattern as in Charts 12,13 and 14.

EXAMPLE 8. ROLE PLAY
A useful way of encouraging children to be observant is through role play. This is not necessarily a way of drawing but a way of changing perceptions of the same environment. The children are asked to look at the environment as if they were

A PLUMBER	A CLEANER
A BRICKLAYER	A SPY
AN ELECTRICIAN	AN ARTIST
A GARDENER	A WRITER
A DECORATOR	A PHOTOGRAPHER

or someone else of their own choosing. The aim is to try to see a building from the point of view of where the plumber has put pipes, where an electrician installs wires, how a writer might use the environment as a setting or how a photographer could photograph in close-up or distance photography. The children discuss, compare and create images as a result of the role play. (Role play could, of course, very easily extend into drama and writing as well as visual art.)

Some useful themes

Through the Door
Early Man
War
The First World War
Sea
Dreams
Inside/Outside
Future Worlds
Space
Outer Space
Personal Space
Solid Forms
Future Transport
Fossils as Evidence of History
Fossil Patterns
Rock Studies
Plaque of the Future
Insects
Nests
Underground
Destruction
Myths
Chaos
Harmony
Gates and Fences
Cell Growth
Distortion
Distorted Faces
Flight
Balloons
Airships
Circus
Games
Sport
Transport
Energy
Machines
Industry
Advertising
Growth
Synthetics
Magic
A Visit
Structures
Clothing
Disintegration by Water
Raw Materials
Prevention
Ancient Egyptians
Holes
Empty
World in Motion
Rotten
Wood
Jewellery
Fairground
The Hobbit
Dragons
North American Indians
Giants
Mythical Animals
Events
Celebrations
Forces
Discoveries
Pollution
Garden Screen
Food
Pattern
Shells
Movement
Change
Accident and Intention
Pattern in the Seasons
The Big Freeze
Touch
The Senses
Memorabilia

The Cotton Trail
Trains and Boats
Inside the Earth
Jungle Life
Services
Windows and Doors
Kings and Queens
Races
Pollution
Shipyards
Solid/Liquid
Sea Defences
Fables
Masquerade
Spirals
People
Nets
Festivals
Networks
Sound
Staircase
Village Study
Time
The Body
Earth People
Air
Fire
Water
Printing
Shapes of Autumn
Infinity
Curves
Rivers
Castles
Photography
Past/Present/Future of a Town
Construction
Embellishments
Skulls Farm
Gears and Cogs
Decay
Fear
Stairways
Contrasts
Surfaces
Ritual
Repeating
Fences
The Planets
Microscopic Life
Topiaries
Stone Circles
Land Defences
Fungi
Trades and Professions
Humans Discover Metals
The Family
Market Place
Entertainment
Religious Art
Religions
Habitats
Buildings
Shape
Stories
Deserts
Beasts
Old and New
Plant Forms
Memories
Turn of a Century
Camouflage
Mathematical Machinery
Musical Structures
Puppet Characters
Colour
Chinese New Year
Volcanoes
Wrappers
Studies
Disintegration
Splash

Gaps and Spaces
Bubbles
Discovery of the Wheel
Turning the Tide
Mystery
Treasure Seekers
City Life
Communication
Windmills
Confrontation
The Vikings
Birth and Death
Prehistoric Surprise
Reflections
Unexpected Happenings
Substitution
Angularity
Racing
Medieval
In a Garden
Musical Instruments
Collision
Lettering and Patterns
Street Fittings
Light and Dark
Fortune
Water-mills
Noah
Railways
Wheels
Measurement
Ways of Fastening Things
Crumbling World
Communication
Fortune
What's It Made of?

Change in creative thinking

A major element of creative thinking is change. For example, if we combine some of these themes we can create further themes such as 'Pollution and Microscopic Life' or 'Treasure Seekers Old and New'. Eliminating words produces variations such as 'Pollution and Life', 'Seekers Old and New' or 'Old and New Treasure'. Alternatively, substituting a word could produce 'Disease and Microscopic Life' or 'Similarities deep within the Earth'.

Alex Osborn (1953) identified a limited number of ways in which any ideas could be changed. His concern was to apply creative thinking (which he called applied imagination) to real life situations. He pointed out that once we had formed an idea it was still possible to

SUBSTITUTE - put another idea in place of the one we had.
COMBINE - put together two or more ideas
ADAPT - change the use or purpose of an idea.
ENLARGE - make larger or more important.
REDUCE - make smaller or less important.
ELIMINATE - get rid of, cancel.
REARRANGE - change the order of, or reverse.

A natural tendency is actually to rule out flexibility at the moment when we think we have arrived at an idea. Perhaps the effort of formulating ideas acts as a brake to further thought. A common failing is to switch off from our search for ideas as soon as an apparently useful idea comes along. Yet it is precisely then that we need to apply these processes of change before making any final decisions. Flexibility means that we change ideas up to the very last possible moment and adapt them even beyond that and we need to indulge in 'professional dissatisfaction' so that we continue to explore ideas. However good an idea seems to be, it will most likely have a limited life if there is no room within it for change and flexibility. It may only fit the circumstances at its moment of birth.

Flexibility often involves the art of the 'U-Turn'. A well-known architect has made good use of flexibility and the mental U-turn in the early stages of his award-winning designs. He first gathers ideas together and consults with clients in as wide a way as possible. He draws the plans and then begins to ask if the client wants the floor plan reversed, rearranged to make use of the west light, a roof-garden added, a courtyard or entrance hall redeveloped. Not until the last possible moment is the plan finally drafted ready for adaptation as the actual building work progresses. By this means he ensures that the most serious problems are solved before the foundations are laid, even making a temporary model of the building to explore his ideas.

The process used here can be described as one of 'controlled uncertainty'. Like any creative activity, the plans are only regarded as a good framework for further change and development. The initial artist's sketch, mental visualization, synopsis of a book, plot of a play or architect's brief are vehicles of uncertainty over which there is a limited amount of control. It is not that we are unable to make up our minds. A well-planned project, topic or theme is so full of ideas and activities that we can select and reject from the abundant resource we have created. We can look at the range of activities which we might include and decide which one we think will prove to be the best starting-point. That activity becomes the seed from which artistic learning will grow and can be as clearly defined and organized as we wish it to be. From there we inevitably meet with uncertainty, which is the price we pay for embarking on anything creative.

6

Creative art in topic work

> We have specific areas of thought that we have to accommodate and these can be enriched by using a topic as a focus. I think I teach topic-work in order to make a relevant relationship for learning from the world itself. Children can relate to historical and geographical scale and there has to be some way of drawing together the different strands . . . but you can't do everything through topics because each area of the curriculum also has its own core, its own special characteristics which don't always touch on other areas of the curriculum.
>
> (*Primary headteacher*)

THE POINT has already been made (Chapter 3) that arts education cannot be the focus when the main concern is something else, especially something involving truth to facts. The implication is that if we are true to facts we are therefore not true to art itself. Truth to art, truth to history, truth to language, truth to maths and so on engages our attention in the 'core' of each subject as the above headteacher comments. That 'core' may well conflict with other factual concerns if its stock in trade is imagination, feeling, expression and fantasy. A more accurate description of topic work is that *the title of the topic describes a focus within which each subject area contributes qualities unique to itself.* The aim is to advance learning across the entire curriculum, through each discipline, yet forge links which ensure that the topic becomes 'big enough to be memorable'. The sum of the experience of topic work ought to be greater than its parts. Knowledge and understanding are not necessarily categorized in real life and topic work breaks down subject barriers which are often artificial.

The many different ways of tackling topic work offer varying opportunities for creativity. There is every reason to suppose that a topic chosen by the children could be just as successful as one chosen by the teacher. Some schools, on the other hand, have an inflexible list of topics which are to be covered during the year so that by a certain age children have 'done' the Romans. For other schools the approach is that each child chooses a different personal topic which they themselves research and carry out. By contrast, an educational visit might provide the substance of a topic, depending of course where the visit takes place and what happens. (It has to be said that some children are more interested in what they had for lunch and who was sick on the bus than where they went.) Alternatively, we can teach historical and social topics by living for a week in the style of the times and art may or may not enter into it. Further, we might stage an event or drama in the school and have the children respond to it by developing a topic. The topic title would not be known in advance but emerge as a consequence of the event or drama. Some schools have a 'whole school' approach with each year-group taking a specific aspect of a wide topic such as 'People'.

These are just some of the well-known ways of doing topic work and there are advantages and disadvantages whatever approach we choose. A class which is doing the same topic may have problems over sharing books, one between four, but collaborative group work and discussion is possible. Children working on their own individual choice of topic might have a considerably wider range of resources on which to call but unfortunately they are working in a rather isolated way with little opportunity for discussion and collaboration. There is no need to share books but their topic has nothing to do with anyone else's. Demands on the teacher of monitoring so many different individual topics can also be considerable and children may consequently find the help they receive is minimal.

Staging an event, such as a drama (historical or otherwise), has the advantage that the topic can begin in an action-packed way. Great excitement can be had, for example, by building a construction in the playground from wood, string and polythene, later developing a topic of 'Habitats', 'Castles', 'Nightshelter', 'Lifestyles', 'Poverty', or 'Constructions'. Events, such as the arrival of workmen in the school, a travelling musician, or an educational theatre company can also spark topics. Topic work which began by solving a problem such as 'What can we do with a hundred bricks?' and led on to a topic of 'Bridge-Building' would be an open-ended way to work. This approach could eventually lead to titles such as 'Railway Bridges', 'The Victorian Builder' and 'The Age of the Railways'.

An obvious advantage of beginning topic work by staging an event in the school is that resource books are not necessarily a first consideration. There is a welcome element of risk and the often criticized 'book-bound' approaches to starting topics are absent. A curious argument advanced in favour of starting with events and not books is that children are typically enslaved by books dealing with such topics as 'The Victorians' or 'The First World War'. If anything, books allow too much freedom rather than too little. The work can become random, unstructured in its learning content and prescriptive in its process. Some children when faced with a book about 'the Victorians' have really no idea where to begin.

> The main area of weakness is in topic work. In common with this type of work in the country at large, teachers leave too much to chance in their planning and are unclear about their objectives and the opportunities for learning that need to be exploited. As a result the work is often over-prescribed, undemanding and lacking rigour.
>
> (*Senior chief inspector*)

> I think as far as art is concerned the trouble is that people rely on images from humanities books and think children have done well if they manage to copy freehand . . . I think you're missing out on looking at projects through art spectacles using the language of shape, form, colour, pattern, line and so on . . . anything else isn't art, it's just superficial.
>
> (*Teacher*)

Topics which emerge as a consequence of some event pose other fundamental questions. If it does not really seem to matter what topic children do, what is the point of doing topics in the first place? The starting-point may be exciting but should the topic develop into absolutely anything we like? Does it matter what ground the topic covers and what children learn so long as the experience is an exciting one?

> Teachers are just ducking the issue if they think there's no progression to consider. You can have as hackneyed a topic as you like and it can be creative and purposeful . . . some teachers will make anything creative . . . others will waste a good idea. I want creative teachers but I'm not sure I want 'exciting' teachers if all it means is I have a school full of gimmicky clowns.
>
> (*Headteacher*)

It is very easy to criticize the twenty or so topic titles which regularly appear in schools. Clichés such as 'The Vikings', 'Flight' and 'The Victorians' are popular largely because they cover particular areas of thought which are considered interesting, productive and wide-ranging. It is not so much that teachers are running around trying to find something to do. There actually *are* topics for which the resources are more abundant and the content particularly useful. For example, Victorian items can often be borrowed and their design examined. Children living near York can visit the Jorvik Viking Centre or the National Railway Museum, opportunities which are well worth taking. Much of the artwork which comes from these visits and resources reflects the scale and excitement of the stimulus children have had.

Occasionally the scale of artwork is lost, however. This is particularly true when small topic work books are used for art. Rarely does 'art in an exercise book' seem to be successful and to work on such a miniature scale and call this art seems to be to miss the point. There is not enough space for artwork of any scale or importance to be put alongside written work. Drawing and painting Victorian objects, for example, lend themselves to the use of larger-scale art media reflecting the grandiose schemes of the times. Studying Victorian paintings, the life of the Victorian artist, Victorian inventions and Victorian fashions deserves displays which cannot be confined to personal project books. Miniature drawings may have their charm but in topic work they tend to be of the crudely illustrative, directly copied kind so destructive of artistic creativity.

As far as clichéd titles are concerned there are clearly different ways of starting even a rather well-worn topic.

> There are ways in . . . I sent the children home one Friday and they all had to make a kite by Monday. Obviously there were parents involved but nevertheless we had a lot of very interesting and varied kites on Monday morning and nobody had yet mentioned the topic of 'Flight'.
>
> (*Headteacher*)

At its worst, topic work becomes a 'cut and paste' activity in which relevant chunks of text and illustrations are copied. It becomes information-oriented and facts loom large as essential ingredients. The central issues, however, are not ones of scale or how clichéd the topic title might be. They concern what we want the children to learn from topics and how we intend to bring this about. Given the same set of books many teachers are able to be inventive and can actually exploit learning by looking at skills, concepts and attitudes rather than information to be learned.

> I think creative teachers are exploitative in lots of ways in that they're good at looking at situations and thinking 'What opportunities are there' . . . I look at the year and look at the context of their experience . . . I look at our school policy and ask what concepts, attitudes and skills do I want to enable. I make lists of things I want them to experience and I work in a structured way so they have the freedom to develop topics yet deal with concepts.
>
> (*Teacher*)

The issue of whether or not to use hackneyed and well-worn titles, books or events need not detain us long. Presentation, discovery,

Figure 10 Elizabeth I. Age 12.

Figure 11 Elizabeth I. Age 9.
(emphasis on lace)

creativity, achievement and self-confidence can be far more important motivating factors in learning than are original topic titles. Some teachers can make almost anything interesting for children from 'The Use of the Full Stop' to 'Onions I Have Peeled'. They no doubt look at development and learning potential rather than the topic title itself.

Events such as excavating a hole, making soap-suds patterns in the playground, drawing with sand, or building a massive construction with cardboard boxes are excellent ways to begin. By repetition, however, even these approaches can become clichés. The reason for this is that many intriguing ways of approaching topic work turn out on closer analysis to be merely different starting-points. Constructing with materials or staging events are often crucial ways to motivate children because they involve such a dramatic stimulus. It cannot be denied that the most critical stage of any topic work is likely to be its starting point. 'Creativity', however, lies more in the process which follows the starting point and exciting work can still be the outcome regardless of how clichéd is the topic title.

Clichés, the 'core' of art, interpretation and the Vikings

A 'cliché' was originally a printer's term for anything which was used over and over again. Words like 'and', 'the', or 'but' would be readily available to the typographer as strips of metal with all three letters on them. A cliché was a time-saver and the letters of the most commonly used words would therefore not have to be set one by one. In topic work repetition within the process of learning can be avoided by means such as:

(1) changing the starting-point
e.g. begin in drama, begin with maths, bring in bricks, collect thirty umbrellas and make a display in the hall;
(2) changing the concept
e.g. change concept of 'time' for concept of 'style';
(3) changing a topic title for a concept
e.g. 'Vikings' becomes 'Invasion';
(4) emphasizing similarities between the past and the present;
(5) emphasizing differences between the past and the present;
(6) emphasizing the use of historical material for poems and stories, art and language;
(7) making a considerable amount of practical artwork a feature of the topic;

(8) making discussion and 'role play' the most important features of the topic rather than practical artwork;
(9) taking each subject in turn and trying to emphasize the development of a specific concept or skill such as 'scale', 'quantity', 'fear' (concepts), colour-mixing, 'vocabulary-development', 'cutting', 'sticking' (skills).

This last variation is almost limitless in its potential and it is within skills and concepts that the 'core' of each subject will emerge. If we turn to the 'core' of art, skills and concepts have their own characteristics which are the key to specifically *artistic* learning. For example, we might say that in art and design we could take the over-worked topic of 'The Vikings' and choose to emphasize skills and concepts such as

(10) learning about line
(11) learning about colour
(12) learning about shape
(13) learning about pattern
(14) learning about design
(15) learning about the medium
(16) learning about a particular technique
(17) learning about texture
(18) stimulating an imaginative response to . . .
(19) developing colour-mixing skills
(20) developing skills in . . . (e.g. sorting, discriminating, measuring, discussing, drawing, arguing, microscope work, visual fantasy)
(21) increasing awareness of . . .
(22) consolidating work in 'contrasts' . . .
(23) exploring the qualities of . . .
(24) expressing the movement in . . .
(25) expressing feelings of . . .
(26) trying out/combining . . .

Each of these (and further variations of them) can be the catalyst to planning an art session. We decide on important skills and concepts and begin to establish the purpose and emphasis within an activity we would like to do. As far as a topic of 'The Vikings' is concerned this might include using the curves from a Viking longship as the start of a pattern. Another starting point is to let children learn about the Vikings through study of artefacts, such as Viking jewellery and pots, creating their own designs based on what they have researched. A third approach is to use events from history to stimulate imaginative paintings. By contrast, illustrating information is rather like copying a diagram or making a chart.

Typically the example of 'The Vikings' conjures up visions such as longships, sails, ropes, villages, houses, animals, utensils, costumes, shields, swords and the sea. In themselves they may suggest using art as factual illustration. Artistic concerns, however, are more those linking 'The Vikings' with mood, feeling, emotion, colour, line, form, texture, shape, pattern, design and so on. Above all, *interpretation* is a necessary feature of any creative artwork. Children might, for example, be analysing and interpreting the structure of boats through drawing. Design features, like the colour and pattern of the sails on a Viking ship, can also provide inspiration for work which interprets a Viking 'vocabulary' of visual images. Fabric designs and claywork can be inspired by Viking and Saxon artefacts such as jewellery and decorated shields.

The shape of a longship can, for instance, be used in combination with water patterns from the sea and waves. Perhaps children will study the designs of Viking helmets or costumes and make their own use of this imagery to decorate their drawings and paintings. Viking decoration on braiding might lead to the study of fabric patterns within a much broader historical context. Studies of a Viking village can stimulate interest in the patterns made by fishing nets, or patterns found on fish, fishing baskets and leatherwork. Children may draw Viking boat shapes which they overlap or superimpose as they develop an image which becomes a network of lines and shapes, a visual artefact for which Viking imagery has been only the initial stimulus.

Within a design, children might use a variety of techniques such as paper collage, wax-resist or printing. Concern might be for the exploration of surface qualities, colours, tones and textures. Artistic decisions might be taken about where to place one visual quality against another, how to make things stand out clearly or merge them into the background. Reading Viking legends could promote imaginative clay modelling as each story unfolded. Alternatively, acting out the drama of a legend might produce a variety of lively paintings, drawings and collages interpreting the feeling of the drama.

Interpretation is not new to art or, for that matter, new to a topic like 'The Vikings'. If we consider painters such as the French Impressionists, they interpreted and expressed their vision through light and colour. The Cubists interpreted through fragmented images in complex structures which used a multiplicity of viewpoints and perspective.

> I think fantasy and imagination in topics are vital. I wouldn't teach from a formula. With a formula you can feel you are covering the whole syllabus but you're not. For me it's creative if they imagine what it's like to be a Viking . . . Personally I don't work from books, set pieces or sets of workcards. I don't just want replicas. History is part fantasy in their minds anyway and I would be more interested in their painting a view from a Viking longship than copying a drawing. If you start from a creative perspective then that's what you'll get.
>
> (*Teacher*)

> I start with drama and get them to role-play what Saxons and Vikings did. That's the time we look at books and pictures. If you stimulate their imagination and get them to think of mood, atmosphere, patterns, dyes, woven and leather clothes, they are imaginative in their drawings and paintings . . . I like to have them think they're on a voyage preparing the ship and thinking what things will look like.
>
> (*Teacher*)

> The children need to look at the aesthetic visual elements of what they see so it's not so much Viking ships as a shape they can use in an inventive way . . . I would ask myself 'What am I doing if I'm thinking artistically?' The representational side of things isn't too difficult but the creative aspect makes you ask questions like 'Have you noticed what kind of curves are used in Viking objects like ships and shields?' . . . 'How can you express things like fire or fear? Might their artwork be something to do with boat design in general or shapes forms and colours we can find in fire or water?'
>
> (*Teacher*)

> I've given two lines representing the prow of a ship and said to the children 'What is it? Where does it go with you? What do you want to do with it?' and someone would put two lines the other way and someone else would want to trace it exactly and print with it, cut it out, change the colour and so on. And then I would reveal its source as part of a Viking ship . . . that approach leads to a lot of creative work. The children find other starting-points in their topic . . . they go outside the classroom and find shapes in the immediate environment . . . something inspires and then you have creativity. You have some movement or momentum in the work being produced.

> Movement means that some kind of process is going on doesn't it? You don't get momentum by saying to children 'Here's a Viking ship, you can draw it big or small and paint it any colour you like.' That closes off the possible art content of what you're trying to achieve.
> (*Headteacher*)

The 'core' of each subject determines many of the concepts which can be taught. Where historical concepts might, for example, be 'conflict', 'consensus', 'change' and 'continuity', artistic ones could be 'contrast', 'light', 'harmony', 'balance', 'line', 'colour' and so on. (Obviously, artistic concepts are concerned with visual phenomena so that 'harmony' and 'balance', in this context, are *visual* rather than musical or historical. We may, for instance, be looking at harmonious colour combinations or a balance of shapes within a rectangular piece of paper.) The very fact that there are marked differences peculiar to each subject is actually a bonus not a constraint. These differences are proof that each subject is a necessary part of the curriculum and we should be aware that ignoring the core concepts of any one of them deprives pupils of a whole dimension of learning. If education is not to be lop-sided, children need a musical or artistic 'core' just as much as they need an historical or scientific one. In a rounded education we should ask questions such as 'Where's the historical content? Where's the artistic content?' and 'Where's the mathematical or scientific content?' We can then begin to ask ourselves about the quality of the content we offer children.

There are various topics or themes which are peculiar to art in the same way that multiplication, geometry and division can be appropriately fostered in mathematics. Some themes, such as 'colour', will overlap art and science. Others, such as 'line' and 'texture' will be peculiarly appropriate for art and design. Whatever the topic title, it will generally fit more than one subject 'core' but cannot fit absolutely everything. A topic such as 'Steps and Circles' or 'Worlds of Fantasy' may be fine for dance, drama and art but to force historical, mathematical and geographical concepts to fit in may not entirely be the best use of topics.

Artistic stimulus

If we are to begin work in art and design there are four possible ways of stimulating ideas.

Photographic Themes
by Thomas Plowman

PEOPLE

Photographs courtesy Thomas Plowman

Photographs courtesy Thomas Plowman

SHAPE

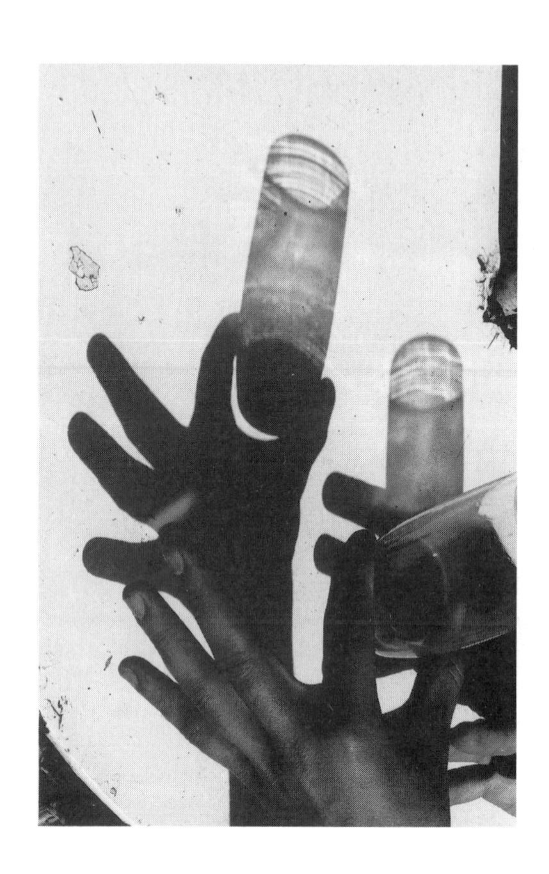

LIGHT AND
SHADOW

Photographs courtesy Thomas Plowman

OBJECTS

Photographs courtesy Thomas Plowman

TEXTURES

Photographs courtesy Thomas Plowman

Work may begin as a response to:

1. something SEEN, FELT, HEARD, or TOUCHED (children actually look at something, feel it or hear it and respond to the sensory stimulus);
2. MEMORY and IMAGINATION (children build up images in their 'mind's eye' and work from these);
3. MATERIALS (children explore a particular material and see what they can do with it);
4. A TECHNIQUE (a particular technique is demonstrated or, if already learned, used as the starting point).

Whichever area we choose, we will be involved in the other three areas quite quickly. As soon as a mark is made on paper we have touched on the first of these areas. We are also using a technique, our imagination and specific materials.

Throughout the art process, 'being exploitative' means thinking of all the possible visual elements there might be. If we are tied to

Four Areas of Stimulus

Example Area 1	Children look at lace, photographs of lace, visit museum, craftsperson visits school. Reference books available, e.g. 'Victorians', 'Queen Elizabeth I', 'Costume', 'Rural Crafts'. Discuss, sort, examine patterns and features.
Example Area 2	Imaginative stories involving elaborate costume, memory of seeing lace, imaginary lace curtains. Designing imaginary lace collars, imaginary tablecloth.
Example Area 3	Provision of string, glue, paper, lace doilies and fabrics as a stimulus for lace designs.
Example Area 4	Demonstration of technique for creating lace effects, e.g. use of pencil, chalk, hole punch, stencils, wax-resist.

Chart 15 Examples of Four Areas of Stimulus (topic of 'Lace')

history, then the art of the times will be a vital ingredient. We need to ask 'What kind of paintings did the Victorians collect?', 'What were they themselves painting?', 'What makes a Victorian painting look the way it does?' and 'Who were the Pre-Raphaelites?' We need to look at the design of clothing, boots, furniture and architecture. Most Victorian architecture is embellished with pattern. Ironwork is a feature and interiors boast elaborate wallpaper. There is also a wealth of visual stimulus emanating from the Victorian theatre. Designs by children could include studies of theatres taken from resource material and they might produce a toy 'peep-show' made from a cardboard box or make a model theatre.

Development of 'lace' projects can include designs based on
looking through layers of lace
sticky-cake doily displays (doily used as starting point for 'still-life' cake display leading to painting, drawing, print, collage)
designing lace bonnets
3 pencil-crayon drawings of lace
a theme of 'lace curtains in the wind'
a theme of 'windows and lace curtains in the Victorian street'
a theme of 'the Victorian table'

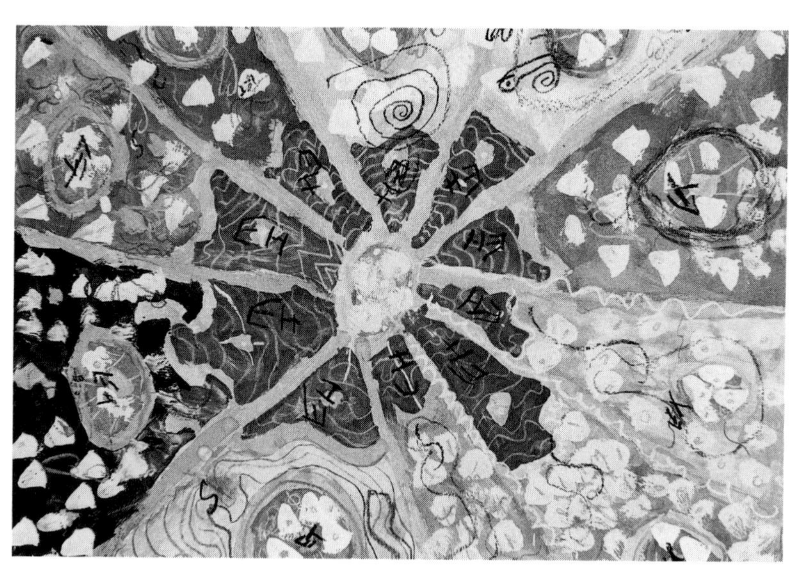

Figure 12 Painting based on Victorian Lace. Age 8.

Figure 13 Lace Design. Age 10.

Figure 14 Lace Fabric Prints. Age 12/13.

a theme of 'the Victorian feast'
a theme of 'Victorian embellishments'
a theme of 'lace-effects in Victorian ironwork'.

Children might explore twentieth-century colours in a Victorian-inspired pattern. They might design Victorian hats, Victorian jewellery, Victorian wallpaper, Victorian samplers or Victorian board games like 'Snakes and Ladders'. The point would be to exploit the patterns, colours and designs and learn something of the style of the period, not illustrate as a visual aid might do.

Further examples of art activities

(1–5, Victorian topics)

1. How many different ways could you use any shape drawn from a Victorian railway station? Examples are: as a relief (lino) print, as a card print, as a stencil, as a silhouette, as a repeated shape on a tablecloth, as a drawing in its own right, drawn many times as the start of an abstract painting expressing 'Victoriana' or as the background for a stage set for a ballet.
2. How obsessed do you think the Victorians were with details in their art? Make a drawing of part of a Victorian building or a Victorian costume and spend a couple of days fiddling with detail like cracks in stonework, the surface of bricks, the embellishment of windows, wood grain, shoes, buttons, button-holes, eyes with lashes, and detail on fabrics. Try to transfer this obsession with detail to something from the twentieth century, such as fashion and fabrics or interiors of the 1930s.
3. Collect and draw three Victorian objects. Use these exclusively as the way to begin a topic called 'The Victorians'. (Alternatively, begin with Victorian pattern and progress from artwork based on this to the topic 'The Victorians'.)
4. Take the theme of 'Cast Iron' and study, research, find examples. Photograph, draw, design e.g. coal-hole covers, drain covers, railway architecture, railings, gates, church fittings.
5. Study the design of Victorian woodwork, windows, fences, doors, furniture. The aim is to extract shapes by studying a small section or detail in wood, e.g. a repeating pattern based on wooden gates, a collage of windows.

Figure 15 Costume Drawing. Age 11.

(6-10 Visual art topics)

6. Bring in umbrellas. (These are 'put up' and displayed as a construction in the school hall.) Make drawings from the umbrella construction and use this as a starting point for a painting or print. Topics of 'Weather Patterns' or 'Floods' emerge. Designs produced for the decoration of golf umbrellas. Umbrellas used in drama, story-telling. Simple science of construction, science of fabrics which repel water.
7. Collect photographs on a theme such as 'People', 'Masks', 'Ourselves', 'Textured Surfaces'. Display the collection and use it as a starting points for artwork. Studies of facial expression, eyes, surfaces, pattern.
8. Study part of a photograph of any natural form and use the resulting drawing as the basis for a painting. Later develop this to include collage, print, modelling.
9. Make rubbings from surfaces, compare, contrast and use for collage. Add drawing, colour-wash or additional crayon embellishment.
10. Using hand lenses, examine and draw from stones, leaves, seeds, flower heads, minerals. Selection of the medium is a decision which influences the outcome.

Where an historical resource is involved, an aim is to become immersed in the art of the period.

> Two or three lines based on a longship say more about the Vikings than three hundred illustrations from a book . . . and if we can only tune children into that and teach them they are actually using an artistic language . . . if the work went off at a tangent and left the Vikings behind altogether it wouldn't worry me at all . . . they would have had a good stimulus for artwork.
>
> (*Teacher*)

> If a topic can take in an environmental issue, even better because you can link with nature and man-made forms which you can actually get to grips with. If a teacher is stuck with books I'd say 'Get out of the classroom into a different environment' . . . they need to respond to things . . . one of the worries I have is that children research things for which there's so little reference . . . we're doing a topic about the building of the new by-pass. That's fine because we can consider all sorts of visual ideas around that experience, go out and actually look at things.
>
> (*Teacher*)

Figure 16 Doing the Lambeth Walk. Age 11.

Creative teachers will choose more than one way to approach topic work. There is much to be said for choosing the starting point after deciding what it is we want children to learn. In the examples described so far, skills and concepts are a priority. Sometimes learning through art will necessitate a school visit, sometimes an event and on other occasions using books and photographs. The aim is to be flexible enough to choose an appropriate way of learning rather than to entertain children and be 'exciting'. Whatever the topic happens to be we should have originality in mind as a desirable aim and, more importantly, interpretation as its executor.

7

Resources and organization

> If you want children to get through your materials fast, then don't encourage them to think about what they're doing. If you want to conserve materials and use them economically you must teach children not only skill in handling materials but how to spend time thinking and planning what they will do . . . the aim is not to reduce consumption of materials but it does seem to be a healthy side-effect of good art experiences . . . I think it's rare to see work of quality which has been badly organized using a vast amount of material.
>
> (*Headteacher*)

PARTICULARLY in the 8–13 age range, resources and materials become increasingly critical as they influence learning at a deeper level. Children have a greater capacity to control media, explore materials extensively and build on their developing skills. Most noticeably they become much more interested in visual detail and are receptive to working from observation of real-life objects rather than relying on symbols to express ideas. As many teachers will recognize, this stage of children's artistic development, from around 8 years of age onwards, is usually called 'visual realism'. That is to say that children leave behind advanced forms of symbolic imagery and become more interested in the conventions of drawing in a visually realistic way. (A more extensive analysis of earlier stages of development is discussed in *Teaching Art to Young Children 4–9*, Allen & Unwin, 1987.)

An excellent opportunity exists at this stage for encouraging children to see in a detailed way yet retain their interpretive rendering of the world. The chance is there for them to become much more spatially aware than before, allowing objects to overlap in their drawings and have some sense of perspective. No longer, for example, do we see people drawn side view with both arms included. One arm disappears from sight if the person is turned away from us. The 'realism' is one of shapes existing in space, detail in eyelashes, buttons, carefully drawn teeth (some of them missing) and people placed in such a way that part may be masked by the detail of something else (Figure 17).

Visually stimulating resources are an essential catalyst to developing children's ability to respond in an artistic way and develop skills in observation. Children are not like art students who are expected to find their own resources. The assumption is that art students have already developed the habit of looking around for ideas. For teachers there can be no such assumptions and many create a display of interesting objects and photographs as part of their ongoing classroom organization. Perhaps they have a collection set up for the whole week or one which is built up over a few months. Children bring in things to study, or each teacher in turn is responsible for providing a display for the whole school.

Figure 17 Schoolgirls in the Garden. Age 12.

> I do a lot of observation work even if it goes into the realms of fantasy . . . I bring in all sorts of things they haven't seen before and I'm trying to make them aware of colour and pattern in their environment . . . very often the car's full of things I want to use later in the week for artwork.
>
> (*Teacher*)

This is by no means an unusual way to work but it brings with it a problem which has been a continual source of difficulty for art education. Developing accuracy in drawing and observation can sometimes exclude creativity, invention and interpretation. The more 'realistic' the drawing becomes the less it may have those qualities which previously gave it expression and a certain unsophisticated charm. The question often posed is 'How can I be accurate yet still interpret what I see rather than represent it?' This difficulty is not helped by the fact that careful representation of objects such as natural forms has a long tradition in art and design. On the one hand we want children to develop accuracy in drawing. On the other, that accuracy must lead to imaginative interpretation rather than study for its own sake. In other words, children need to use resources in an interesting and expressive way if they are not to become bored by mindlessly drawing twigs, shells, minerals, seed heads, bottles and crushed drink cans.

> It's a question of attitude. They're studying seed heads in order to find out about natural forms . . . and in the end I want their drawings to have a special personal quality and be selective rather than generalized . . . you get too many children trying to put line and shading absolutely everywhere so they don't express anything in particular. I try to get them to use their drawing to aim for things like 'contrast', 'surfaces' 'variety in lines' or 'magnification' and then you have something special . . . I want them to look carefully but see so much that they can't possibly put everything in.
>
> (*Teacher*)

Paradoxically, the more accurately children observe, the more interpretive and expressive the drawing can actually be. They no longer generalize by trying to include everything they can but look for details which suggest particular qualities which might be there. It cannot be said too often that artistic expression is ultimately about *qualities* and gathering resources for art involves considering

Figure 18 Stones - mixed media. Age 12.

qualitative characteristics of both natural and man-made forms. Such qualities might include

the delicacy of petals
the symmetry or asymmetry of a seed head
the flowing line of a twisted tree root
the softness of fur and feathers
the balance of shapes when objects are placed on a mirror
the sharp-edged quality of minerals
the reflective quality of shiny surfaces
the complexity of surface pattern
the contrast of strong lighting
the contrast of silhouette against complex pattern
the contrast of colour.

If we want working from resources to produce *artistic* results there has to be an *artistic* emphasis in the way the resources are observed. This crucial point is summarized by a teacher who says

> We develop work from the local environment, things I bring in or personal experience and usually the children are set a task such as looking for lines or concentrating on such things as shapes, patterns and so on . . . or expressing atmosphere or mood. There *has to be something in particular we look for.*

A good example of resource material which is stimulating can be seen in Figures 19, 20, 21 and 22 showing still-life groups which a primary school teacher sets up in the classroom for the whole week. These are no ordinary still-life groups and her approach is to find patterned fabrics and decorated objects for the children to draw and paint. There is already an element of interpretation and imagination evident in the way resources have been selected. Each group of objects contains strong 'artistic' elements even before the observational work begins. The groups are heavily loaded with pattern and the work which results reflects the highly specific content (see Plates 4, 29). Given that the children have already developed some skills on which to build, the equation here is a simple one. Aesthetically stimulating objects equals aesthetically interesting artwork.

Figure 19 Still-Life Group.

At this crucial age of visual realism the children who are working in this school are challenged to draw things which overlap in such a way that the space on the paper must be organized to take account of the space within the group of objects. It is very difficult for children to make an inspired drawing of, for instance, a solitary teacup or a pair of pliers, let alone make them expressive and interesting. An obvious reason for this is that to draw a solitary object on a blank sheet of paper takes no account of its relationship with anything else. 'Draw

Figure 20 Still-Life Group (see also Plate 29).

Figure 21 Still-Life Group.

Figure 22 Still-Life Group.

me a plum' is hardly as exciting as drawing plums on a decorated dish accompanied by other fruits and using patterned fabrics as a background. The elaborate collection of objects allows for discovery of special qualities which, in turn, find their way to the drawings.

A parallel experience to this is one of learning to play a musical instrument. We can practise indiscriminately or practise in order to develop a particular quality or skill. How many amateur musicians know the first page of a sonata very well but flounder as each subsequent page is practised? Practising the same piece of music over and over again without focusing on qualities, especially the same first page, can result in rehearsing the same mistakes. Having a purpose in mind for each practice session, such as improving sound quality, developing contrast, concentrating on rhythm, attending to dynamic markings, giving attention to the last page of music as well as the first or aiming for accurate tuning informs the search for improvement. There is some focus to the practice and, as the art experience was concerned with 'looking', so in music there *has to be something in particular we listen for.*

Resource areas, such as the extensive one in Figures 23 and 24, are a valuable alternative to taking children out to draw and gather material for themselves. This particular arrangement of resource space became an important feature of the classroom environment. A resource area is still second best, however, compared with children finding their own resources but it does serve to bring attention to specifically interesting features and visual qualities. After all, looking at a fragment of bark or a stone inside the confines of the classroom can influence the way children see these in the rest of the environment.

Artists continually respond to things around them but a very important function teachers have is to bring visual resources to children's notice by talking about them in detail. Clearly we cannot follow children around pointing things out to them all the time and a resource area in the classroom (however small is the resource) gives teachers the chance to use an artistic language of shape, pattern, colour and so on. The very fact that these words are used reinforces a particularly artistic vision.

Enthusiasm for looking at things with the eye of an artist can be infectious when aesthetic qualities are discovered. Intricacies of shape and design cannot be described very well unless we have examples to hand. In that process of discovery, nature offers the artist an apparently infinite variety of forms from which to learn. Curves, decoration and above all light and shadow have considerable impact. The effects of weather, for example, especially the changes of light, dramatically accentuate the natural forms around us. Fundamental to art education is the need to heighten our perception of what is already there and absorb visual phenomena as they become evident. We cannot force children to respond to natural forms but we should take account of the fact that they are undoubtedly fascinated by them. Possibly their curiosity is an extension of early learning when they bumped into objects or chewed them to discover what they were like.

Close-up photography of natural forms illustrates the way in which nature can inspire imagination as well as being worth careful objective study. A sense of scale is removed in many of the images reproduced here and they invite us to imagine caves and caverns, imaginary planets and environments. In practically any natural form we care to magnify there are hints of the landscape or ocean-bed from which it came. Nature repeats its forms and patterns from the microscopic to the gigantic in scale. Often a fragment of rock holds the key to an entire cliff face as its essential form encapsulates a much grander scale.

It is no surprise that using hand lenses to draw fragments of natural form is popular with art teachers. The absence of scale and many of the clues which allow us to recognize things fire the imagination. It is as if the essence of nature is in the imagination. Certainly the painters Edgar Degas and Georges Braque (see Goldwater and

Figure 23 A Resource Area.

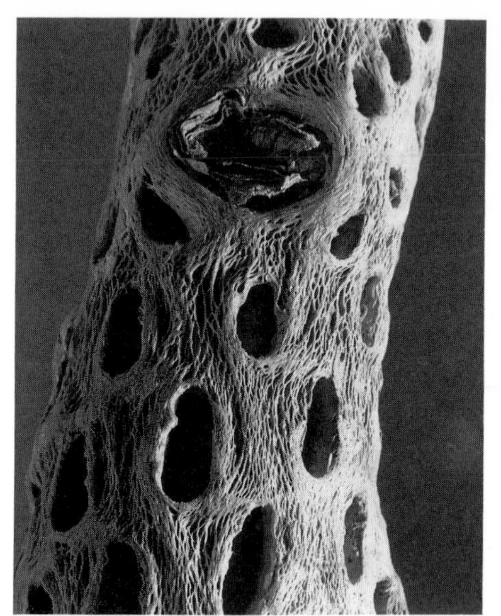

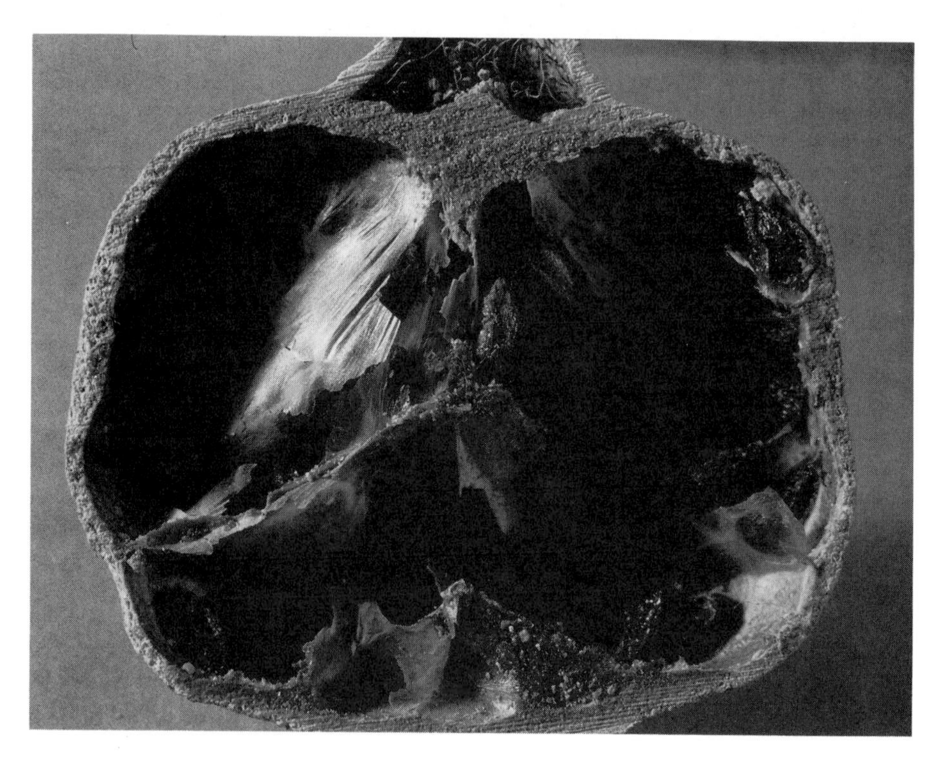

Figure 24

Treves, 1976) wrote about their art in relation to the importance of imagination. They were concerned with making our imagination work as spectators of their art as well as observing nature accurately. Their cryptic comments on nature, imagination and imitation are worth including here.

> The artist does not draw what he sees, but what he must make others see. A picture is first of all the product of the imagination of the artist; it must never be a copy. If then two or three natural accents can be added, obviously no harm is done. The air we see in the paintings of the old masters is never the air we breathe.
>
> (*Degas*)

> One does not imitate appearances; the appearance is the result. To be pure imitation, painting must forget appearance. To work from nature is to improvise.
>
> (*Braque*)

This is not to deny the value of studying nature accurately and undertaking work which is still in the realms of representation. Braque's comment that to work from nature is to improvise may seem too subtle to make immediate sense. Yet children respond creatively when experiences have real meaning for them and there is no better teacher than nature whether for study or to stimulate the imagination. Studying nature accurately in Braque's terms stimulates the mind to add something personal to the artwork. He does not make too sharp a distinction between the real and the imagined.

Within the environment itself, however, there are also man-made areas of special interest which can similarly fire our imagination. Railways are evidence of our industrial past as are ageing warehouses and factories. A specific focus such as 'the coast' provides abundant resources in the shapes of stones, weathered sea defences, birds, feathers, flotsam, fish and insect life. Any one of these can act not simply as something to be recorded, but as a springboard for developing artwork (Figure 25).

A further resource is to be found in the work of other artists. Either in reproduction. or as originals, many local authorities have built up collections of work which tour the schools. From these some excellent children's work has resulted. Studies of reproductions can lead to pieces of work on the same theme (see Chapter 10 and Figures 26 and 27). The focus of attention is on learning how artists have used materials, colours and visual ideas to interpret their world. (See also Plate 26 for an example of work based on that of the artist Robert Delaunay.)

Figure 25 Development from Feathers. Age 9.

> I got some large colour reproductions of Rousseau's 'Jungle' and I'd ask questions like 'What's Rousseau done with colour? How has he organized pattern . . . a lot of teachers don't really ask enough detailed questions . . . you have to inspire them with your own joy of looking at things and it does take time . . . it's a bit like learning to read and it happens gradually.
>
> (*Teacher*)

The elaborate set of resource 'boxes' in Figure 23 is only marginally different from setting up a school museum or making use of the local museum service. Handling real museum exhibits is sometimes possible through contacting museum curators and their staff. Often they are very willing to help and there are in some cities special school's collections set up specifically for children to handle. Exhibits can even be borrowed occasionally by the school. Curators may not always be prepared to talk to a whole class of children but are usually willing to be brought in on discussion groups. The real strength of a local museum service, however, is that a visit can extend to other

Figure 26 Magic Jungles. Age 9/11.

Figure 27 Painting based on the work of Delaunay. Age 9/10.

areas of the curriculum besides art. Once the children return to the classroom creative ideas can begin to take off and further visual interest be generated.

Stretching the idea of a resource 'box' further, buildings other than museums are also resources boxes, so are rooms, cupboards, drawers and the garden shed. Ordinarily these resource areas may be rather random in their organization of space. Yet part of teaching children art and design is to teach them to select from the 'visual jumble' of what they see and bring to our notice something they have used as a focus for interpretation.

Materials and groups

Success or failure in using resources for artwork largely depends on how well children have learned to handle art materials. It follows that demonstrating how to use materials has its part to play. Children must certainly discover for themselves how materials behave but they also need to be taught how to develop skill in handling media. They tend to waste materials when they first try them out but the teacher's attitude to this apparent waste is influential. The initial 'discovery' stage of using materials is unfortunately viewed by some teachers as being a disaster instead of a tentative attempt to try something new. In fact it is an important stage in the development of control over the media. Of course, teachers' attitudes vary but there is a considerable difference between regarding a new material as a good 'discovery' experience in itself and deliberately attempting to build up skills as the discovery proceeds.

When we give children a thorough understanding of how materials behave we are giving them the skills necessary to create and be expressive. There is actually nothing wrong with extending their experience by demonstrating a skill or a technique so long as this does not prevent innovation. Demonstration is usually necessary in order to give pupils a range of techniques relevant to the materials they use and the experience of many teachers is that when children are left to try out material for themselves they seldom exploit the medium to the full. They remain in ignorance of a whole variety of possibilities. The aim in demonstrating what materials will do is ultimately to enable children to be independent of their teacher. In the interim, we need to bring the full potential of each medium to their attention.

Are children really in any position to choose the medium best suited to their work? If they have not experienced a wide variety of materials how can they possibly know what to choose? Variety is a prerequisite for choice. Unfortunately, in the quest for introducing children to a wide range of materials, it has often become an aim in itself. The point about building up skills is that it requires repeated use of the same materials to achieve any noticeable refinement of skill. Children should not experience so much variety that they use a different material each week; that would be to encounter variety at the expense of repeated efforts to learn how to control media. They would simply forget what they had previously learned. A one-off session in claywork, for example, is of doubtful value because continuity is necessary. We should think carefully about the number of sessions needed to make the experience meaningful.

The properties of materials themselves can provide children with worthwhile discussion topics. Some of these have already been mentioned and we can ask 'Does the material stretch, cut easily, wear out or bend?', 'What are the properties of natural materials like wood and clay?' and 'What are they best used for?' Questions such as these are a significant way of introducing children to design education (see Chapter 9) and serve to extend the purpose of their art activities. A personal view is that children and teachers spend far too little time discussing artistic concepts, skills, materials and methods than they might. If children are not extended in their thinking through using an artistic vocabulary they are missing out on a whole area of learning. Time spent, for instance, discussing why clay will or will not join together when it dries is fundamental to claywork. But understanding why materials respond as they do is also fundamental to understanding their value to the designer. Developing understanding of materials not only widens the choice available to children but it can give them confidence to explore the same idea in several ways.

It goes almost without saying that if art materials are to be organized effectively, the children themselves should learn to look after them. Good classroom practice is to teach children how to find materials, use them properly and return them in a fit state to be used again.

> I think a lot of teachers just don't organize their materials properly. Children have to learn how to look after materials and they must be in order. You can't have a free-for-all . . . from the very beginning they have to learn about materials, what they're called and how to use them. They'll learn about the different kind of paint we've got . . . thin

> brushes, thick brushes . . . they even learn the numbered size of the brushes and we have whole sessions devoted to learning how to use things . . . they do develop great care if you give them a pride in what they do.
>
> (*Teacher*)

> It took me about three years to realize that making racks for everything was worth it . . . now we lose very little over the year. The children don't have to count things like paint brushes and scissors because they know the racks are always meant to be full.
>
> (*Teacher*)

Organization of group activities is something which many teachers find difficult. Some teachers solve this by organizing art for the whole class at once. This does have the advantage that there is a sudden surge of artistic activity and there is nothing quite like seeing an entire class working enthusiastically. Other approaches include having small groups of children working on projects most of the time. Whatever the preference in style of working there is little reason to suppose success can be had without good organization in respect of time, space, materials and children.

The idea of working in groups is that co-operative ventures can be tackled and activities can be divided between subject areas. It follows that to free the teacher to deal with a group of children the remaining groups must be engaged on familiar tasks. These might range from practice tasks to using an historical resource area, from finishing off work to practising handwriting. Clearly there have to be ground rules made so that there is a 'teaching group' and the other groups are expected to get on with established work until it is their turn to be taught. A particular advantage with topic work is that activities such as looking for information and making maps or diagrams can be balanced with teaching an art group.

An alternative to having 'practice' groups is to organize a number of ongoing activities such as the still-life or interest table which is there for the whole week. The session might be organized so that one group writes about its art while the other does it. In any case the teacher cannot hover over the art group all the time and watch. Art requires concentration and there are periods of independent working necessary if original artwork is to be forthcoming. Well-organized teachers are usually the first to admit they have discovered that being organized makes teaching art easier not more difficult. Invariably this means they teach the children to be independent of them.

The following examples are well-known practical solutions to group organization which some teachers find will work for them.

Examples

(1) Teach one group how to use a particular medium and the following day have children working in pairs, one child from the group showing another what they learned the previous day.
(2) Explain an idea to three groups at the same time (for example, a drawing and painting project). Then change the rules for each group so that there are limitations as to how each group uses materials. For example, one group might use black and white paint, another collage, a third use felt-tipped pen. The purpose of this would be to use the results for further discussion on art and compare the different responses each group had.
(3) Demonstrate a new technique to the whole class but have only a small group tackle it at a time, each group taking it in turns. An advantage here is that when each small group comes to try out the technique, less repetitious explanation is necessary.
(4) Set children a task such as finding circular shapes in the school when they are in areas other than the classroom. Make use of their observations after two or three days. Alternatively set them the task of collecting photographs of circular shapes from newspapers and involve them in starting off a group topic or theme on 'circles'.
(5) Divide children into groups of three and provide each group with a readily available object such as a cup and saucer. Let each group discuss its shape, colour and any special characteristics they can see. Later in the week, assemble a still life using the objects from three groups. The nine children exchange descriptions of their own group's object and make drawings, paintings or collages of the collection of three objects.
(6) Try three short practice activities like (a) a two-minute drawing, (b) trying out different grades of pencil, (c) making ruler and pen patterns, followed by an extensive piece of work which uses all three practice ideas.
(7) Begin a drawing or painting which has to be worked on at a later stage with oil, pastel or collage. Make this a piece of work which is meant to be continued over a period of a whole week using lunch times or odd moments when other work is finished. (This

Figure 28 Parrots - group mural. Age 9/10.

is not a case of suggesting that art is a spare time activity.) The value of these extended pieces of work is that children can learn to develop other work they do and appraise its progress over a period of time. For this to be successful, the principle that the work is extensive, and not to be completed quickly, has been laid down in the first place.

Group activity suggests large-scale work to many teachers. Most often this takes the form of a mural or frieze. The word mural is perhaps better if only to rid us of the time-worn idea that someone will paint a background and the children stick down their own contributions to make a frieze. There are alternatives such as can be seen in Figure 28 (see also Chapter 10). Here the children each took a section of a design and worked on it. They might use this technique to study a section of a photograph cut up into six or eight pieces.

Alternatively we might decide to emphasize the background as the main feature of a mural. A highly decorated background could contrast with blank silhouette shapes in themes like 'People at a Fair-ground' or 'Figures in a Supermarket'. The mural might be abstract, in which case the strategy could be to have children working out ideas on scraps of paper first. Anything which involves the assemblage of units, one from each child, will need to be organized so that children are quite sure where their unit fits in.

Displaying work

Sometimes topic work or artwork based on a theme such as 'Insects', 'Colour', or 'Holes' lends itself well to a special display. One of the main reasons for producing a display of work is that it presents work in a new context. The relationship between various pieces of work and the space they occupy affects the final impact of the display. Teachers also demonstrate the value they place on children's work and the class environment by the quality of their displays. Occasionally, however, the mechanics of display are quite out of hand, double, triple and quadruple mounting of work being a major feature. Of course, work looks better mounted but the triple-mounted work is really quite unnecessary. Knowing where to put the work on display is just as important as creating an elaborate border around it.

In the teaching day there is never enough time to give to display. Even so, a number of very elementary points can be made here and what follows should be regarded only as very general guidelines. They are included for those teachers who are less experienced in the techniques of good display.

There is a distinct difference between 'window-dressing' the school and taking care over displays. The very best primary school environments are not overloaded with masses of children's work. The corridors, display areas, school entrance and classrooms are carefully considered, often under a whole school policy for display. Some artwork will be framed. Other displays will not always be of artwork but will come from other areas of the curriculum such as mathematics and language. There is also a case for a very temporary display such as having a display of paintings on the classroom floor and gathering children round to look at them.

In their enthusiasm for display, many teachers put up far too much work in the space they have available. An obvious reason for this is to try to include work from most of the class without worrying too much about overcrowding the exhibition. Yet far less work can often have greater impact. We need to allow plenty of breathing space around work or objects displayed if they are to be seen to the best effect. The space needed is rather like the space we need between ourselves and someone else, in order to carry on a conversation. We need space in which to focus our vision. An overcrowded display board does little for the eye. The exception may be work which is all the same size and on the same theme because it has a unity which allows for displaying it much more closely.

Displays which include the original source material as well as the work which has grown from it have great impact. There is a sense of exploration and an element of 'time' encapsulated by the juxtaposition of objects and work done from them. We can see what the inspiration was and how inventive the outcomes are.

Displaying two-dimensional work is sometimes like doing a jigsaw. The outside edges need to be considered before the middle. Where possible, some attempt should be made to place the top edges of various pieces so that they create a level top line to the display. Similarly the bottom edges can be aligned. Alternatively the work can be organized in a symmetrical pattern. A sense of balance is the aim (notice the small display above the resource area in Figure 23). For this reason it is essential not to rely on scissors to trim work. A trimmer or guillotine is necessary because the work can look square when it is being prepared but prove not to be when the whole display has been arranged on a wall.

If work is mounted (for example, on black paper) the margin all the way round generally needs to be between 10 and 20 mm.

Coloured mounting paper occasionally detracts from the work as does wallpaper which has a strong pattern. Once a piece of work has been put up on a board it needs about 50 mm of space between itself and its neighbour to allow it to be easily seen. Obviously this amount of space will be exceeded for the purposes of balance but is a rough guide to establishing visual 'breathing space' within a display.

Titles and headings are best not lettered freehand even when we are experienced at lettering. A card strip which acts as a guide to the height of lettering or drawing ruled lines is necessary to ensure the height is consistent. Good displays are often spoiled by freehand lettering and, unfortunately, it is very easy to learn to live with hurriedly lettered titles. Many experienced teachers whose lettering is poor are actually quite unaware of the effect it has on the appearance of their displays.

Lettered questions included in the display can help make it much more active as a stimulus to thought. Questions such as 'How do you think . . . ?'or 'What makes this . . . work?' All these headings and questions need a good margin around them to avoid their looking cramped. As much as half the height of the letter is a guide for the margin around a title or label. Paper can always be trimmed off afterwards if the margins surrounding headings are too large.

Three-dimensional work brings particular problems of display. The main consideration here is to try to organize a display which has some variety in its height. Claywork, for example, can be displayed using bricks painted white or cardboard boxes covered with paper to give the necessary change of level. Often it is far better to group objects or pieces of claywork together in twos or threes rather than have an equal amount of space between them. A further point to consider is that a background which visually distracts the viewer from the three-dimensional work is not helpful. Items like pots need breathing space behind them and drawings and paintings should, in any case, be given their own space well above or to the side of 3-D work.

Ultimately good display is a question of being sensitive to the needs of the artwork or objects being displayed, which is why these are only guidelines. There are many teachers who break all the accepted rules yet still manage to display work successfully. Their lettering is freehand and contained in cut paper shapes rather than rectangular labels. Space between the work varies considerably but they have one thing in common with teachers who display in a more orderly and conventional way. They are still sensitive to the overall space they use and the work they place within that space.

8

Developing children's drawing

DRAWING records the way we think. Unlike a camera, which records whatever it can, our perception of the world is far more selective and drawings show the capacity we have to sift detail from the complex images we see. We filter out anything which we do not think is important yet perceive a far greater range of tones and colours than can be captured by photographic film. Any artist who has tried to work from a photograph knows just how much information is actually missing. Far from recording everything, the camera records a fleeting impression of what is there. The artist David Hockney (1988) comments:

> the only thing a photograph might be able to convey with some degree of truthfulness would be a flat surface, as in the reproduction, say, of a painting. When it attempted to depict space, that's when photography seemed to me to get into trouble. The camera, although people think it sees everything in front of it, cannot see the main thing *we* get excited about in front of us, which is space.

A drawing is essentially an image which coincides with something we already recognize or can imagine. From approximately the age of 8 years upwards, children's drawings follow more closely the conventions of our own artistic culture. Unlike the ancient Egyptians we use devices such as perspective and a sense of space which gives an illusion of much greater depth. We should remember, however, that these conventions of the artist are still illusions and we learn to understand them only gradually. When children between the ages of 8 and 13 are learning to improve their drawing ability they are involved in a process of creation whereby they adapt to the Western way of depicting the world. Marks made by a pencil are meaningless until they exist in relation to each other and describe shapes, forms, surface qualities, light and shadow. The relationship of one mark to another creates the illusion that we come to recognize as a drawing.

Drawing is by no means an automatic extension of children's looking. Just as they learn to use a language or a musical scale so they learn to give meaning to the marks they make. The rules are more fixed in language and musical scales but drawing still has its agreed conventions. Children experience a wide variety of images in books and on television and have no doubt traced and copied many drawings by this age. Conventions of perspective and shading are familiar sights even if learning how to use them is still a mystery.

Hockney has pointed to the most difficult hurdle children have to overcome. A three-dimensional world existing in space is being interpreted on two-dimensional paper. Small wonder that before this age children solve this problem by drawing symbols, some of which are highly sophisticated. The young child's organization of forms in space is comparatively primitive and characterized by the absence of shapes which overlap one another. Subject matter is surrounded by empty areas and nothing is left obscured by another object. The bottom of the paper often serves as the ground and the most important subject matter is usually drawn the largest, especially if a self-portrait comprises part of the drawing. Objects are often drawn facing the child who draws them as if they were lined up to be seen.

Spatial organization is a good indicator of how well children's perception and drawing have developed. Teachers can glean information about children's perception from looking at drawings in this context. Throughout the history of art the depiction or interpretation of space has dominated drawing and painting alongside a concern for light and shadow. Fortunately children develop various ways of solving the difficulty of representing space but their transition from symbols to visual realism is often accompanied by acute dissatisfaction with their own skill. (These earlier stages of development in drawing are more fully documented in Kellogg, 1969, Gardner, 1980 and Barnes, 1987.) A crucial role the teacher has is that of guide and enabler, questioning the appearance of things and teaching children to *look* carefully for themselves.

A noticeable difference between 8 year-olds and much younger children is that the older children are, the more they want their drawings to be understood by other people. Most 5 year-olds are

Figure 29 Figure Study. Age 13.

satisfied so long as their symbolic artwork makes sense to themselves. In contrast to this, 8 year-olds are at exactly the most receptive stage for learning to study through direct experience of real objects, like those seen in the still-life groups in Chapter 7. Objective drawing is in many ways the most appropriate activity for them to do. They have usually developed enough control over a pencil to tackle studying some natural or man-made form in an elaborate and detailed way and they have a growing sense of scale, proportion and shape which can be developed to a far more sophisticated level.

The dilemma for many teachers is whether or not to try to preserve the innocent symbolic drawing of earlier years or encourage the more culturally acquired 'adult' approach to drawing. Do we continue to praise symbols in the face of obvious dissatisfaction from the child? Do we point out the way objects cannot be seen if they are overlapped or that the sky meets the ground?

To a certain extent these problems resolve themselves. Encouraging children to look carefully is its own taskmaster. Children explore through drawing so long as we bring visual resources their way and continue to point out details of shape, colour, pattern and so on. There is in the end no system for drawing an eye or a nose, only ways of seeing. Children discover that the sky meets the ground when they genuinely perceive it that way and not before. Part of the joy of drawing is discovering how to give the illusion of space from sky to ground. When Hockney describes being excited about space he reflects something many artists feel.

Can children see more than they can draw? There is certainly a mismatch between what they see and whatever mechanism is learned to produce a drawing. Children can recognize objects illustrated in books, which must mean they are able to cope with Western conventions of illustrative style. Yet they cannot draw objects with the same facility with which they recognize them in a drawing. Obviously this is also true of adults. The artist includes details and shapes which no doubt coincide with our experience at a more subconscious level. Like recognizing people we know, we refer to buried memory of shape and form which matches the face we see before us.

An important aspect of understanding how differently a class of children learns to interpret through drawing is one of making comparisons between the various attempts they have made to draw the same thing. A glance through drawings done by a group of adult art students attending the same life class reveals much the same phenomenon. Each drawing records the individual perception

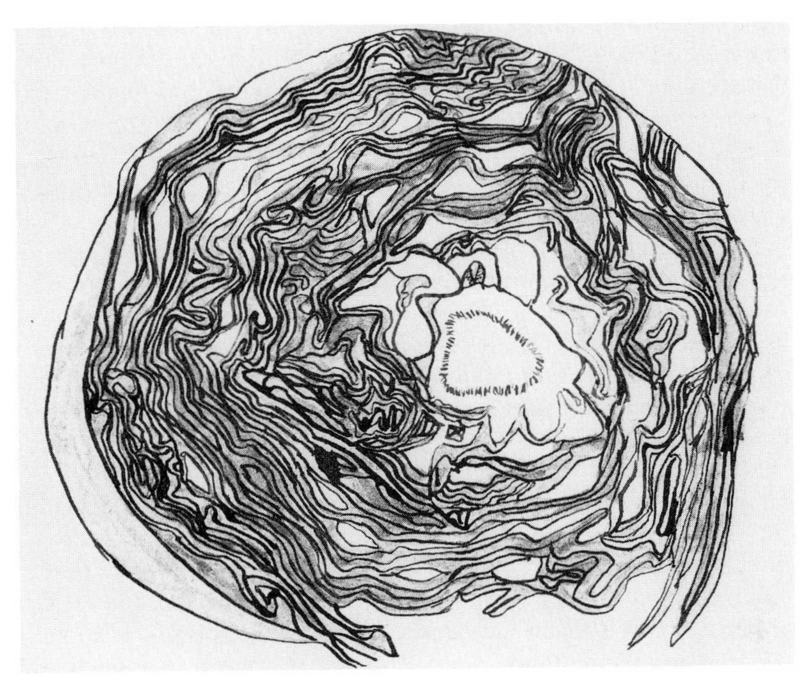

Figure 30 Cabbage. Age 10.

of curves and proportions. All are different yet all refer to the same model who has posed. In day-to-day life we have all at some time met people whose perception of life's events is different from our own and, as we have little else to trust but our own perceptions, it is not surprising that we see our view as truth. The danger is to assume that other people's *visual* perceptions must be the same as ours. Children cannot draw anyone else's perceptions because we happen to trust what we see. We can only try to awaken theirs.

Perhaps more than in any other age range, 8–13 year-olds need continual encouragement to draw. Their spontaneous and delightful symbols are behind them and there is often a sluggish period of development (sometimes referred to as the 'latency' period) as they adjust to new ways of seeing. Realizing that shapes overlap and exist in space is quite different from confidently telling a story through symbols. Stumbling attempts at a more objective drawing can undermine the most confident of children.

One way to destroy children's confidence is to present them with an adult drawing as their goal. 'I can't draw' often means 'I can't draw as well as an adult'. It cannot be overemphasized that children do not draw like adults. They show qualities of lively expression which are as valid as anything an adult produces but the way to develop drawing ability does not lie in making children think they are inferior to adult artists. They need acceptance and praise for the quality of the drawings they have made.

An assortment of particular drawing problems emerges in the 8–13 age range. There is confusion between what should be drawn in plan and what in elevation. A room window, for example, will be drawn in elevation whilst a rug or perhaps a bed is drawn as if it is seen in plan. Questions are asked like 'How do I draw noses? How do I draw somebody sitting cross-legged? How do I do the shadows?' and 'How does perspective work?'

Many of these questions are prompted by a shift away from imagination in drawing. Imaginative subjects, or drawings based on memory have featured strongly in the early years from age 3 to 6. A concern for realism and objective drawing consequently pushes out much of the fantasy we associate with younger children. The tragedy of this is that objective drawing can become an end in itself and children thereby lose sight of imaginative work. A remedy can be found by asking ourselves what the objective drawing is actually for. What is the point of studying through accurate drawing if it cannot inspire special qualities of expression? What is the point of drawing unless it teaches us more about interpreting what we are looking at?

At one level of experience there are maps, diagrams, or line drawings which merely give factual information. Much more interesting is the kind of drawing which conveys personal feelings about something which has been seen or imagined. The difficulty for children is that a certain amount of careful, rather straightforward objective study is necessary for them to draw in a more expressive way later on. Attempts at 'information-gathering' and accuracy through drawing should not entirely be swept aside. Like the musician who practises scales and exercises, the artist must find out about the world in ways which are not always exciting and expressive. However, the comments of Degas and Braque (Chapter 7) about artists drawing with their imagination are also relevant. Previously mentioned 'qualities' which children search for, such as 'balance', 'contrast', or 'delicacy', are crucial to their retaining expressive and imaginative modes of drawing.

Figure 31 Newspaper Portraits. Age 12.

Imaginative drawing can occasionally help more objective ways of drawing. There is a well-known game children play when they are young.

> My sister and I used to play a game when we were little. In fact it was more of a competition between us. We'd each scribble lines round and round on a piece of paper and exchange our papers . . . then the other person had to find creatures, faces, objects, buildings or landscapes within the lines. We never had any difficulty finding something there.
> (*Art collector*)

The game is good practice for identifying shapes. It also may help to encourage the mind to see how shapes which are slightly distorted by the mass of lines can still have certain qualities of expression. The shapes are made to fit the available lines but they turn into cartoon faces, monsters and imagined cities, often having a strongly emotional appeal. Accuracy in drawing shapes is sacrificed for the rewards of invention, fantasy and expression.

Drawing requires considerable concentration. It is not unusual to find that children will draw carefully for a short period of time

Figure 32 Pencil Abstract. Age 12.

then become quite careless and a meticulous drawing may well be followed with scribble or very sketchy work. The concentration needed to sustain a drawing is often too much to expect from children all the time. Repeated experience of concentrating on looking and drawing, however, teaches children to pace themselves and adjust to the demands which are made on them. They can begin to experience a sense of achievement in drawing which has been bought at a price of intense effort.

The least helpful way to teach drawing is by giving children stereotypes. A stereotype is anything which is a fixed way of drawing such as a perfect oval for a face or a zigzagged shape for a Christmas tree. (A puzzle is that at Christmas time zigzagged trees usually have their branches portrayed as pointing down. In reality the branches of most room-sized Christmas trees point upwards.) Other examples of stereotypes are cartoon characters, pin men and fashion drawings such as are found in magazines. Children are sometimes shown how to draw birds by joining two circles together and adding a beak, or drawing a fish by adding fins to an ellipse. All these are fixed methods and bear little relation to studying the real shapes and forms which exist in the environment.

Stereotypes prevent further searching inquiry and they encourage children to repeat themselves instead of looking for new challenges. We do not need to give children stereotypes because they develop enough of their own for drawing things like eyes and noses. They seldom realize, for example, the extent to which each eye is actually slightly different from any other eye and is invariably seen from differing angles or viewpoints. For some children the stereotype of two arcs enclosing a small circle becomes a sufficiently satisfactory way to draw an eye and there seems no further need to look more carefully.

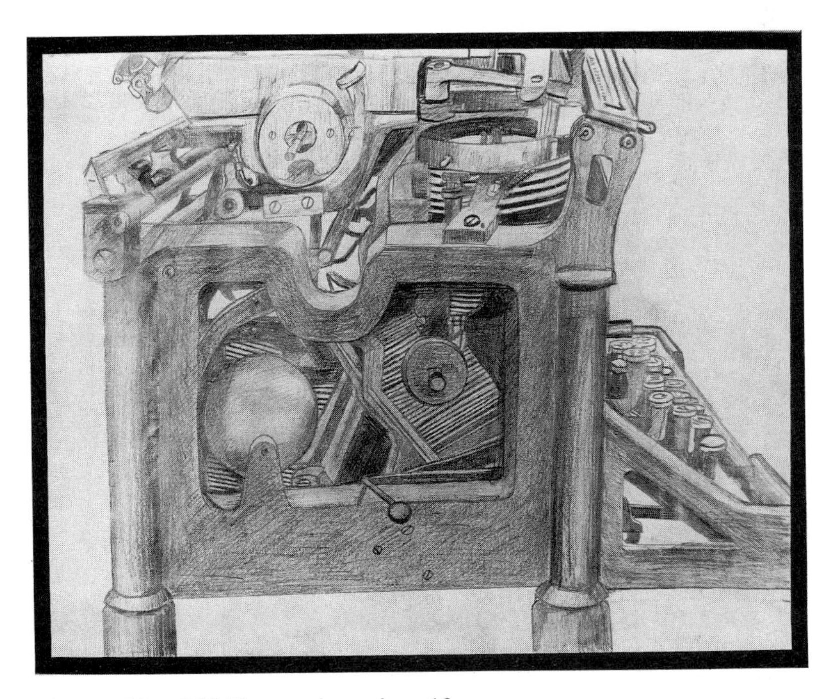

Figure 33 Old Typewriter. Age 13.

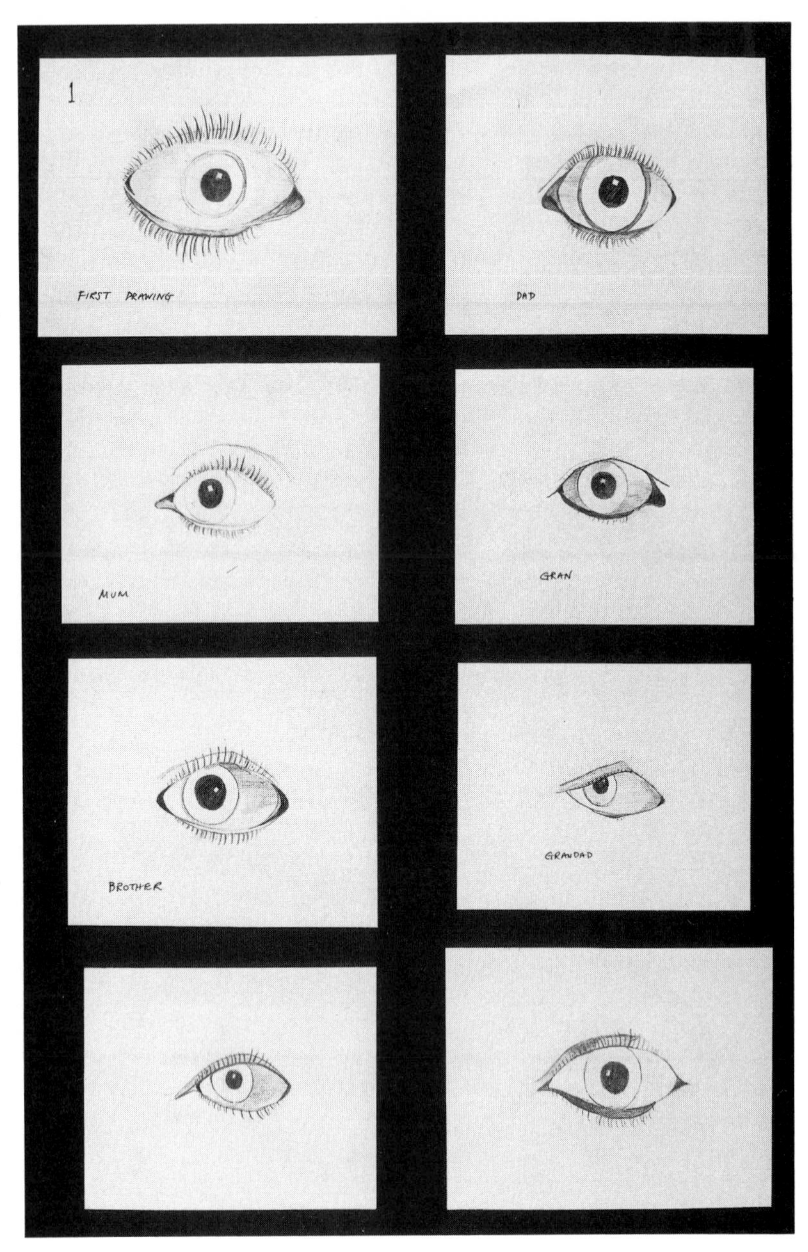

Figure 34 Drawings of Eyes. Age 12.

Figure 34 shows eight drawings of eyes by a 12 year-old boy. The first drawing indicates the stage of his own stereotype for an eye. (There are, of course, much more crude stereotypes than this and his first version of an eye shows he already has some experience of drawing eyes.) In common with many children he draws the circle of the iris so that it is in full view giving that 'surprised' look. Normally we do not see the full circle of the iris because it is covered by the upper eyelid. We tend to see the lower three quarters of the eye. He drew the remaining eyes over a period of a week and the only instructions given were these: he had to pay particular attention to the amount of the white of the eye visible, its shape and how much (if any) was above or below the iris; the eyelids should be observed for the way they vary from one person to another and the iris of the eye similarly studied to see how much of it was covered by flesh.

Notice the way the eyelid in the 'grandad' eye covers far more of the eye. In subsequent drawings the stereotype has begun to disappear and traces of it remain only in the treatment of highlights in each iris. A development from this piece of observation would be to draw two eyes from the same person but with the head turned slightly to one side so that the 'whites' of the eyes were at their most different. Study can also be supported by comparing the way famous artists have drawn eyes, discovering, for example, that many of the eighteenth-century portrait painters had their own stereotyped method of painting highlights in the eyes. One of their aims was to draw eyes in such a way as to flatter their sitters.

Most of us understand the difference between being asked to read ten pages in two days or a whole book in a month. Reading ten pages seems less arduous. In drawing, children can cope with very complicated problems so long as they do not face them head on. Asking children of this age to draw the whole face may well be too threatening. A better approach can be to isolate part of a face such as eyes or mouth and begin by drawing those. Another example is where children are working outside drawing a building. They will very often respond far better if they are asked to begin by drawing just one window or the part which interests them most. From there, the whole building gradually begins to emerge on paper. It is the thought of having to draw the entire face or the whole of the building which seems so daunting. The temptation to give cursory attention to looking at eyes is bound to exist if children know they are expected to draw the whole face in the time they have been allotted.

The principle of isolating a small area can be extended to using hand lenses or making small cardboard frames through which to look at the world. Studying eyes can absorb children in looking for changing shapes of the 'whites' of the eye, dark and light lines in the iris and reflections of light in the pupil. Eyelids, lashes and the overall size of the eye can similarly demand attention.

Teaching children to draw does not mean the teacher has to be good at drawing. In many cases this is a handicap because it leads to the tempting strategy of demonstrating stereotypes. Worse still, the teacher might draw for children instead of accepting their less sophisticated but more honest efforts. Some of the best teaching takes place where children are finding out alongside their teachers and no one thinks they are an expert.

Essential to teaching drawing is looking at pattern and shape. Practice in drawing patterns and shapes is a first consideration because it temporarily puts problems of drawing three-dimensional space on one side. Most children can manage to draw the pattern of a tiger's stripes, a zebra, cat fur, or the bark of a tree, for example. Decisions about lines, stripes and other patterns can be taken without having to consider an outline. An effect of this concentration on pattern is that it inevitably leads on to the search for shape. Skill in finding shape within pattern can stimulate the awareness of outline or silhouette.

Patterns which have been drawn from real-life objects can be cut into silhouettes later on so that an outline shape is created. Using scissors is a way of drawing in itself (see the cut of the clown's jacket in Plate 23 and the cats in Figure 35). The activity of making outlines is another stage in the process of learning to see and, although it may not be so commonplace as looking at pattern and shape together, it helps children to discover about outlines. Before long they begin to find outlines in which to put their patterns and the two elements come together. The drawing problems have once again been broken down into manageable stages.

There must be a million different shapes for a cat to be. Far from learning a stereotype children need to see and imagine a cat in as many positions as possible such as

sitting hunched up on the top of a wall
side view, front view
sitting with head up, alert
cleaning its fur
back arched and aggressive
stretched out in the sun

Figure 35 Black Paper Cats. Age 12.

curled up asleep
asleep on the arm of a chair, legs dangling
with head poking out of a cardboard box
sitting on a dustbin lid

As has been mentioned, there is really no system for drawing eyes and noses; there are similarly no methods such as 'how to draw cats', 'how to draw faces', or 'how to draw plants'. There may be slightly different approaches needed for each subject but drawing is drawing, not something specific to subjects. The drawings of sheep by Henry Moore are very personal in style. Yet there is no step-by-step way we could learn to draw sheep like Moore. These drawings are the product of his own vision just as children's drawings should be an outcome of theirs.

When children are learning to draw *they are making comparisons with what they already know*. Just as we recognize a friend by subconsciously comparing with previous experience of the shape of the facial features, so with drawing any shape we compare with known shapes. Drawing involves

looking for shapes which are circular
looking for rectangles and squares
comparing shapes against verticals and horizontals
comparing length, width and height
comparing curves with straights
looking for triangular shapes

Figure 36 Looking for Shapes.

looking for angles, pointed or spiked shapes
looking for the direction of lines and changes of direction
comparing dark shapes with light.

Figures 36 and 37 show photographs of the same group of objects. While many other shapes could be found there is an indication here of some comparison with known circles and triangles. Figure 38 shows the results of an exercise in a more subtle comparison using black paper shapes. The aim is not only to say which shape most coincides with the glass bottle but why the others do not. The exercise can easily be developed to consider proportion, height, scale and so on.

There are useful guidelines for drawing which children can discover for themselves. One of the most easily recognizable or 'readable' shapes is a profile or side view of something. (Signs and symbols tend to make use of this fact.) In comparing the shape of a horse with a cow, for example, the shape of the body of a horse (seen in profile) is most like a kidney bean, whereas the shape of a cow's body is rather rectangular. Both shapes are in reality nothing like kidney beans or rectangles but the comparison serves to point to how much and how little they might deviate from these known shapes. Earlier,

Figure 37

the stereotype of a bird which was constructed from a larger and a smaller circle was mentioned. This stereotype works simply because it is possible to imagine these shapes within a bird as seen in side view. But we know there are actually many species of birds and a far more extensive comparison must be made between them in order to distinguish one from another. The bird stereotype is ultimately not much help unless we ask ourselves 'How different is this bird from the stereotype?' or 'What are the differences between this species of bird and that?'

Judging what shape things are is largely a question of comparing extremes, such as straight against circular, long against short, or dark against light. We may know that something is curved but we need to determine which part is the *most* curved, which the *least*. How curved is it compared with a circle? Which is the straightest part of the curve? All comparisons are relative and whether or not something is fat or thin, curved or straight, depends on the context of the drawing. Central to learning how to draw is that we are not seeking to make things look like triangles or circles. We are looking to discriminate the quality and extent of 'triangularity' or 'circularity'.

Figure 38 Comparing Similar Shapes.

> I remember trying to help a boy who was drawing a buffalo from reference in a book. The drawing he was doing gave him problems and he was stuck with the idea that a buffalo was like a cow or a horse. On closer examination of a picture of a buffalo we found that the shape of its body is actually rather triangular with a very narrow part of the triangle towards the tail and a large head attached to the front side of the triangle . . . somehow if you can help them to get started they will usually have a go at drawing anything. Mostly all they need is a way in.
>
> (*Teacher*)

A major aim is to encourage children to develop a 'vocabulary' of shapes which includes ellipses, circles, rectangles, triangles, cones, pyramids and cubes. Letters of the alphabet can also prove to be useful reminders of shape (like the letter M in Figure 40). We know that accounts of Picasso's childhood tell of his difficulties at school and the way he saw numbers as shapes after struggling with an examination.

> On the way home, he imagined the pigeon he would paint, describing it in terms of the numbers used in the examination: 'The little eye of the pigeon is round like a 0. Under the 0 a 6, and under that a 3. The eyes are like 2's, and so are the wings. The little feet rest on the table, as if on a horizontal line . . . underneath it all the total.'
>
> (*Gedo, 1980*)

Further, an awareness of directions and angles is a significant contributor to sensing spatial relationships within a drawing (Figures 41, 42). Quite a number of drawn images can also be reproduced from memory as children try to conjure up the vocabulary of shapes they previously drew. By drawing from memory, we can discover the underlying nature of the object or experience we have had.

Sometimes the description of an object needs to be a group effort from the class. Each person remembers some minor detail or other which triggers a stronger mental image than individuals might construct by themselves. The vocabulary of shape grows until no drawing problem is too difficult. The circles, ellipses and cubes have become part of memory so that they are future points of reference.

Of course, there are situations such as drawing a landscape or a person where there may be no vertical or horizontal lines with which to make comparisons. The sixteenth-century draughtsman Albrecht Dürer would have solved this by using a wire and wooden frame in

Figure 39 Finding Shapes and Letters.

Figure 40

Figures 41, 42 Finding Angles and Directions.

order to reduce the scene to squares of a known size. The squares would coincide with those on his drawing paper. Similarly, artists will draw squares on a sketch and scale it up for the canvas. The process is yet another simple aid to finding relationships, proportions and sizes with which to compare. The artist who checks sizes by holding a pencil at arm's length, and sliding a thumb up and down it, is also comparing proportions and making measurements.

Sometimes the only way to check that shapes are accurately drawn is by constructing verticals and horizontals of our own. Vertical lines (like the uprights of a doorway or the side of a building) are usually easy to find and do not present problems of perspective unless, for instance, we are looking up at a skyscraper or down a lift shaft. Horizontal lines exist only if they are absolutely level and directly opposite us. Otherwise, eye level and perspective become a consideration. One solution is to make a drawing frame to which we can refer.

The wire-framed device in Figure 44 can be used as a guide and if necessary the paper on which the drawing is being done can have a similar number of squares drawn on it. Cake trays used in cooking are an obvious substitute for spot-welded frames and other very easy ways to make drawing frames are to take an old picture frame and stretch rubber bands across it or to use an overhead projector acetate. The frame and the subject can be accurately aligned each time by closing one eye. If all this seems very elaborate we should remember how

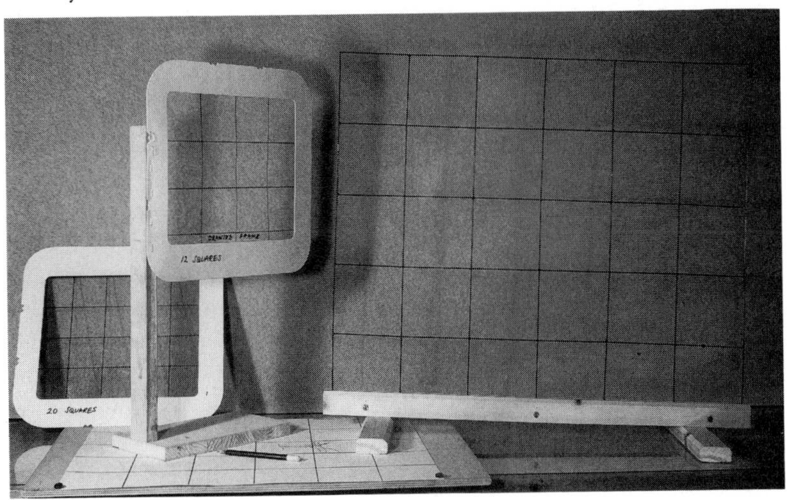

Figure 43 Drawing Frames.

Figure 44 Drawing Frame in use (after Albrecht Dürer, 1525).

well Dürer could draw, yet he still found it necessary to use various devices to 'see' what to draw.

Two strong contenders for very different approaches to drawing are these. We can draw things from the outside shape (the outline) or from the inside (by imagining the structure or bones of things). Clearly the difference in emphasis between the two approaches is important. The outline is more accessible for children to see but the imagined internal structure is sometimes just as useful a way of looking at things. Drawing a twig, for example, may not offer much in the way of an outline but we can construct pencil lines which begin almost as an armature inside the twig. This is probably the origin of drawing 'pin men' and adding padding to the shape. Certainly this approach found favour with artists at the turn of this century. The painter Sickert (Goldwater and Treves, 1976) was prompted to remark that artists 'draw and then . . . upholster their drawings'. The tradition in art schools was to learn anatomy and draw the human figure by first sketching the 'bones' of the drawing. People were not so much drawn in outlines but as bones clothed in flesh.

These two ways of looking at things are not exclusive of one another. Children's drawing skills will develop by using both 'internal structure' and 'external outline' approaches. In fact *any device which helps children to see is valid.* Some pupils will respond to using a drawing frame, others to looking for circles, rectangles, internal structure and so on.

The 8–13 age range (as has been pointed out earlier) is not one characterized by a very advanced awareness of tone. The ability to shade meaningfully with a pencil is perhaps one of the most elusive aspects of drawing. Line is much more basic to drawing and the effect of light and shadows is the very thing which can destroy linear drawings. Once shading meets with line, the line disappears. Line can define pattern and outline whereas shading often fades in and out gradually and the artist has to decide how much or little will retain the strength of existing lines.

Awareness of tone, coupled with attempts at shading a drawing, pushes children well into the business of assuming adult artistic conventions. There are additional problems to face like whether or not to shade something heavily because it happens to be a dark colour. Should the artist merely find the shadows, regardless of how light or dark colours are? In what direction does the shading go?

Children who are keen enough will look at drawings by artists to find out what they did. They will also try out shading to see what effect it has on their drawing. The results of these explorations are stored as part of a growing memory of what action has a particular effect. Yet being able to express tonal values is the consequence not so much of looking at drawings as of becoming aware of light and shadow. Here, magazine photography is particularly helpful and children can make excellent photographic collections which demonstrate a range of lighting situations.

Figures 45 and 46 show two photographs of plants. The photographs were taken in very different lighting conditions and the effect of the light consequently would demand two different approaches to drawing. In one photograph the emphasis is on the silhouette or outline of the group of plants. The other photograph has been lit from one side and the form of the leaves themselves is more clearly highlighted. Forms in this picture have strongly contrasting light and shadow within the same leaf and the outline is slightly less evident. The 'lace' curtains behind the plants also have a different emphasis. From the point of view of the artist, shifts in the lighting present different challenges and children gain considerably in perception by exploring and discussing how light changes the form.

Strong lighting, especially from the side or behind, automatically gives a useful contrast to objects. Shadows become clear shapes rather

Figure 45 Effects of Lighting.

than fading very gradually and light and dark can be stated with some contrast. There is still a pattern of light and dark to be seen. Diffused light, on the other hand, or light from above and the front, tend to have a flattening effect. Forms melt into each other and it is much more difficult for children to see what three-dimensional qualities are there and decide how to shade with their pencils.

We can see from the painting in Figure 47 that artificial light is not necessary to articulate form. Light from a window is quite adequate. Natural sunlight can also bring shapes into sharp relief but it too can have a flattening effect, especially on the landscape at midday in high summer. The early morning and late evening light work in the way the photographic floodlights have done in the plant pictures. Long shadows, clear light and a low angle in relation to the form define it in a manner which can be helpful to the process of drawing.

When we stop to analyse children's thinking as they draw it is surprising just how much logical thought is going on. They will make

Figure 46

measurements and reason that part of what they see is longer or shorter so the lines must be longer or shorter in the drawing. This shape is larger than that one, this is lighter or darker and the corresponding perceptions are put down as drawn images. They also reason that certain parts of their drawing must be made more important, other parts less so, or that a line must go at a particular angle to suggest something is leaning to one side. In this context, drawing is by way of a test in logical thinking as children work out the translation to pencil marks from what is there.

We cannot assume children will automatically make comparisons of shape, pattern and light by themselves and they need to be on the receiving end of a teacher's skill in asking questions. This is not only a matter of responding to questions but beginning to experience the way they might ask themselves about what they see. A group of 8 year-olds was looking at a teapot. Just how much they compare with what they already know can be seen from this exchange.

Figure 47 Figure by the Light. Age 11.

Teacher: When I hold the teapot up can you tell me what shapes you can see?

Caspar: A round shape . . . like a ball.

Teacher: If you could see this teapot and had to describe it to someone who had never seen a teapot before how would you describe it?

Elaine: A sort of semi-circle shaped handle and a round sphere shape.

Caspar: I think the bit that you pour with to make the tea looks like a seal or a slug with its nose up.

Teacher: Oh yes . . . it does doesn't it? . . . this time I want you to look at the spaces around the teapot . . . yes, Alex?

Alex: The inside of the handle is like an ear.

Lizzie: The spout looks a bit like an elephant's trunk when it goes up.

Caspar: The lid looks like a Chinaman's hat with a bobble on the top.

Teacher: If I said to you 'This is like a circle but it's not quite a circle . . . '

Lizzie: The top and bottom are not like a circle . . . there wouldn't be a bump at the top and the bottom is straight.

Elaine: I'd draw the middle bit first, then the handle.

Teacher: Anyone do it a different way?

Alex: The top first.

Caspar: Sometimes I do things as if I'm planning them. I'd do different drawings of the views.

Teacher: There are lots of curves on a teapot . . . are they all the same?

Elaine: Well, the one on the spout isn't the same as the curve on the handle . . . it's a bit steeper.

Teacher: Where is it steeper?

Elaine: When it comes up to the opening.

Caspar: Well, I think the curve on the top is different from the handle because it goes up and over like a mushroom and the other one is a semi-circle.

Teacher: Can you look carefully from the rim here to the bottom? Describe what happens.

Lizzie: It gets bigger.

Caspar: The rim is like a cliff . . . it starts at the bottom and comes over.

Teacher: Now, if I get you to look at the lid it's like a circle isn't it? . . . but if I move it upwards . . . tell me how it changes.

Elaine: It's sort of oval shape.

Teacher: Is that an exact circle on the bottom?

Children: Yes.

Teacher: Anyone disagree? (Silence.) Watch it as I tilt it . . . what happens? How does the circle change?

Elaine: It goes oval.

Caspar: It's like an eye . . . it starts looking at you then it goes like an eye looking down at the ground . . . as if someone was telling it off.

Teacher: I wonder if our eyes go like that . . . you have to take it in turns . . . have a look.

We often talk about feeling in drawings. We mean expression and emotion but sometimes children literally need to find out about what they are drawing, by feeling with their fingers. They need to discover in a tactile way by running their fingers over the object to explore its shape.

> We've been looking at all sorts of things today . . . bones and flower heads but I brought in that curly cabbage and most of them had never seen a cabbage quite like that before . . . I'll ask 'What can you see? What shape is it? What direction are the lines going in?' I let them trace their fingers round the crinkly edges of the cabbage and feel it . . . look for fat lines, thin lines and how it's dark on the outside and paler in the middle.
>
> (*Teacher*)

No mention has been made in this chapter of techniques of perspective. There are two reasons for this, the first being that there is not space here for the complexity of rules to be described in sufficient detail, the second that perspective needs to be understood very thoroughly if it is not to enslave children. As soon as straight lines (usually ruler-drawn) put buildings in perspective, children can be enraptured with the 'adult' look their drawings suddenly acquire. Perspective becomes its own stereotype. Despite eventually needing to know something about perspective children need to understand that it is still an illusion which does no more than point the way to organizing space. The very greatest drawings do not make us aware of perspective as a technique and there are many artists, such as Picasso and Hockney, who have periodically abandoned perspective as a way of drawing. Try, for example, showing children reproductions of a Cubist picture or some of Hockney's work from the 1980s. Both defy the conventions of perspective yet are regarded as being great and famous examples of art.

The best that can happen is that children learn to use perspective thoroughly and come out of the other side of the experience taking it for granted. Otherwise it ranks with stereotypes like oval faces and zigzagged fir trees. Drawings had no accurate perspective until the fifteenth century when artists began to establish the illusion according to rules. Uccello and later Piero della Francesca particularly had developed perspective and it was to become almost standard practice to use this in the following centuries. Now we cope with Picasso and Hockney in their deliberate rejection of such artistic conventions.

Drawings which have been found in caves are thought in some cases to be 50,000 years old, testifying to a long-established need we have to express our ideas through making marks and lines. Differing styles of drawing down the centuries exemplify the way human beings have changed their drawings as they have changed their perceptions. The conventions for drawing a galloping horse, for instance, in the days before photography, meant all four legs were portrayed extended in the gallop. Photography simply taught us to see the horse in a different way. As teachers we have the opportunity to open children's eyes

Figure 48 Two Heads - etching. Age 12/13.

to the way they themselves perceive the world. In the process of learning to draw they will no doubt teach us to look more carefully at the shapes and forms which surround us. They will rarely find drawing is easy but they can still make enough progress to feel a sense of achievement and pride in what they do. If we find that they stumble we should not be surprised. They are trying to cope with a dimension which is as much a cultural illusion as it is an assumption that what they see is the truth.

9

Art into design

ARTISTS HAVE always been designers in the sense that their paintings and sculptures are designed. Fifteenth-century artists would have thought nothing of designing a piece of jewellery, a fountain, a ceiling, a religious painting, or a front door. It is in the twentieth century that distinctions like 'graphic designer', 'industrial designer' and 'fashion designer' have come to the fore. Design has had much more interest paid to it in art education in the last few years than ever it had previously, particularly through the Design Council which has recognized that design education is inextricably bound up with being an artist. In its report *Design and Primary Education* (1987) the phrase used is 'design-related activities'. The point which is made over and over again is that design education is by no means an activity separate from art.

Just as 'pottery' became 'ceramics', 'handwork' turned into 'craft'. 'Art and craft' has changed so much that now we think of 'art and design' being a more appropriate description. The surge of interest in CDT (craft, design and technology) has also nudged art towards taking on a more design-conscious role. No longer are children expected to learn craft as distinct from art. They use art and craft skills in solving design problems and learn how design permeates and affects our working lives. Design-related activities very often centre on a theme or topic and are therefore another piece of the jigsaw of art in relation to topic work. Like topic work, design-related activity can cover the entire curriculum as children are calculating, problem-solving, decision-making, drawing, making, evaluating and writing. Where learning involves creativity across the curriculum, art, design and topic work are almost inseparable.

Examples of activities give some insight into the nature of design.

The Design Council's 'Big Paper', published from 1987 termly for schools, has described projects such as the London school which decided to create a department store. Each class took an aspect of designing and made badges, shop notices and a logo for the store. The history of shopping was studied as was toy-making, fabric design, furniture design, and making specific items like desk tidies for the stationery department. The book department had a new alphabet book designed for it. Tie-dye vests and appliquéd tops were 'for sale' in the clothing department, all made by 10 and 11 year-olds. There was a fashion show and the design project culminated in a two-week exhibition for parents and governors of the school.

There have been examples such as designing a children's play area which involved making models of play structures from wire and paper. Animated films have begun by making a 'flick book' of images. Simple puppets with moving parts have been made in the topic 'How the Human Body Works' and discussion has centred on

Figure 49 Design for a Throne for a King's Palace. Age 10.

Figure 50 Design for a Vehicle which can Fly and Travel Underwater. Age 10.

original designs for teapots including one designed as a 'Mad Hatter'.

Design-related activities strongly emphasize function. Activities explore how things work and what are the best new solutions to long-established tasks like drawing a map, making a poster, or designing a working model. A particularly noticeable feature of any design-related project is that it lends itself to three-dimensional work. The Department of Education and Science for years has expressed its concern that far too little three-dimensional work takes place in primary schools and if there is a crucial bonus for schools, it is one of bringing three-dimensional work out of obscurity.

Much primary school artwork has in the past been limited to flat drawings and paintings, with the addition of occasional pieces of claywork and historical models. The surge of interest in design-related activities has meant constructing and model-making are now indispensable aspects of the curriculum. Finding out how to make a spacesuit, or how to build a model of a suspension bridge, involves design problems generated by what we want the models to do. Children have to try out ways of sticking things together, folding and assembling, if they want to solve design problems. Moving parts may be involved and technology is needed to make models work. Decisions about what materials will best suit the needs of the project have to be made. Children may have to decide whether or not to change their original plans and discuss how to improve on their design.

Materials themselves are explored, not only in terms of how expressive they might be, but how appropriate they are for their function. Discussion of why metal parts are made a specific thickness and shape, why wood is used the way it is and why certain things are not made of sand or glass are relevant to learning about design. Two questions especially recur in design-related activities: 'Why are things the shape they are?' and 'Why are they made of this particular material rather than something else?'

Questions like these highlight problems of form and function in design. Not that the one always follows the other. The styling of motor vehicles in the 1960s, for instance, often divorced appearance from function to incorporate the prevailing fashion for chromium-plated embellishments. Form does not always follow the mechanical or electronic function of consumer goods because commercial considerations such as a 'saleable shape' impinge on the rationale for the design. The forms which designs take, however, are usually related in some measure to their function. Advertisements on hoardings must attract the eye and be easily read from some way off. A hammer must be a certain shape and weight for the job it does and a telephone handset must have mouthpiece and earpiece at an appropriate distance.

The priority of excellence in design is to achieve a balance between functional and visual elements so that neither takes over from the other. In Victorian times, decoration and embellishment were often used to disguise the mundane function of objects and ornament frequently made them less efficient. For example, many decorated cast-iron handles were distinctly uncomfortable to hold. Designers like William Morris were inspired to lead a revolt against the imbalance which was taking place as design sense became a nonsense. This balance between function and appearance has always taxed the designer, from the invention of the blast furnace to modern-day plastics. New materials have new properties and qualities which provide potential for new shapes and forms. Elegance is not something which can simply be added like pouring milk on a breakfast cereal and it must go hand in hand with function.

The dividing line between art and technology becomes blurred when function is a factor. Unfortunately aesthetic considerations are often swept aside in the haste to make things work. A large number of promising school design projects have been sacrificed to rubber-band and drawing-pin technology, a style of problem-solving which often ignores the final appearance of the products. In reality, not everything needs to be made from scrap materials and the final forms which designs take must surely be the result of thinking about pleasing shape and finish as much as function. Even if techniques for achieving a fine finish to designs are not available, drawings of the intended style and shape can be a major part of the design detail. Rubber bands, electric motors and commercial technology kits are not necessarily the best ingredients for learning about design.

A good reason why the appearance of things tends to be put on one side is that products which are meant to function in a particular way cannot merely look satisfying to the eye or feel good in the hand. Although designing must involve considerations of shape and form, to disregard function eventually leads to inefficiency. This is not the case with aesthetic appearances, however. Temporarily ignoring the appearance of products does not mean they will not work well. Competition between manufacturers of the same product (a kettle, for example) makes aesthetic qualities of design more important. If the function of a dozen kettles is identical, and the prices similar, we can be left with largely (though not entirely) aesthetic considerations about which one to buy. Over and above this choice there is another possible long-term aim which is that we might improve the environment if we were to consider more carefully the design of the objects around us.

Teachers of the 8–13 age range can introduce children to design by talking about it as part of their everyday teaching. Apart from being asked questions like 'Why do you think it is this shape?', children need to have technical processes brought to their notice. Pasting layers of papier-mâché, for example, relates to fibreglass techniques. Joining slabs of clay with a 'weld' joint relates to jointing metal. There are also design-related questions to be asked like

> What would happen if this was made of another material such as . . . ?
> What else can you think of that is made of the same material?
> How do you think the designer has solved the problem of . . . ?

What do you think of the shape of these two steam irons?
How suitable is the decoration on this . . . ?
What else might this be used for?
If you were to change anything in this design what would it be and why?
Why is the neck of this bottle wider than that one?
Why is this the size that it is?
What would happen if this became half/twice its present size?
Why is this heavy/light?
Why does this jug pour better than that one?

A vocabulary which uses words and phrases like 'proportion', 'balance', 'fitness for purpose', 'lines', 'economy of shape' and 'clarity of form' can grow through discussion. At first children may not be particularly good at discussing design but we can expect that much later in life they will begin to appreciate differences between good and bad design, given practice in looking and discussing. Good design should give us the feeling that no other way of solving the problem was possible. We should feel that nothing needs to be changed in the shape or function of what we are examining. If we see bad design we should know why it is bad and what might be done to improve it.

There is also the dimension of design which adds a special quality to functional objects. Where the function is relatively straightforward, like a door handle or a chair, there is often the potential for bringing variety into designs. The glassware in Figure 51 and the wooden

Figure 51 Comparing Shapes in Glassware.

Figure 52 Light-Pulls influenced by Architecture.

light-pulls in Figure 52 are examples of the designer's ability to be creative yet sensitive to pleasing shape. These qualities can emphasize the refinement of form which gives pleasure in handling shapes or drinking from them.

An intriguing facet of design is the way one form influences another, as in the light-pulls which are, according to the designer, influenced by architecture. We see this phenomenon time and again as glass lamp shades which hint at the 1930s look like flowers or shells.

Developing a design sense follows naturally from anything that might be said about drawing. Children can use drawing as a way of 'thinking aloud' on paper and, like drawing a cartoon strip, a sequence of design-related ideas can be presented. Drawing for design is often a case of prediction, especially if it is the work of a professional designer, such as an architect. The architect has to be able to predict what a building will look like because trial-and-error designing, using building materials, is inefficient. The architect resorts to elaborate means of organizing space on paper, developing a sequence in which to construct and adapt the design as one proposal conflicts with another.

Sequencing the stages of designing is central to developing an understanding of design. The same is evident when children are predicting in science. Discovering 'how things work' usually involves understanding various stages of their function and, for this, drawing is a vital ingredient of the designer's thinking process. An obvious way to learn sequencing and prediction is through story-telling and a useful design exercise is to make a story-board or strip of pictures showing the sequence. Topics such as 'How a Deck Chair Folds up', or 'How to Build a Bridge' are examples which children can draw as a sequence of pictures.

Further, we must not ignore drawing as a way of comparing one finished design with another. A very basic design activity is to make a drawing of one object and compare it with a similar design (as might be done with the light- pulls or the glasses). We can then begin designing more shapes of our own in response to what we have already seen. In historical studies of designs for tableware, door handles, windows and all manner of household goods we can make effective use of drawing as a means of comparison. Discussion of the relationship between materials and shapes, curves, style and fashion can highlight the design dimension of each period of history.

Television is particularly good at this in the way it highlights periods of history through drama and films. Extraordinarily accurate research is demanded of costume and set designers, who must discover not only what people wore, but factual information such as when string was abandoned in favour of self-adhesive tape, or when the first polythene bag made its appearance. As television dramas unfold, shapes and patterns in period fabrics and furnishings are complemented with the trivia and objects of the time.

Design is rarely something which ignores style and good design is therefore difficult to discuss unless it is seen in the context of its historical period. What, for instance, makes an eighteenth-century table or a well-proportioned seventeenth-century candlestick a good or bad design? Many designs of the 1970s which were hailed as excellent now look very outdated. But does that indicate they are examples of bad design? The growing fashion for collecting the furnishings and objects of the 1940s and 1950s will probably mean that the worst as well as the best could eventually be revered. The collector's insatiable taste for the future antique often begins to obscure questions of quality. Nostalgia and current fashion enter into the equation.

It would be a mistake, however, to think we should teach children our own personal taste or preference in design. Matters of taste in colour, shape and form are like matters of taste in the rest of the arts. We might bring to children's notice the famous designs of William Morris or the Bauhaus design school. After all, classic Bauhaus chairs are still sold throughout the world and the influence of Morris has long permeated floral fabric designs. We can champion what we believe is excellence in contemporary design but the spirit of what we teach lies in exploration rather than brain-washing. Design sensitivity is not a matter of pointing to a few selected items and taking them as a standard. Like sensitivity to music or literature, design-awareness grows through looking at design frequently enough for its principles to begin to make sense.

Contemporary designs grow from contemporary needs. A Victorian lace iron (Figure 53) which contained a heated slug of iron was an excellent design so long as there was a need for ironing lace and an absence of electricity to heat the iron. The lace iron was small, lightweight and had no sharp edges which might become tangled in the lace. The sliding partition (shown lifted) at the back of the iron meant the slug could be exchanged for another which was already being warmed in the fire. Now the lace iron has become a collectable piece and has the additional though incidental charm of illustrating manufacturing methods which we no longer use.

Five distinct aspects of designing are shown in Chart 16. Each one is part of a cycle of design activity. No aspect is more important than any other and though they are not intended to be in a particular sequence, 'idea generation' and 'information gathering' clearly come

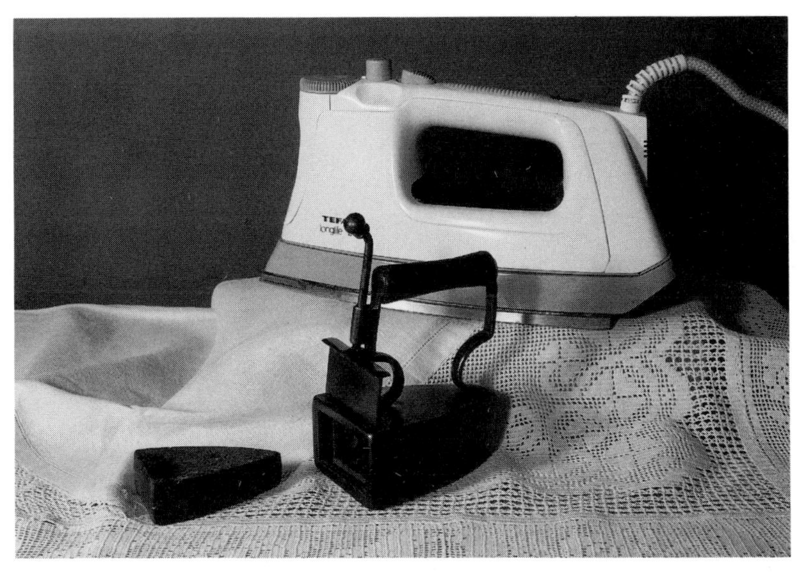

Figure 53 Victorian Lace Iron and 1980s Steam Iron.

before 'making', 'evaluating' and 'modifying' in the order of events. The point here is that for designing to be creative the process must be flexible and will repeat itself many times. Part way through designing we may, for example, need to gather more information or generate more ideas.

Gathering information and generating ideas can include finding out such things as

Who is going to use the design?
What is the design expected to do?
What similar designs already exist?
What problems need to be solved?
What materials do I need?
How might the design be made?
What skills are needed?
How long is it expected to last?
When is the design to be finished?

At this stage it is important to develop as many ideas as possible so that there are enough from which to select and reject. One of the hardest aspects of designing anything (as was pointed out in an earlier chapter) is that having a good idea prevents further thought. The natural tendency is to stop thinking when we have discovered a potentially good idea. When we want to generate more ideas we may have to think of what might happen if we modified the present design by

combining two or more ideas
substituting one part or one idea
eliminating part of the design
using a concept from the design for another design
reversing or changing the arrangement of design features.

Construction of a design may involve crude prototypes. Evaluating and modifying will take us back to the initial identification of the problems we were trying to solve. 'How well does the design fit the original brief?' 'What changes were necessary and how did that affect the design?' Evaluating a design can be very positive and need not

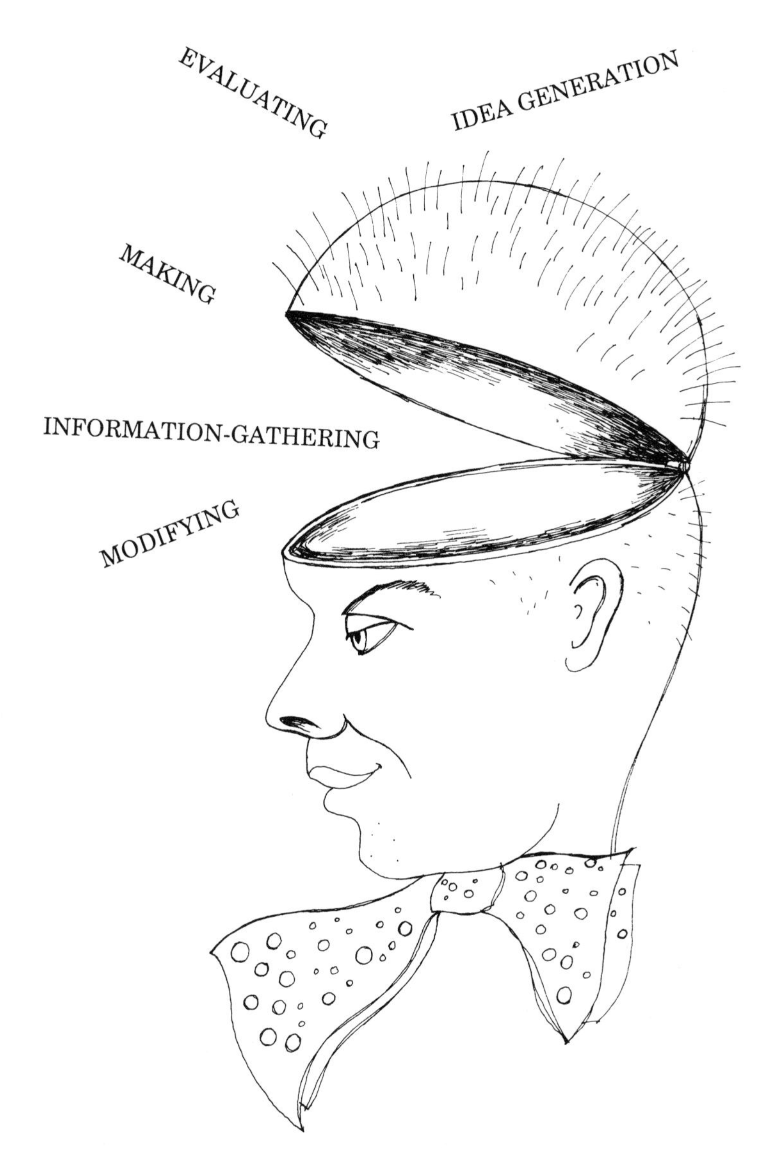

Chart 16 Five Aspects of Designing

destroy children's confidence. It is important not to concentrate on the least successful aspects of their design. We can ask:

What is the best feature of your design?
What would you change if you could?
What do you think of the style and appearance?
How would you add something else to the design?
What are the main problems of construction?
How could fewer materials and stages of construction be incorporated?

If the aim is for children to learn through design-related activities we can see that further development and discussion is an important element of teaching. Children will not automatically think about design unless we use the word often enough and ask questions related to design concepts. Discussing the properties of different adhesives, shapes, decoration, materials and techniques is almost as important as using them. Design-related activities are not particularly new or revolutionary as part of the school curriculum but the important factor is that they are there at all.

Practical examples in art and design

The following examples of projects fall into the design-related and fine art categories. However, there will be ideas triggered for other parts of the curriculum and for that reason no real distinction is drawn here between those activities which are design-focused and those concerned with art, science, or technology. The aim of these examples is to give some idea of a possible range of well-tried art activities.

EXAMPLE 1. THE FABRIC DEPARTMENT

Note: This is a less extensive project than a department store, though a number of variations can be explored using this topic.
Concepts Difference, similarity, variety.
Learning Potential Designing, analysing, comparing, inventing. Drawing, colouring and constructing.
Skills Lettering, painting, drawing, cutting, constructing.
Stimulus Children discuss visual aspects of a fabric department, designing displays, taking photographs. Collecting examples of lettering, packaging, advertising material.

Options Study fabric design, history of a store, fashion.
Materials Children choose from a range made available to them. Some emphasis on limiting colour and shape.
Practical Session Begins by designing lettering and a logo for the store. Children take this theme as a design project involving architecture, furniture, technology. Fine art 'events' in the store.
Development Logo used to promote fabrics, other goods, displays, furniture design studied, drawings from fabrics at home. Development of a particular advertising promotion for the store.

EXAMPLE 2. BLUE AND ORANGE EYES MURAL

Concepts Shape, colour, scale.
Learning Potential Awareness of shape, contrasting colour. Flexibility in designing small-scale preliminary collage for later use. Experience of working with limited range of colour.
Skills Colour discrimination, cutting, sticking, drawing, designing.
Stimulus Children make collections of photographs of eyes from magazines and newspapers. Draw eyes in different positions (use mirror, each other). Also collect blue and orange papers and fabrics.
Options Colour-mixing activity could precede this project. Mural might grow from work using geometric shapes.
Materials Paper, glue, pencils, paint, fabric.
Practical Session Construct a collage from magazine eyes and drawn eyes using this as a preliminary design for a mural. The structure of the mural collage could be based on a geometrical shape, a grid of rectangles, a spiral, a shape derived from drawing an eye and so on. Mural coloured with a variety of mixtures of blue and orange paint, papers, collage. An alternative would be to enlarge drawings of eyes and incorporate different scale from large to small.
Development Other murals using drawn and collaged shapes, e.g. 'Oil Lamps', 'Bicycles', 'Fruit and Veg'. Different range of colours used.

EXAMPLE 3. LOOKING AT PART OF A TREE

Concepts Shape, isolation, invention.
Learning Potential Developing awareness of line, organization of space.
Skills Drawing, decorating.
Stimulus Children look at collected tree bark, twigs, leaves, reference books. Make visits.

Options Preliminary drawings of tree section done outdoors, rubbings of surfaces, drawings of leaves used previously as a pattern. Children look at richly decorated fabrics (decorated with leaves, plant forms).
Materials Paper, pencils, hand lenses.
Practical Session Children examine small section of bark or a small area of the upper branches of a tree. The aim is to make a drawing where line is the most important element. Consider linear patterns on bark or directions of branches. Wood grain.
Development Add small quantities of gold/silver foil. Design painting using only leaf shapes. Use similar process for examining plants, seed heads.

EXAMPLE 4. TWENTY SQUARE CENTIMETRES

Concepts Scale, awareness of detail.
Learning Potential Develop an awareness of how much can be found in a tiny area of our environment.
Skills Magnifying, observing, translating, drawing.
Stimulus Deliberately limited area of visual material.
Options Natural form or man-made? Pencils or paint? Clay or collage?
Materials Pencils, paper.
Practical Session Children choose an area of the environment which is 20 square centimetres in size. Using magnifying lenses they make drawings on a much larger scale. The aim is to search for shapes and patterns within this very small area.
Development Drawings displayed, collages made from structure seen within drawings, abstract paintings, poems. Clay modelling.

EXAMPLE 5. STAGE DESIGN FOR 'SPACE TRAVEL 2001'

Concepts Applied design, function and imagination in combination. Contrast, practicality.
Learning Potential Designing for a dramatic purpose, learning about lighting and colour.
Skills Model-making, painting, drawing, designing a sequence of sets for the story.
Stimulus Drama, creative writing, television series. Photographs, books on volcanoes, geology, minerals, 'astronomical' resources, books on space travel.
Options Design sets and next move into drama or begin in drama? Group work or individual?

Materials Card, paper, pencils, junk, glue, scissors (workshop materials available).
Practical Session Children discuss similarities, differences between planetary landscapes and earth volcanoes. Work in drama. Begin drawing out a sheet of possible designs. Make a story-board. Construct models (group work).
Development Designs developed to be used in puppetry, colour transparencies taken and later projected, science of space travel, use of lighting on models.

EXAMPLE 6. COLOUR-MIXING

Note: By the age of 8 years children should have experienced something like this. It is surprising how many have not.
Concepts Awareness of colour and shades of colour.
Learning Potential Discrimination of colour, use of paint.
Skills Mixing, drawing, painting.
Stimulus Demonstration of mixing different reds and greens using yellows as well as white and black to vary the tone and colour. The aim here is to show that red, for example, can be changed slightly by adding one drop of any other colour so that the change appears to be negligible. Children are given the topic 'A Thousand Vibrations of Red or Green' and asked to think of seeing a fire or fruit through a window made of frosted or distorting glass. Shape is not a main consideration in this project. When their painting is finished, there should be no more than a few brushstrokes which are exactly the same colour.
Options Different mixtures for each few brushstrokes. Red becomes pink, green becomes shades of pale green/white. Painting on top of previously painted sections of the work.
Materials Paint, brushes, crayon, pencil.
Practical Session Children mix colour until it is thick enough to cover newspaper without showing the print through the colour. They attempt to cover the entire paper with different shades of each colour. Add crayon, pastel.
Development Transfer mixing skills to topics such as 'Stage Lighting', 'The Vegetable Patch', 'Leaves', 'Sea Coral'. Other colours explored. Change the medium.

EXAMPLE 7. COMPARING THE BATHROOM WHITES

Note: This project assumes white bathroom fittings. Children could use paint instead of paper but the experience of trying to work with collage techniques is a particularly valuable one. This project and its development section follow on from the previous experience in Example 6.

Concepts Whiteness, tone.

Learning Potential Awareness of the variety of whites found in the environment.

Skills Discrimination, cutting, collage.

Stimulus Collection of assorted white papers from different manufacturers, e.g. writing paper, kitchen paper, printing paper, cartridge, card, duplicating, wrapping, tissue. Photographs of advertisements for bathroom fittings.

Options Paper, chalk, paint.

Materials Paper, scissors, pencils, glue.

Practical Session Children compare various white papers to see the range of the slightly different colours we accept as being white. Make collections of photographs or make drawings of baths, wash basins etc. Draw and construct a collage such that almost all pencil lines are absent. Image appears entirely through subtle differences in white paper or card.

Development Collect black papers, use mixtures of black paint adding minute proportions of other colours. Make images from different black and white newsprint and from magazines.

EXAMPLE 8. BUILDING CONSTRUCTION

Concepts Structure, colour.

Learning Potential Discovering textures, assembling images, discriminating.

Skills Observing, drawing, sticking, comparing, evaluating.

Stimulus Walls, windows, doors and fittings.

Options Collage, paint, clay.

Materials Chosen from the above.

Practical Session Children look at external walls, windows, doors and fittings, photographs; imagine walls. Make drawings, rubbings, study shades of colour in brick and produce a piece of work where the aim is to emphasize one main feature of a building. This might be a window, an elaborate door, a section of wall, a gateway or a roof. It must have some special feature (such as its shape) which renders it worth using as a stimulus for artwork.

Development Study design of walled gardens, climbing plants, graffiti, distortion through glass, reflections in plate glass, wrought iron designs.

EXAMPLE 9. FIFTY-FIFTY CONTRAST

Concepts Contrast, balance.
Learning Potential Awareness of shapes in contrast.
Skills Drawing, cutting, assembling.
Stimulus House plant with interestingly shaped leaves.
Options Paper collage, paint, charcoal.
Materials Black paper, white cartridge, glue, scissors, pencils.
Practical Session Leaf shapes of different sizes are cut from the black paper. Stems of different thicknesses also cut. The children have to arrange the stems and leaves on the white paper until they think there is exactly half white, half black in areas of the two contrasting papers. Glue them. An obvious way to do this is to measure the black paper and make it exactly half the size of the white. However, the children should be encouraged to estimate the balance between black and white for themselves.
Development Look for examples in the environment of half black half white areas of contrast, e.g. in buildings and clothing. Use any remaining scraps of paper for a further collage. Paint designs using black paint on white paper to achieve equal areas.

EXAMPLE 10. GEOMETRIC TEMPLATES

Art educators deplore the use of templates for drawing such things as animals and faces. Geometric templates are quite another matter, however, and can be used to produce designs like those described in Chapter 12. Perhaps the most interesting approach is to take a shape such as a circle and make a template which is derived from compass lines intersecting or running parallel with the circumference. The template which is cut from card is then based on a circular shape (and may have some straight lines as well as curved ones) rather than being just a smaller circle. Children can experiment with a variety of templates which began as a geometric shape and have been adapted. The advantage of using a template, rather than drawing a shape each time, is one of being able to produce repeat patterns fairly quickly. As a design aid, templates have advantages but considerations of scale, colour, decoration and media are also important. Some of the most effective designs are those which behave according to mathematical rules and restricted use of colour.

EXAMPLE 11. MACHINE ROBOTS

Design a robot which has various functions such as arms which extend, rocket-propelled feet, instant transporter button, potato peeler and entertainer screen. List the various activities the robot might be expected to perform and devise a collage, clay model, drawing, or painting which gives some idea of this activity taking place.

EXAMPLE 12. PHOTOGRAPHIC FACE MAKE-UP

The aim here is to take a well-known idea and refine it. The children find parts of photographs from colour magazines and adapt them to make faces. For example, a central heating radiator might become teeth, a transistor radio an ear, a car wheel an eye. Flesh might be made from pictures of food, a tongue from a green pepper. The aim is to let the imagination construct something new from familiar objects. The less obvious it is that, for instance, a wheel was used for an eye, the better. Children should not become too easily satisfied and find only a few examples from which to choose. A development might be that they make drawings from their collages, murals or a group project. Advance collection of magazines is essential. The children need to have far more resources than they will use so that discrimination is possible.

EXAMPLE 13. NEWMOBILE

Design a vehicle which is built entirely for leisure. It should have every desirable leisure facility incorporated. Its method of propulsion should be shown. Written comments, diagrams and so on are part of the design process.

EXAMPLE 14. SPOONERISMS

As Speckled Frogs became Freckled Spogs (Chapter 2), so there are other creatures to draw and paint from the imagination.

Great Big Lion	Late Big Grion
A Wee Mouse	A Mee Wouse
A Conquering King	A Kingkering Kong
A Tunny Fish	A Funny Tish
A Brown Fox	A Frown Box
A Wriggly Eel	An Iggly Reel
A Wombat	A Bombwat

EXAMPLE 15. COLLAGE DIFFERENTIATION

Find fragments of patterned fabric and choose one of them to cut into a shape. This is glued down on a much larger card somewhere near the centre. The aim is then to find papers, mix paint, crayon or any other suitable medium (except fabric), to match any qualities, such as colour, shape, texture and so on found in the chosen fabric. These eventually constitute the matching background around the central fragment. Learning points are concerned with discussion of qualities, how media change those qualities, how repetition of shape affects the design, search for pattern and shape, balance of the whole design and blank areas contrasted with more complex ones.

EXAMPLE 16. DESIGN A COMMERCIAL

This takes place in more than one session. First, study package designs and design a new product such as 'Shrinkwaste Dustbin' which makes rubbish smaller so that the dustbin lasts for longer without being emptied. Each design must fulfil a function. Create a story-board sequence for selling the product. Take this into drama and from there return to designing posters which remind consumers of the product.

EXAMPLE 17. DOUBLE DOSE DRAWINGS

This drawing project relates to Cubism, a feature of which was to create a drawing or painting which depicted objects from more than one angle. A drawing of a group of objects is made using one colour, e.g. in red pencil crayon. The objects are then rearranged and a further drawing superimposed on the same paper (using a different coloured crayon) as if the previous drawing did not exist. It would, of course, be worth superimposing a third drawing if the children's interest could be sustained. Further options include using the drawing as a design for a 'Cubist' collage or painting.

EXAMPLE 18. WOODEN FENCES, GATES AND GARDEN STRUCTURES

Children make rubbings from wooden surfaces, collect reference material for fences, pergolas, trellis, look at photographs, visit, draw. These rubbings are turned face down and the shape of fence panels and wooden gate structures drawn and cut out. Children have to decide on structures for fence and gate. The value lies in exploration of the local environment and designs based on studies which are made. Other problems which are to be solved include perspective and scale. There are also options such as colour of background, collage or paint, 2-D or 3-D. These designs could be based in mathematics, particularly the wooden gates or garden structures.

10

Responding to works of art

It may not be Van Gogh but it's the best sky I've ever painted!
(*10 year-old*)

LIKE THOSE teachers of English who cannot spell, there are many art teachers, even at a highly specialized level, whose training did not include art history. Many have never heard of artists such as Chardin, Velásquez, or Bernini, yet have, all the same, gained a degree or diploma to teach art. Their concern was producing artwork rather than setting it against any cultural context. Particularly in the art schools, exhibitions of work by contemporary artists assumed greater importance than 'old masters' as an influence on students' work. Few students who were frantically searching for their own style wanted to emulate art which was a couple of centuries old.

An increasingly important aspect of art education is one of responding to works of art. Not every child will grow up to be an artist and it is recognized that responding to art in later life is still part of being educated. This is not solely to do with art history or art appreciation. Sensitivity to the environment and being able to discuss what we see are a major part of visual awareness. Developing critical skills in children can begin through learning to respond to their own and each other's work, discussing this in the same way as any other major work of art might be discussed.

Responding to world-famous and original art has unfortunately meant in the past that children learned a few facts about painters and their work. Art history sessions were often infrequent and supported with reproductions, books and the occasional slide lecture. Children were not always expected to take an active part in the events but were listeners and absorbers of historical information. The possibility that they might develop independent critical skills was not something which informed traditional approaches to what was called 'art appreciation'.

Now we expect that children will develop a broader awareness of their cultural heritage of which art history and criticism are a part. Projects, such as 'The Critical Studies in Art Education Project' (Taylor, 1986) have highlighted the relevance of working in galleries and taken account of the inspiration that such experiences can give children. Although the project was aimed at older children as well as the 8 to 13s, the practical involvement of primary-age pupils in this project is carefully outlined. Taylor describes four common threads which run through schools' use of works of art. These are: discussing works of art (whether originals or reproductions); making drawings from a description of a work of art; making studies directly from a work of art; and setting up poses or still-life groups similar to work by famous artists.

An important point Taylor makes is that children can very easily be put off going to galleries if the preparation for their visit is poor. He comments that there is nothing more likely to provoke our regret than 'seeing children pass by things which we admire as masterpieces without even a second glance'. Clearly they need some help and explanation before they set off if they are to be interested, let alone inspired. How might we begin discussing works of art? What features are there to which children can feel able to respond?

The business of looking at anything with a critical eye is rarely as straightforward as it might seem. Marcia Pointon (1986) writes:

> Obviously, to look at stained glass only through binoculars is never to see it as it was intended to be seen. On the other hand, however, the full quality of colour and the effectiveness of technique cannot be appreciated without a closer look. The art historian wants to know not only what it is but also how it has been made. Similarly, the magnifying glass is not only used by art historians to authenticate a work or to examine a signature but can assist towards knowledge about how a picture was painted.

This 'closer look' referred to does not necessarily involve binoculars and magnifying lenses. We can also find out about works of art through television, film and reproductions besides visiting a gallery. Although the quality of the original work cannot be adequately reproduced, there are activities such as painting which are more difficult to organize in a gallery and may best be set up in a classroom. Galleries, however, have long established the importance of their educational programmes and many of them run practical courses for children. The limitations of photographic reproductions are easily discovered when we try to find out what exactly was the medium used by an artist. Some reproductions give no idea whether or not the artist has used oils, acrylic, screen printing, or coloured etching. Colour reproduction does little justice to the subtleties and intensity of colours in an original work of art.

The 'guided tour' of major exhibitions is now a regular feature. The implication is that seeing works of art can be more worthwhile if there is information and discussion as part of the gallery visit. In truth we need to be educated to almost all the art we see, especially as the context in which it was produced can easily escape our knowledge. It is probably just as difficult without knowing the context to discriminate between two eighteenth-century Dutch portraits as it is to compare two contemporary works of art.

Children's own work

Any work of art, whether it is by a child or a famous artist, presents certain visual qualities which can be pointed out. Knowing how to look at a painting is an important part of children's own development as artists and they can often make a start by looking at their own artwork and referring to the work of others. Naturally, with experience of looking at works of art, we develop a special sensitivity to qualities of expression which fall quite outside any arbitrary list we could make. Even so, we can discuss

what we asked the children to do
further ideas around the theme on which they are working
feelings evoked by the artwork
their use of fantasy and imagination
shapes, colours, lines, patterns, tone, texture
scale, size of the design
handling of materials
a particular technique
the effort put in
ways in which ideas could be used in another medium at another time

Composition - the arrangement of shapes within a rectangle, a circle, and so on.

It is far more worthwhile to look for specific qualities than it is to take a generalized view of the work. All too often, teachers are unable to find much more to say than 'That's good', or 'I like that', as if general encouragement teaches children about what they are doing. They need some idea as to what they might do next time to improve on their work. What could they have added or changed? What pleases and displeases them in their work and why? There is no way to avoid influencing children by what we say. But if we are to help them to understand the visual qualities in their work then clearly we must refer to these by discussing them because to do otherwise is to avoid the issue. Of the possible qualities we could find to discuss these are some examples:

well-drawn shapes
good use of colour, line, tone
carefully selected detail
atmosphere
balanced design

Figure 54 Fantasy Trees. Age 13.

inventive pattern
inventive ideas
creative interpretation
sensitive use of media.

All have their more negative counterparts such as badly mixed paint or poor use of colour and it should be remembered that no single piece of work will include all of the above qualities. (A drawing in pencil, for example, can hardly exemplify good use of colour.) The fact that they are discussed at all is important in the development of visual discrimination and an obvious outcome of considering these visual qualities is that teachers are likely to develop their own artistic 'vocabulary'. The task is not so difficult as it might seem because the responsibility for seeing qualities ultimately lies with the children we teach. We can comment on the care with which shapes have been drawn without knowing much about art. Developing a personal artistic vocabulary can also be a process learned alongside the children rather than explored away from the classroom.

Commonly used words like ceramics, kiln, firing, mobile, collage, brushwork and mural can be introduced to children, as can adjectives such as embellished, vibrant, abstract, dramatic, subtle, ominous, or lively. Further than this, creative teachers will generate a vast repertoire of discussion topics which they enjoy developing just as much as do their children. Examples might be: 'How a Sculptor Makes a Maquette', 'Why Painters Often Use Long-handled Brushes', or 'What Differences there are between Water-based Paints and Acrylics'.

Two ways of looking at works of art

Critical responses to artwork can obviously be elicited through asking children questions. Factual information about the lives of painters illuminates character and gives some insight into the artists as 'people' but need not necessarily give much insight into their work. Looking critically at works of art and putting them in context is often far more important. Van Gogh once lived in London but that fact does not necessarily bring us much closer to understanding his work. Most schoolchildren know that Van Gogh cut off his ear but details about the oil-lamp days in which he lived, and information in his letters to his brother Theo, can perhaps tell us more about his work. He wrote about his use of colour and his development of artistic ideas saying that he was an arbitrary colourist who would exaggerate the fairness of the hair using orange tones, chromes and pale citron-yellow. (Again, we are likely to touch on artistic elements of colour, shape, pattern, line, tone and texture.) If we are to understand Van Gogh's work are we not more concerned with the qualities of expression, his use of colour and his painterly brushstrokes than details about his problematic life?

Gaitskell and Hurwitz (1970) identified four very useful areas in which to discuss a work of art with children. This was discussed in a previous publication (Barnes, 1987) but their model remains an excellent and understandable focus.

(1) What do you see? (Description)
(2) How are things put together? (Analysis)
(3) What is the artist trying to say? (Interpretation)
(4) What do you think of it? (Judgement)

Tempting though it is, we should not give children our own insights before we have discovered theirs. A major source of difficulty is to encourage children to look at works of art yet restrain ourselves from pointing out features which we think they would otherwise miss. Children's critical awareness needs to be extended but not at the expense of losing independence in their acquisition of these personal skills. If there is a fine balancing act to be achieved it is between informing children and relying on their ability to see for themselves. How similar this is to any other part of the curriculum. Education, in its broadest sense, is nearly always a combination of understanding and information, self-discovery and taught knowledge.

The four areas already mentioned deal with the work of art as a physical object. Context is hardly touched on in these four but is also important in trying to discover what the artist is saying and in making some judgement of the work. Rembrandt's use of colour, for example, would have to be seen in the context of the colours he had available to him at the time. Bright reds, greens and yellows were practically unknown until the discovery of aniline dyes in the second half of the nineteenth century. A critical study of a Claude Monet *Lily Pond* needs to take account of the aims of the French Impressionists and be compared with Monet's many other paintings of his garden pond. In looking at famous paintings such as these, art historians are just as likely to emphasize the political and artistic climate of the time as they are the physical artefact. Pointon (1986) identifies further areas of analysis when looking at a painting. The political, artistic and social contexts are evident in the kind of questions she asks.

What is it?
How did it come to be here?
Where is it?
What did people think of it?
When and where was it made?
What is going on in it?
How is it organized?
For whom was it made?
Is it effective?
What condition is it in?
What does it mean?
What did it mean?
How is it presented?
What is it made of?
How much did it cost?
Is it the only one of its kind?

The intriguing aspect of this second way of looking at art is that it can, to some extent, be applied to objects found in nature, to architecture and even to the bric-à-brac of the attic. Responding critically also includes being aware of the aesthetic qualities of those forms which have not necessarily been produced by an artist. The point about having some means of analysing what we see is that although it may not be perfect, using a set of questions is a very good means of getting to know how we respond. Hildred (1987) comments that aesthetic experience involves 'an attitude of particular attention to ongoing experience – noticing that you are noticing'.

The samurai of ancient Japan would spend his day off contemplating a stone. He did not think he was wasting his time. Every form found in nature or work by an artist will have its own particular characteristics quite outside any formal analysis. However, wide-ranging questions like 'What can you see?' are likely to highlight the especial qualities of, for instance, light in a Monet or despair and jealousy in a painting by Edvard Munch. Brain-coral and seed heads may have jewel-like intricacy whilst we may feel that stones can have qualities such as dignity, smoothness and serenity.

Practical activities associated with critical studies are most likely to be aimed at close study of original works of art and reproductions.

Setting up a pose from a famous painting has already been mentioned as one example of a practical project. Studying the style of a painter like Van Gogh is another. In Figures 55–60 we can see some of the results from a project undertaken with 9 and 10 year-olds. They began by looking at reproductions of paintings by Van Gogh and particularly studied qualities of brushstroke and direction of line. The first piece of practical work they did was to make drawings which explored the swirling marks which might have been used by Van Gogh. Some of the children followed this by creating collages which had a 'directional' quality. Others explored colour-mixing and the way in which Van Gogh built up his colours, brushstroke by brushstroke. The aim was to try to understand rather than copy a particular Van Gogh reproduction.

Next session, the children each studied a fragment of a reproduction as accurately as they could. The reproduction had been cut up and each piece numbered. A corresponding number on the back of the child's artwork identified the section of the reproduction and the results were finally put together to make a mural. The use of fragments for study and production of the mural was informed by the two previous activities concerned with brushstrokes and directional lines.

What did the children learn? In the paintings based on brushstrokes they had to make sure that light and dark mixtures of colour were clearly separated. They obviously learned a great deal about colour, especially through trying mixtures made up of pale yellows as well as whites. Different qualities of blue were explored, not simply lighter or darker blues. Those doing a collage had to organize how much space they would leave blank and what they needed to make a collage have 'direction' or movement.

A key feature of sessions was to keep returning to the reproductions of Van Gogh's work to discuss them. The production of a mural, interesting though it was, formed part of the project rather than the main focus. If children knew more about the way Van Gogh worked then the session had been successful in its aim. It was not even necessary that paintings and collages should look like the work of Van Gogh when they were finished because the whole experience was important as a way of developing children's own artwork. Its value was best summed up by an excited child who said, 'It may not be Van Gogh but it's the best sky I've ever painted!' Even when the project was over, the children's teacher was keen to make further use of their experience.

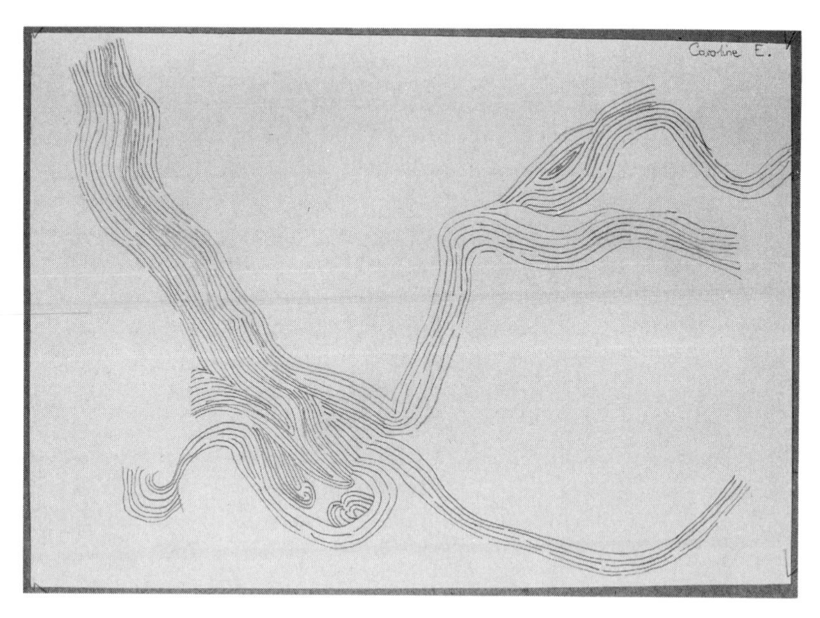

Figures 55, 56 Drawings based on Van Gogh's brushwork. Age 10.

Figure 57 Study of brushwork from Van Gogh. Age 10.

I think I'd want to get the children to write about this experience next . . . They seemed to grasp the qualities of brushstroke and very quickly developed a 'painterly' way of working. I want to follow this up with a similar project next term and see how much they have developed.

(*Teacher*)

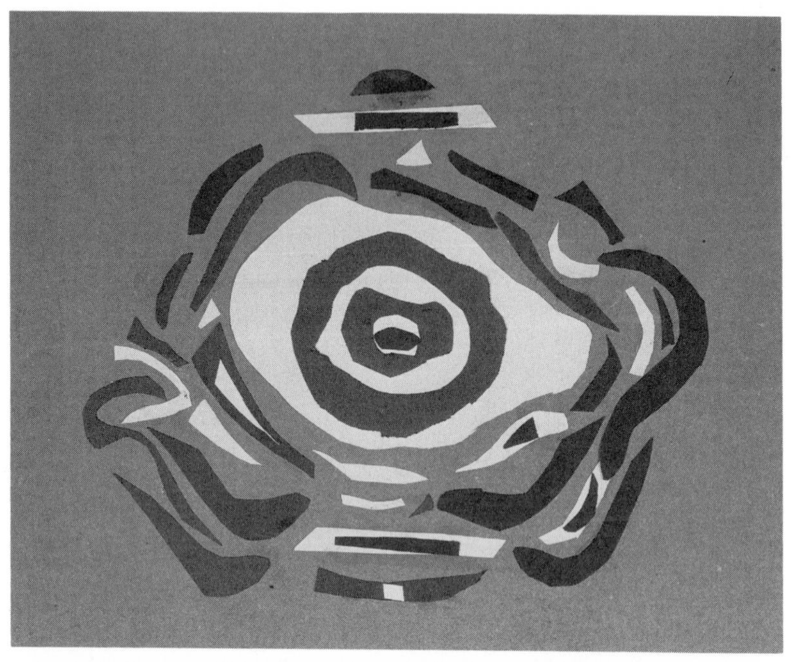

Figures 58, 59 Collages based on 'directional' lines in a Van Gogh. Age 9/10.

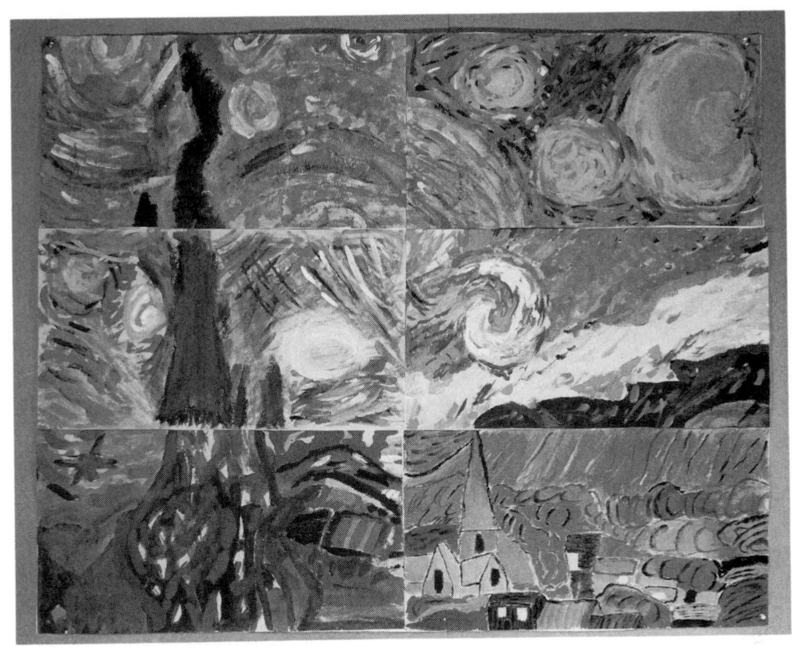

Figure 60 Group mural based on a Van Gogh painting. Age 9/10.

Evaluating artwork

A natural consequence of trying to develop critical skills is that we are involved in making judgements. Space permits only a summary of a model for assessment of children's work (published previously in full, Barnes 1987). Five categories are proposed which can be assessed against known criteria. These are

(1) process of working (e.g shows initiative, independence)
(2) handling of materials (e.g. able to mix paint to a good consistency)
(3) use of media (e.g. discriminates when using colour)
(4) critical skills (e.g. can point to similarities, differences in things seen)
(5) stages of personal development (e.g. has confidence in producing artwork. Drawing advanced for age).

Evaluation, by contrast, is taken to mean making a judgement about the educational value of what we have done, not assessing children or their work. Evaluative questions are those such as 'What did the children gain from the project on Van Gogh?', 'How well is children's drawing developing?' or 'How independently are they working?' Questions such as these focus on the learning content of our own teaching and are useful in that they influence future planning.

It is important to take a positive view of evaluation for two reasons. First, children generally progress in their artistic learning if we emphasize their successes rather than their failures. Secondly, as a social group, teachers are perhaps one of the most self-critical in our society. A crucial aspect of artistic learning is that teachers and children invest a great deal of their own emotional energy in what they are doing and are therefore vulnerable to critical comment. It follows that evaluation must emphasize the good as well as the bad if it is to be worth undertaking.

The job of teaching is in reality an impossible one if we consider the demands from the various authorities, parents and children. The illusion of perfection is sought by many conscientious teachers and it is all too easy for parents, the government, the media and teachers themselves to be highly critical of apparently imperfect standards of achievement. In the arts we witness teachers and children taking risks and frequently they have to live with their own failures. Yet it is in the nature of art teaching that if we are not prepared to make mistakes we will actually achieve very little.

There is also a sense in which evaluating anything gives us an impression of having done final justice to a project, a term's work, or perhaps an in-service course we may have helped to organize. Yet good practice is to evaluate continuously rather than wait for specific occasions where evaluation can be a group affair. Teachers of art and design, more so if they are specialists, tend to have quite personal approaches to their teaching, and their children's work is characterized as much by what is missing as by what is there. There may, for example, be very little except painting, no print-making, little three-dimensional work, or a peculiarly narrow range of materials available. It should be remembered that this is not necessarily an abnormal state of affairs. It is not possible to cover every conceivable permutation of teaching style. There are, however, a number of agreed areas in art teaching which are regarded as essential. They have been reduced here to a set of minimal indictments.

The inspector's torpedo

You are hereby charged that in the course of the year of your present duties you did fail to teach art, design and topic work adequately and are guilty of the following commonly known offences.

(1) That you made no mention of artistic qualities such as 'intense red', 'subtle shades', 'balanced design', 'contrast', 'movement' and so on. Children were unable to use an artistic vocabulary which included words like 'kiln', 'glaze', 'firing', 'brushstrokes', 'linear', 'vermilion', or 'repeated shapes'.

(2) You failed to use any white paint in your range of colours, thereby depriving children of the discovery that colour is not simply to be watered down to make it paler. In many instances children were only able to use colours which were mainly in a dark tone and the work had very little contrast where it really needed to demonstrate a full range of tones from dark to light.

(3) On closer inspection it was discovered that the range of colours you had ordered on the school requisition contained only one red, namely crimson, instead of a minimum range such as two reds (e.g. crimson and vermilion), two blues (e.g. ultramarine and Prussian blue), two yellows (e.g. yellow ochre and a bright yellow), a black and a white. In mitigation it is recognized that you did supplement this range with orange, brown, purple and green.

(4) You further did make no attempt to encourage children to mix various shades of colour from these basic ingredients. They dipped brushes in whatever was available. Consequently all paintings in the class were similarly red, yellow, blue, green, purple and brown, usually all in the same painting.

(5) White paper was the only colour available on which to paint. Coloured papers were only used for making posters for school events. You had no intention of showing children how to mix paint thickly enough to cover print on a newspaper without it showing through. This would have ensured it was sufficiently well mixed for children to paint over coloured papers such as grey sugar paper.

(6) All pencil drawings seen were executed with very blunt yet hard pencils. At no time was any drawing articulated in sharp and distinct lines. Though there was a pencil sharpener of impressive technological complexity this was never used.

(7) Resources in the form of interesting visual material, objects, reproductions and photographs were entirely absent from your classroom. Children were expected to work from memory.

(8) Fantasy and imagination were not allowed in any work. Drawings, paintings and collages were produced only to represent facts in topic work.

(9) Children were not allowed the opportunity to vary what you asked them to do. The concept of 'change' in their work did not enter into your teaching strategy.

(10) You failed to see any relationship between one piece of work and another. The phrase cross-curricular was unknown to you.

(11) The children were unable to try any work in a special medium such as is used in print-making or claywork.

(12) No other three-dimensional work was evident. The idea that children could be problem-solvers and designers was never considered. Only one type of glue was available and some half-used rolls of sticky tape.

(13) Children were unable to draw without copying or filling in outlines provided by you. They consequently made frequent requests for you to draw outlines of things you were quite unable to draw.

Failure to rectify this sorry state of affairs will result in this authority condemning you to teach facts alone in the style of the schools of the late nineteenth century.

Taylor (1986) mentions that many pupils become interested in art as a result of some particularly 'illuminating experience'. Earlier (Chapter 2) the phrase 'moments of poignancy' was used. We cannot make such experiences happen but we can evaluate the experience we provide for children and the quality of teaching which might bring illumination their way. The process of evaluating calls for interpretation and few areas of the curriculum lend themselves more readily than art to the criticism of being subjective. Yet all areas can have that charge levelled at them as soon as there are questions of quality to be determined. Discoveries in science still have to be interpreted. Numbers and symbols in mathematics have no meaning until we attach a meaning to them (Best, 1985).

Where subjects such as art, dance, literature, drama or music are concerned their currency is *meaning or knowledge beyond fact*. Evaluation, therefore, is a matter of learning to make professional judgements in the light of our own teaching experience measured against that of interested colleagues, educationists, advisers and inspectors. There is often a remarkable consensus amongst teachers about the qualities to be found in children's artwork. This is all the more surprising when we consider that we are trying to deal with our judgement of someone else's vision expressed through a work of art.

11

Working in 3-D

IN THE 1950s children were taught 'handwork', which usually meant following instructions to the letter and making the same model as everyone else. Now we would expect them to put much more of their energies into expressing their own ideas and finding solutions to construction problems. Skills learned along the way can be transferred to other situations and links made between model-making, sculpture and construction techniques. If children are making sculpture they are exploring form in relation to space and a prime concern is that of expressing a three-dimensional world in a three-dimensional way. It is noticeable that most children spend their school days working in two dimensions rather than three and the reasons for this are many. Two of them are that classroom space tends to be invaded by 3-D work and considerable time is taken to complete it.

From a purely organizational standpoint any work in 3-D is going to be more demanding to teach than is flat 2-D work of the pencil-and-paper kind. On the other hand, good 3-D work which is tackled over an extensive period of time can be the most memorable of all art experiences for children. They learn the limitations of each material, whether or not it will bend or glue to another surface, and how it encloses or defines the space around it. In two-dimensional work we tend to use the word 'shape' (often associated with outlines) and reserve the word 'form' for something more three-dimensional. Occasionally there is confusion because we can use the word 'form' to mean something we have represented in a painting or drawing. Children can begin to develop a concept of three-dimensional form, however, by working round a sculpture, construction or model, and this experience is an important aspect of their art education.

Some sculptures are meant to be viewed from a particular side but most do not have a front or back view to them. A major contrast with painting is that 3-D work is usually meant to be seen from a multiplicity of viewpoints and, in some instances, the work should be explored in a tactile way by being touched or handled. We can experience seeing expressive qualities which actually change as we walk around the 3-D work or turn it round in our hands. Nuances of form and shifts in the balance of shapes all contribute to a total experience of the characteristics of the sculpture, construction, functional object, ceramic form, or assemblage.

The nature of most 3-D work is such that it consumes time, including 'drying time' or 'setting time' when certain materials are used. Often the best way to work with three-dimensional materials is to embark on projects which children clearly understand from the outset will extend over two or three weeks. In the first instance, however, it is important to produce something which does not take that length of time so that children are not bored by waiting for the final results of their work.

One reason why teachers will show children a puppet or a model which has been made in advance is that they want to motivate children to try their hand at making something similar. Provided the model is used to discuss construction techniques and is not held up to be copied the practice is an understandable one. Children cannot work for an extended period of time entirely without knowing what they are aiming to produce. Extending children's 3-D work is a matter of attitudes and the hurdles of coping with time taken and space available must be overcome early in the process.

Sequencing 3-D activities is also important because skills need to be reinforced and developed from project to project. Children are unlikely to develop any expertise in 3-D work unless they build up some basic skills such as how to cut, fold, glue and model in media like card, wood, papier-mâché and clay. The aim of developing skills, as with other art activities, is to teach children to work independently rather than step by step with their teacher. They need to be able to make connections between one technique and another, one idea and a variety of ideas.

A start can be made by taking an idea which is essentially two-dimensional and turning it into three dimensions. Figure 61 shows a birthday card which began as a two-dimensional design problem and was resolved in this interesting way. What could have remained as a fairly flat piece of artwork has been designed using an approach which can be applied to a range of activities involving decorated paper or card. Simple prints or a paper collage could be produced. Very little imagination is needed to turn these into cylinders or to use shapes which are cut and folded to make a pattern which decorates a plain white card cylinder (Figure 62). Many twentieth-century canvases have three-dimensional qualities and the division between painting, relief and sculpture is by no means clearly defined. Sticking three-dimensional forms to a painting is one way in which this mixed-media work can first arise and there is much to be said for translating an idea from one dimension to another.

Collage techniques and 3-D work have a great deal in common. In a collage, a central aim is to sort out one material, area, or colour from another so that it looks as if it was placed intentionally rather than by accident. Children need to make sure shapes do not merge together or the resulting collage may become so complicated that it lacks unity. The same applies to working with three-dimensional materials to make a sculpture. Discrimination, intention, contrast, unity, balance and so on are considerations. The work needs to have a 'readable' quality so that contrasts are clearly realized and shapes

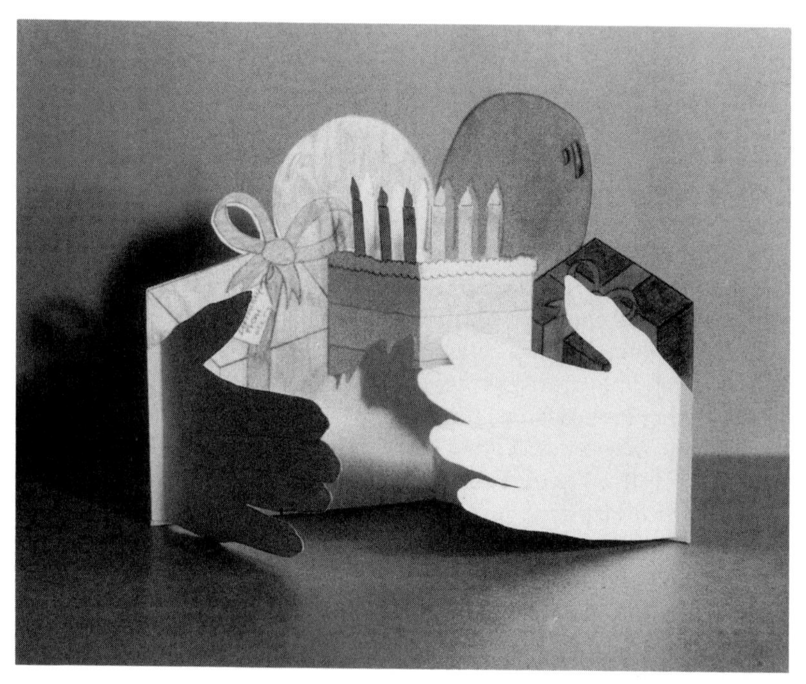

Figure 61 Birthday Card. Age 13.

Figure 62 Cylinders and Shapes.

have a power and clarity which can be registered by the eye from a short distance.

The National Portrait Gallery's education courses, run in May 1988, made a profitable link between collage and sculpture. Sessions were organized to complement an exhibition by the contemporary sculptor Eduardo Paolozzi who is known to design his sculptures using collage 'fragments', translating these into three dimensions. An aim was to understand something of Paolozzi's work by trying techniques related to his work methods. Children on the courses were asked to make drawings of portraits in the twentieth-century rooms of the gallery and the results formed a 'lucky dip' of drawn features. Each student then reconstituted a face from a mixture of other people's drawings, thus making their own collage and 'fragmented face'. A worthwhile follow-up to this might have been for children to make sculptures from their collages when they returned to school.

Of the possible range of skills necessary for 3-D work these listed here seem to be particularly important. They are included to reinforce the view that teaching children skills of construction is a far more flexible approach than making specific predetermined models. They are:

learning to fold card along a scored line
knowing how to curve paper strips, pleat paper and twist it
being able to join clay so that it does not fall apart when it dries
cutting shapes in card, paper, or clay exactly to a drawn outline
learning to saw timber (such as pieces of dowel) without disaster
learning to use a hand drill, screwdriver, hammer and nail
learning how to smooth and polish wooden shapes
knowing which glue is the appropriate one to use
being able to use exactly the right amount of glue to stick things together
knowing how to cut tabs to fix a cardboard cylinder to another shape
being able to measure and cut with more than average accuracy
learning several ways to join materials together

There is nothing very new or revolutionary about these skills but how well they are learned fundamentally affects what can be achieved. Gluing a tab of card and cutting exactly to a drawn line are two examples where being skilful has obvious spin-offs for later work. The teaching point to grasp about learning a skill is that it can hardly be described as 'skilful' if there has been no attempt to try to improve on the accuracy and care which are taken. It ought to be obvious (but is far from obvious in practice) that learning to construct things is doomed to failure if high standards of measuring, cutting and gluing are not insisted on. Even if the highest standards are not actually achieved, their achievement should still be a worthwhile aim.

> I learned what accuracy meant when I was an apprentice shop fitter. We did some very high-class work fitting churches and the best shops in the city. The foreman was a man called Mr Bodger. He seemed determined to live down his name and if a piece of wood had to be cut to an exact length, or we had to measure an exact angle, then that's how it was. You didn't aim to get things more or less accurate. They were either accurate or they were not.
>
> (*Teacher of Craft, Design, and Technology*)

A remarkably simple but effective practice exercise can be done by children to increase accuracy in using scissors. Each is given a small piece of scrap paper and draws a curved line across the paper with a sharp pencil. Next, they take the scissors and attempt to cut along the length of this line in such a way as to split it in two down its entire length. If they veer off the line the advice given is that they slow down until they can cut more accurately. Ideally it should be possible to find traces of pencil line along the curves of both cut pieces of paper when they are closely examined. The natural tendency is to cut accurately for a short distance and suddenly speed up in the haste to reach the end of the pencil line. As in many other skills, children need to learn not to let their minds race ahead of their practical ability.

Figures 63 to 66 show stages in the construction of papier-mâché figures. (See also Plates 23 and 25.) These models were made by 10 and 11 year-olds and the figures boast names such as 'Deadly Dan, the Sausage Man' and 'Ricky the Rocker'. They are excellent examples of how a simple technique can be developed to become more sophisticated. Strictly speaking the models are a combination of wire, rolled paper and layer upon layer of paper, though other modelling materials were used for details. Wire is fixed to a small wooden base to form an armature and two tubes are glued to it to construct legs. The design of the clown's suit, for example, became part of the underlying structure from the very start and thinly rolled paper was strengthened with newspaper and glue. The model was finished with hard toilet tissue of the very old-fashioned kind. When the figures had been painted with liquid tempera paint and poster colour (mixed with a little PVA glue), they were varnished with polyurethane clear varnish. Sticking paper around a wire armature, however, is only one consideration. Before that stage we have to think:

Who might the characters be?
What will they *do?*
What movement, twist of the head, raised arm might there be?
What position most expresses the character of the figure?
How might it balance?
What action might be seen in the face?
How might the style of the jacket or skirt look?
What opportunities for colour and decoration are there?

Questions like these can continue to influence the design when the models are still under construction. It cannot be emphasized too strongly that responding as an artist means that judgement is deferred and changes are made so that the models can develop as they are

Figures 63, 64 Stages in Papier-Mâché Construction. Age 9/11.

made. Changes of mind and additional ideas are all part of keeping the process alive and creative, as this teacher describes:

> Once the basic body frame has been constructed there is no limit to where the imagination can lead . . . The whole project caused much excitement and conversation with children swapping ideas about what their character was going to be and how they would design it . . . some children became experts in making hats, sausages or spectacles and were willing to share their experience . . . the models almost became real people to the children, many of them giving them names . . . any

Figure 64

> problems happened in the initial stages . . . it was difficult to get the figures to stand up straight if too many stages were attempted all in one lesson without allowing enough drying time . . . some tubes got too wet and collapsed but all the problems were easily resolved once the tubes had dried again. I think in future it would be possible to work on much larger figures, say, three times the size and to work in groups and make a group model like a circus scene, sporting event or a fairground.

Using papier-mâché is not always a matter of sticking layer upon layer until the form is thick enough to withstand handling. The process can be accelerated by making hollow paper tubes beforehand, covering them with more paper later on. Having two kinds of paper (e.g. tissue and magazine) also helps to see which layer is which. PVA (white woodworking) glue, however, is not particularly good for papier-mâché because of its very sticky quality and does not dry well enough to harden the construction. It can be used with paper as a modelling medium but some experimentation is needed with this way of working. Cold-water paste (school paste without harmful fungicides) produces much better results and the models are unlikely to stick to their owners each time the children try to put them down.

Figures 65, 66 Finished Models. Age 9/11.

Constructing from paper spills is also a useful approach (Figure 67) because it produces very lightweight structures. The forms can be covered with paper and the structure still remain light enough for use in activities such as mask-making or large-scale sculptures. The spills photographed here are in pyramid form, which is very strong, but there are also alternatives to using these geometric shapes.

Almost any object can be used as a former to be covered in papier-mâché. The traditional clay and Plasticine formers can be smeared with soap or grease to recover them later. Corrugated card, wire, wire-netting, balloons, lollipop sticks, dowels, rolled newspaper, crumpled newspaper and adhesive tape all make good starting-points and where the papier-mâché is cleverly used the technique need not be evident. Powerful designs should command the attention so the construction technique appears to be almost an afterthought. Like accuracy, technique should eventually be taken for granted.

Papier-mâché work can also be approached in a quite different way. Traditionally, a pulped mixture is made from torn pieces of newspaper

Figure 67 Newspaper Spills.

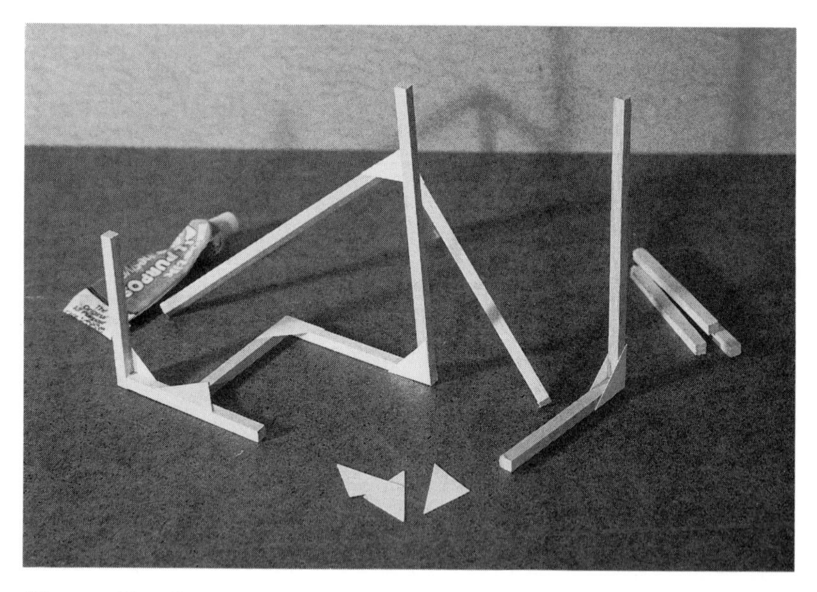

Figure 68 Construction Method.

and paste. This is how papier-mâché (mashed paper) became known in the first place. The paper is put in a bucket and left to soak for a day with paste or PVA glue as a binder. Newspaper is better than glazed paper from magazines as the latter is difficult to break down into fibres. The resulting soggy mixture is squeezed out in a sieve or wrapped in a cloth and wrung out to remove most of the moisture. It then becomes a modelling medium in its own right and almost any shape can be formed. The method is very versatile but drying time can be critical.

Ways of joining a variety of materials are in themselves a learning experience for children. David Jinks (Williams and Jinks, 1985) has pioneered simple ways of constructing things from wood, cans and assorted junk. Particularly useful is the method he suggests for making simple card joints (Figure 68). As can be envisaged, this approach could also be used to make sculptures.

Various diagrams and instructions on making models appear in magazines. A few are excellent but most are so inflexible that they actually rule out creative thought. Once we are locked into trying to follow a carefully mapped out plan, there is little left to the imagination unless we disregard the step-by-step instructions and go our own way. Where one teacher might see these diagrams and instructions as a good project to undertake, another teacher's approach will be far more ambitious. The question which most naturally occurs to the ambitious teacher is not 'How can I do this?' but 'What can I do with this method of constructing?', and maybe this should be the first question we ask ourselves rather than the last. Published instructions and diagrams should not be seen as sacrosanct but as indicators of ways to construct.

Ever since Picasso began assembling sculpture from wood scraps in his Cubist period of 1910–14, 'assemblages' have fascinated artists. Assembled sculpture usually demands very simple woodworking techniques to make the pieces stay together and the scraps may need to be adjusted and modified on a school woodworking bench. The nature of assemblages is that they are, for the most part, abstract works of art. One reason for this is that the shift of emphasis is away from representing something as a church stonemason might have done, and towards allowing the qualities of the scraps to be expressed as they are. In other words the assemblage becomes an object to be looked at for its own qualities. Assemblages are often monumental, balanced, witty, emotional, rhythmic, contrasted, or fragile and can also be figurative like the one in Figure 69.

One way to approach the business of assembling is to have a theme in mind before beginning. A theme such as 'symmetry', 'tension', or 'rhythm' can give the assemblage some unity. A common failing in children who are working on assemblages is that they try to assemble too many pieces. Their overall design becomes confused and complicated unless there is a strong shape to contain a miscellaneous collection of parts. The teacher's role is one of encouraging children to discriminate between qualities which already exist in each piece which has been collected. There is not much point in finding a piece of driftwood (which has its own aesthetically pleasing 'eroded' appearance) and covering it with so many pieces of bric-à-brac that its qualities can no longer be experienced.

The reason for making assemblages does not rest solely in learning to construct. Poems, drama and the history of twentieth-century art also have their part to play. Figurative assemblages like the 'Robotic Man' can become starting points for writing or drama. Like the one which is photographed here, they may be quite temporary and could be assembled, rearranged, or dismantled at the end of a day.

Figure 69 Robotic Man. Age 13.

Working in clay

Some of the same concerns which were important when using papier-mâché are also relevant to clay-modelling. Movement and action are particularly critical yet they need not always arise as the work progresses. Sometimes in 3-D work, movement is evident before any modelling or carving begins. Figure 70 shows a carving from Indonesia. The craftspeople carve creatures according to the shapes suggested by this variety of tree parasite, which grows like a fungus and is quite hard to the touch. The photograph is included as an example of the way in which an artist can respond to the natural movement of the form and turn it into action. A novel approach to claywork might be to create a sense of movement in a piece of clay and begin to fashion the shape in response to whatever it suggested. Twisted tree roots, plant forms, or driftwood might suggest imaginative creatures which could be modelled.

Figure 70 Fish 'Parasite' Carving from Indonesia.

Another source of inspiration might be found in the natural forms suggested by photographs in Chapters 6 and 7, especially where they suggest movement. Many natural forms have a sense of life within them and can prove to be an excellent starting point on which to base designing with clay. Looking at forms which have abstract qualities can take us on a journey of the imagination. We are the ones who invent from the abstract shapes, much as we might find a stone on the beach and discover that it looked like a creature, or as the two sisters (Chapter 8) scribbled, exchanged papers and found something to draw within the existing lines.

Creating shapes without first knowing what they will be contrasts sharply with making carefully planned models. It is doubtful if looking at lumps of clay and turning them into creatures will sustain children's interest for ever. They also need to find out what clay will do by trying to make it fit their intentions. In their early years they will probably have discovered that clay is different from Plasticine and that it can be pushed and pulled about until it becomes hard and 'tired'. It begins to crack and if mixed with water will form a sticky slurry known as 'slip'. Making clay models explores the limitations of the medium and influences the final design. Children discover that certain clay shapes simply fall apart. They find that the detail they expected to incorporate is not so easy to achieve as it is with a pencil on paper and must learn particular techniques and skills if they are not to become frustrated.

Stimulus for modelling is just as crucial as it is in any other media. Collections of photographs, pictures of faces or books on animals are typically useful resources. Children may also wish to act out a drama as if their clay model characters were characters in a play. They might imagine something like 'Making the Tea', 'Mending a Bicycle' or 'Having an Argument'. Particular characters might fascinate them such as 'Old Man on a Windy Day', 'Pop Star with her Mouth Open', 'The Cellist', 'Tug o' War for Six Footballers', 'An Opera Singer', 'The Surgeon', or 'Clowns Falling Over'. These topics are lively examples which demand a sense of movement and vitality somewhere within their construction.

Of course, using movement is not compulsory and there can be very straightforward 'passive' models of houses and figures in repose. Yet a sense of 'something happening' in the model makes the problem a more ambitious one for children to solve and helps them think their way to expressive claywork. It is difficult to imagine children trying to portray a mood without putting some action in the model. 'A Sad

Face', 'An Angry Cat', 'An Excited Cockerel' or 'A Frightened Horse' are examples. Modelling human faces is also an option, if only because humans are apparently the only animals capable of smiling. However much we might like to think otherwise, the smile of the crocodile or the domestic pet is imagined and relates to how we see a smile. No other creature has the facial muscles necessary to produce a smile.

The surface of clay lends itself to being decorated by impressing shapes into the soft clay or by adding pieces and 'welding them'. Patterns and textures can be added by scratching the surface when it is semi-hard. Once dry, however, scratching with abrasive tools or smoothing the surface by scraping is a health hazard and the dust from clay should not be inhaled. Potters, more recently, have begun to use face masks to ensure they do not breathe in clay dust and glaze. Scraping and smoothing dry clay has always been a useful technique and it still can be if sensible precautions are taken.

Technically there are three main ways of joining clay. First, we can push or smooth one piece of clay into another so that each becomes part of the other. Secondly, we can smooth a thinly rolled stick of clay along a butted joint (say, in the corner which is made by two pieces of clay at right angles to each other). This 'welded' join becomes particularly strong on firing the clay. A third method is to roughen the two surfaces to be joined and glue them together with 'slip' (clay slurry) applied with a brush. Without doubt the most successful way to join clay is to make sure two pieces of clay become part of each

Figure 71 Two Seated Figures. Age 11.

other. This is why a model of a cat will probably have the tail welded to the side of the body or a hand-made milk jug will have a handle which has become part of the main vessel.

Many forms made in clay have had to be adapted for sound technical reasons. Using a flat, rolled base-plate of clay for a model is useful. Clay animals' ears need to be thick enough where they join so as not to fall off and this often results in a cone-shaped ear which is thick where it joins the rest of the model. Legs, tails, eyes and so on must be stronger than might be expected if they are to survive firing in the kiln and a relevant learning point is to look at more professionally made clay models to see how artists have coped with these problems.

Another teaching point is to explain to children why pieces of clay will not stick together when they dry out. Moist clay shrinks at different rates as it dries and a piece of clay may seem to be stuck when it is wet but later drop off as it shrinks. When clay is used carefully, and by an artist who understands its limitations, its inherent properties can be stretched to the limit. We can see this in the professionally made porcelain figure by Paul Jackson (Figure 72). The figure stands 280 mm high and shows elaborate use of detail in the figures and tree.

There are a number of commonly found problems which need to be resolved when clay is being used in schools.

A second torpedo from the inspector

(See Chapter 10 for a first visit.)

You are hereby charged with failing to take account of the following basic problems when using clay.

(1) That a polythene bag of clay was left open for an hour and the clay began to dry out.
(2) That the legs fell off the aardvark, cow and gorilla because you failed to join the clay properly.
(3) That some animals, such as the giraffe, collapsed before being fired because the bodies were too heavy for the legs. Next time make sure the body is hollow and you put something under the body such as a block of wood, lump of clay or tea-cup until the clay has dried out.
(4) The entire collection of work from the class blew up in the kiln because the clay was not sufficiently dry, the clay was too

Figure 72 Stretching Clay to the Limit – porcelain figure by Paul Jackson.

thick, there was a fragment of Plaster of Paris in the clay or there was air trapped in the clay. In future, models which are hollow must have an air-hole to release any gases during firing.

(5) You allowed children to scrape clay which was dry and breathe in the dust without wearing a safety mask. Clay dust is not safe and you are likely to find yourself in hospital (possibly with the entire class) as a result of regularly breathing in the products of enthusiastic scraping.

(6) You threw away dry clay instead of reconstituting it (see below).

(7) You had no idea how to keep ongoing work moist (see below again).

(8) Children were allowed to let clay tread into the floor. They also discovered that pellets of clay were first-rate missiles, especially when they stuck to window panes.

(9) You did not realize that non-porous laminate surfaces were unsuitable for claywork. The models consequently all stuck to the surface of the tables and had to be left there until they dried out. Small pieces of wooden board, large enough for an individual model, would have been better.

(10) You failed to smooth the sharp edges off the base of your model and it is consequently razor-sharp now it has been glazed.

(11) You dipped clay models in glaze and failed to remove the glaze from the base before placing on the kiln shelf. All models are stuck to the shelf and are virtually impossible to remove. You need new shelves.

You are required to attend several in-service courses on claywork where these problems can be experienced and solved at first hand.

Clay can be reconstituted by soaking it in a plastic bucket which has a lid. A small amount of water is needed at first and after a day or two, the clay should have absorbed the water. The clay should then be taken out on to a dry wooden surface and manipulated even if it is very sticky indeed. After manipulating it, leaving it for an hour or so and further manipulating it, the clay will become usable. The technical term for pushing clay about is 'wedging' and the clay should not be full of air pockets when it is finally ready for use.

When clay arrives from the manufacturers it can accidentally become hard through not being perfectly sealed. A solution is to take out a lump as big as a tennis ball, hollow it with the thumb and fill it with water. Leave it wrapped in polythene until the water has been absorbed and then manipulate it. Manufactured clay called 'crank mixture' is especially useful for schools, as is red terracotta, and 'crank' is easier to reclaim than some other clays because it absorbs moisture more quickly. Crank mixture has tiny fragments of broken pot mixed with it and this acts as a binder, consequently surviving better in the kiln than clay which is smooth.

Unless it is possible to complete models in one session some means of keeping them moist is needed. The most straightforward way is to spray with water and cover with a polythene bag. A garden plant spray is excellent for this purpose and wet paper towels are occasionally useful for preserving the moisture in the rim of a pot. However, a discarded fridge makes an ideal storage cupboard. An area will need to be set aside for storage even for finished models as they remain fragile until they are finally fired.

In this chapter, emphasis has been given to modelling. Other techniques for building in clay, such as slab-building and coiling, are well known but cannot adequately be described here. The value of in-service courses has been mentioned because technical points have to be learned by using clay, not simply reading about it, and the emphasis on modelling has been there to reinforce the appropriateness of this approach with children. Teachers do not need to be experts to emphasize ideas such as movement, action and careful consideration of shape and form. Children can and do make 'pinch' pots, firing them in a sawdust kiln. They can (if we want them to) make teapots and mugs. Yet clay-modelling links much more closely with drawing and imagining. It is not that functional objects are less creative. They usually require an approach which is appropriate to the upper end of the 8–13 age range. Wood, plastics, metal, clay, paper, card and assorted junk are only the means to understanding the range of possibilities for three-dimensional work and, as with all works of art, creative ideas count for far more than the media and techniques which produce them.

12

Art from mathematics

> I feel very strongly that other people need to see that maths is not dull. It all comes down to how they feel about doing it and I try to get children to develop a positive attitude to what we do. We're not just colouring things in . . . it's not just an exercise but they're looking critically at what they've drawn.
>
> (*Mathematics teacher*)

ARTISTS, unless they happen to be someone like the Dutch artist Escher (1972), are not very often thought of as being mathematical. Mathematics has rules and formulae. Art, though it has rules concerning perspective and proportion, does not usually set out to test whether anything is true or false, right or wrong. A mathematician will say that a square is an abstraction from reality (four lines of no thickness meeting at points of no area, satisfy certain precise rules, with logically deduced properties which are stated with a certainty that exists in no other field of knowledge). For many artists language is less precise and something 'squarish' can be regarded as a square. The use an artist makes of a 'squarish' shape is often a distortion of a square and the language used by a mathematician could probably describe it as 'a wobbly rhombus' or 'a bent parallelogram'.

By applying logical argument, axioms and theories of mathematics, mathematicians are able to deduce the properties and relationships of the abstract objects they deal with. Theories they evolve are tested to see if they work and, if they do, can often be applied to such areas as engineering, architecture, science and industrial design. In mathematics, as in art, exploring a variety of changes to an idea is very much a way of life. A shape changes perhaps, or a mathematical term no longer means exactly the same as it did before. Exploring what happens when changes are made creates new dimensions or new meanings to which the mathematician or artist can respond.

The two subject areas become intriguing when art begins to look mathematical and mathematical ideas become artistic. Escher is famous for his tessellations along with other distortions and illusions of reality. Constructivists such as Naum Gabo and painters like Mondrian have given 'mathematical' order to their art. What they have in common is a desire to explore and experiment through themes and variations, both of which were discussed in Chapter 2 as essential characteristics of creativity. Creative people are rarely satisfied with one version of an idea but must try out as many permutations as possible.

Richard Dunne of Exeter University calls this a 'What if not?' principle. A simple example is to draw a two-dimensional shape, such as a square, and ask 'What if it were not two-dimensional?' or 'What if it were not a square?' The question '*What if not*?' begs variations which are *unspecified* and the mathematician or artist has to think of possibilities in an open-ended way. There are no clues given. Alternatives like asking 'What if it became a triangle?' or 'What if one side changes?' are still interesting questions, yet specific enough to restrict invention if they are asked too soon. Asking 'What if things are *not* as they are at the moment?' has obvious parallels with design and invention of all kinds. We find ourselves having to speculate by asking our own 'What if?' questions.

Speculating on this or that alternative is central to most forms of creative thinking and, indeed, all problem-solving activities. The 'What if not?' principle becomes an influential motivator of ideas and a questing instigator of change. There are obvious examples of speculation in life. Architects are speculators, as are politicians, and decisions made on the 'What if not?' principle generate yet more speculation. Changes in policy, or adjustments to the laws governing a society, have effects which can be far-reaching, though we should recognize that these are not necessarily creative, even if they invite us to speculate. (It is hard to believe, for example, that Marie Antoinette's 'Let them eat cake' response was a particularly creative reply to the problem 'What if no bread?') Teachers regularly use the 'What if not?' principle to explain ideas because children's understanding often depends as much on knowing what things might be as it does on what they are. There is value in discovering a thesaurus of alternatives in order to pick the best or find the one which fits a particular rule.

The following examples use mathematical rules to generate pictures. The aim is to try them out in as many variations as possible to see if this produces anything which is of aesthetic interest. Some of them are variations on grids of lines and these provide a useful way to explore colours, shapes and surfaces.

Chart 17 is a diagram generated by a triangle drawn inside a rectangle to which some mathematical rules have been applied. Around the sides of the rectangle are marks measured anticlockwise from the corner P with the distance between each mark increasing by a unit of three. Starting with 10 we have a sequence of measurements in the sequence of numbers 10, 13, 16, 19, 22, 25, 28, 31, 34 units. This is an arithmetic progression obtained by starting with 10 and successively adding 3. Similarly, the triangle has marks measured in this sequence, though in a clockwise direction from Q. The perimeter and the unit of measurement in the rectangle are double that of the triangle. Each mark on the rectangle is first joined to the corresponding mark on the triangle: 10 to 10, 13 to 13, and so on. Then each of these marks is joined to a mark on the triangle so that the numbers joined total 44: 10 to 34, 13 to 31, 16 to 28 and so on.

A further rule, established to explore a more artistic area, is that shown in Plate 27. Here the rules are that each part of the grid of lines must be either red or green and should change in tone from light to dark. Measurements are made in the sequence 1, 3, 6, 10, 15,

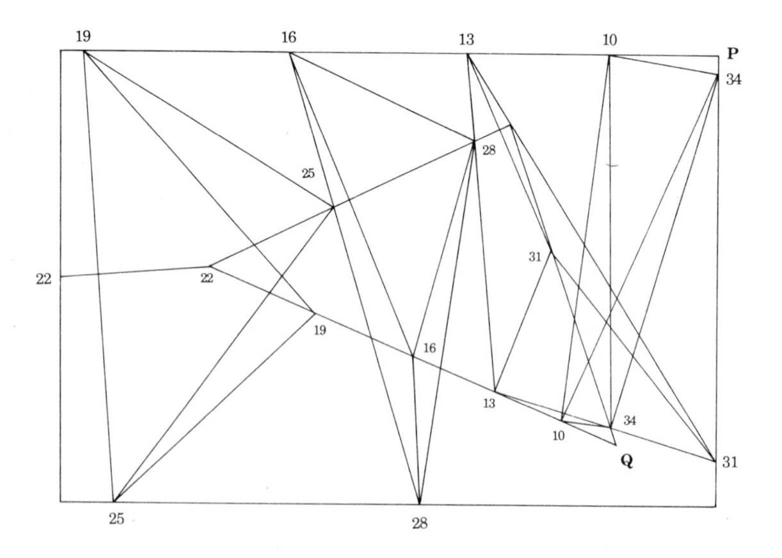

Chart 17

21, 28, 36, 45 and demonstrate that mathematical art still involves 'artistic' judgement about which areas are the ones to be filled in. Applying Dunne's 'What if not?' principle there are further variations we can explore.

What if not double the perimeter?
What if not double the measurements?
What if not red and green?
What if not light to dark?

We may end up with a 'What if?' of the kind that says

What if patterned surfaces?
What if the circle is moved?
What if in ratio 1:3?
What if shaded in pencil?
What if worked as a collage?
What if a mirror-image of two triangles?
What if we try the same idea with equal measurements?
What if a cube?
What if filled in like a chess board?
What if we made a 3-D construction of this using wood, a drill, card and some thread?

We can also explore *concepts* through art and maths. A concept of 'circularity' is explored through work similar to that of the artist Robert Delaunay (see Chapter 7 and Plate 26). Other concepts can include 'progression', 'disintegration', 'change', 'harmony', 'discord', 'balance', 'order', 'discontinuity', 'randomness', 'regularity', or 'irregularity'. It is easy to see how applying the 'What if not?' question alters the nature of a design. Adapting the same mathematical rules, or rules of colour progression, we can introduce a new concept into the task and explore it. For example, if we had produced a very balanced design and wanted to introduce an element of *discord* we might distort two of the measurements. If not two then three? If not three then why not four? If we wanted to introduce *regularity* we could measure and divide the design by establishing marks of equal distance from each other or angles of equal size. Questions which might arise as teaching points are 'What does progression mean to a mathematician?', 'What does it mean to an artist?' and 'Where are there major similarities and differences?'

Figure 73 was constructed as a development of paper-weaving (Figure 74 shows the reverse side). Chart 18 shows the basic principle

Figures 73, 74 Cut Zigzagged Patterns. Age 10.

Figure 75 Woven Zigzagged Pattern. Age 10.

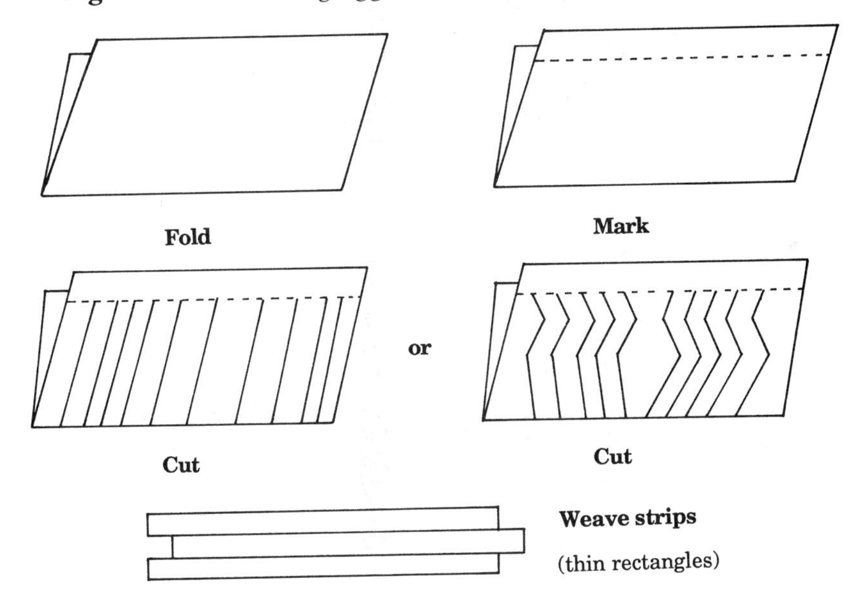

Chart 18 Method of Cutting the Basic Design

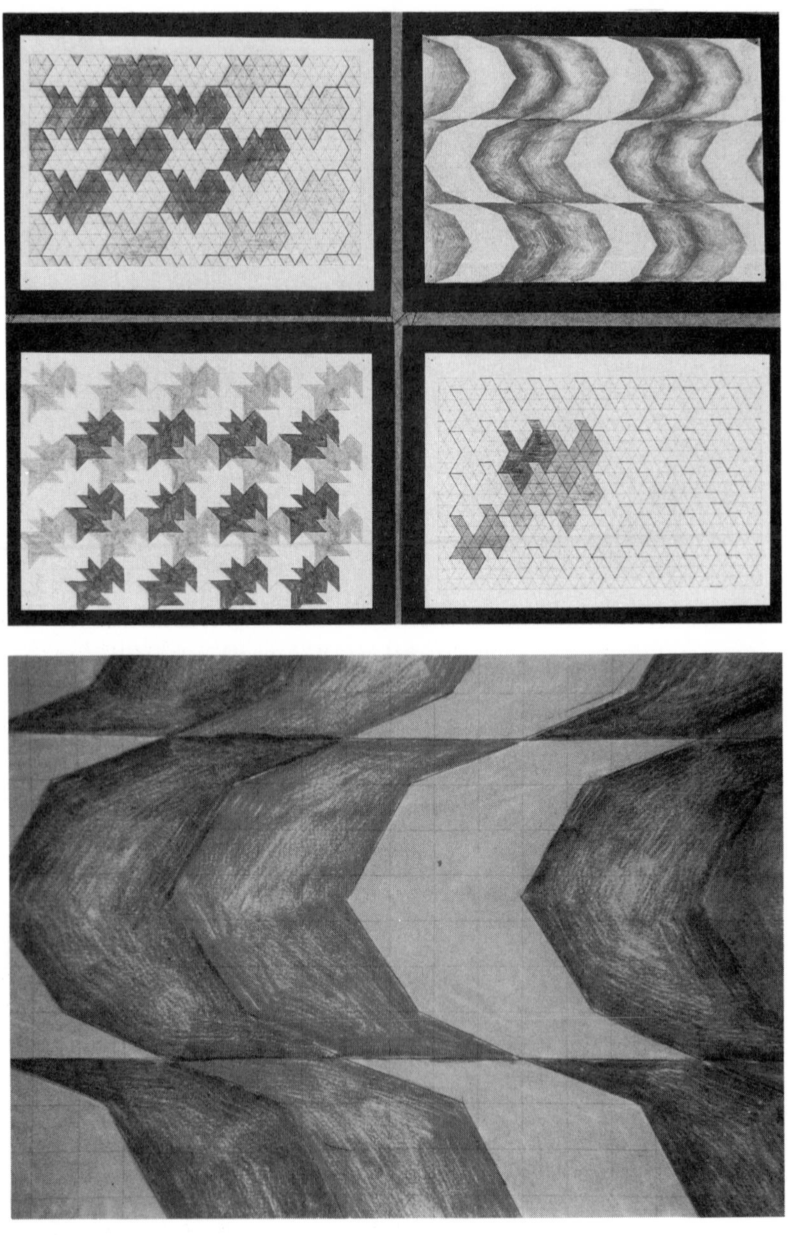

Figures 76, 77 Shaded Tessellations. Age 11.

of folding and cutting the necessary zigzagged lines for these designs and, in this example, black paper was used and strips of a contrasting paper woven in between. The varied width of strips (thin rectangles) gives the illusion of changing the triangular design.

Where then is the artistic content of mathematical designs such as these? Figures 76 and 77 show tessellations. The strongest element which can be associated with art is obviously one of pattern as is demonstrated by many of the constructions suggested so far. Mathematical variations produce number patterns but these can also be useful to the artist as a way of exploring space. Constructions, such as in Figure 73 and Plate 27, exemplify certain mathematical rules. Yet in the process they also happen to have visually aesthetic qualities. In other words, they work visually because of their shapes, tones, colours, surface treatment and overall impact. It is not enough for the artist that there are shapes because, to be called art, they must have qualities which are familiar to the visual arts. They may interpret themes, explore colour for its own sake and express ideas connected with design. As in the detail shown in Figure 77, constructions could have especially interesting surfaces using line, shading and texture.

Decoration may become one of the main features as in Plate 28. Even here there are still mathematical rules for using colours on these hexagons. Further variations of surface might be these:

Use fragments of colour photographs in a collage.
Emphasize contrast from one surface to another
Decorate the surfaces like engravings.
Devise a colour scheme.
Decorate hexagons with hexagons.
Decorate hexagons with triangles.
If not hexagons . . . ?

Tessellations become more interesting once they actually do more than tessellate. Escher was able to transform his tessellations from one creature into another. Birds became fish and fish became frogs as shapes degenerated and regenerated from one to the other. Children in the 8–13 age range would obviously find difficulty in achieving that level of sophistication. They are more likely to produce designs where shapes do not gradually change into something else. Tessellations can become artistic, however, by more simple means such as gradually changing them from one colour to another. Similarly, there can be variation in the tone from one side of the paper to the other, as in Figure 78. Further developments of surface pattern are possible, as

Figure 78 Changes of Tone.

is varying the scale of each tessellation. Though not tessellations in the strictest sense, Figure 79 shows variation in scale produced by increasing the underlying grid of lines by 10 mm each way, beginning at the centre of the paper. Measurement is involved and the process presents children with interesting problems of reproducing their design within new boundaries of scale.

Geometry is so closely allied to art that it is perfectly possible to use geometric shapes in their own right as an art form. (This is quite apart from basing designs on a geometric shape. Sir Joshua Reynolds, for instance, would often have designed a portrait as a triangular composition in the eighteenth century.) What, for example, could we produce as a design inside a triangle? What designs can be produced using a triangle as a template? Chart 19 shows triangles arranged according to two constraints. The triangles must repeat from left to right by moving one corner by 10 mm and a second corner by 15 mm. As is shown here, there are still choices open to the designer and decisions to make. Chart 20 applies two rules: first that the length of the three sides of the equilateral triangle increase according to the number sequence 1, 1, 2, 3, 5, 8, 13, 21 and so on. Secondly, the triangles are rotated anticlockwise keeping the left-hand corner fixed, but moving a corner through distances of 1, 1, 2, 3, 5, 8, 13 and 21

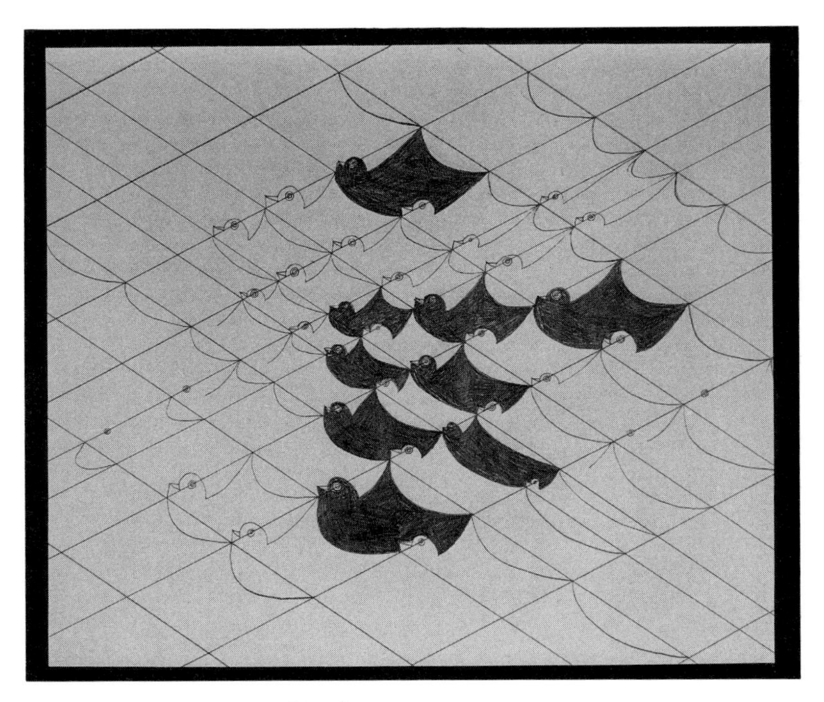

Figure 79 Changes of Scale.

units. Suddenly the triangles imply movement with something of the feel of a 'Futurist' painting by Marcel Duchamp.

The number sequence used here is the well-known Fibonacci series discovered as long ago as the thirteenth century. Fibonacci wrote his book on mathematics in 1202 and the sequence of numbers is obtained by starting with 1, 1, and then each subsequent term is the sum of the two terms which immediately precede it. The first two numbers are always 1 so we have 1, **1**, 1+1=**2**, 1+2=**3**, 2+3=**5**, 3+5=**8**, 5+8=**13**, 8+13=**21**. The sequence is significant for being found in nature, in spiral shapes and plants particularly. The numbers of petals of many flowers are Fibonacci numbers, including daisies, for example, some of which have 89 petals, others 55 or 34. The sequence is also found in such diverse examples as the pattern of the family tree of the male bee and a piano keyboard (Jacobs, 1970).

Musical structures have often used elements of the Fibonacci sequence and its much older consort the 'golden section'. The Greeks knew of this magical ratio and it can be found in their architecture

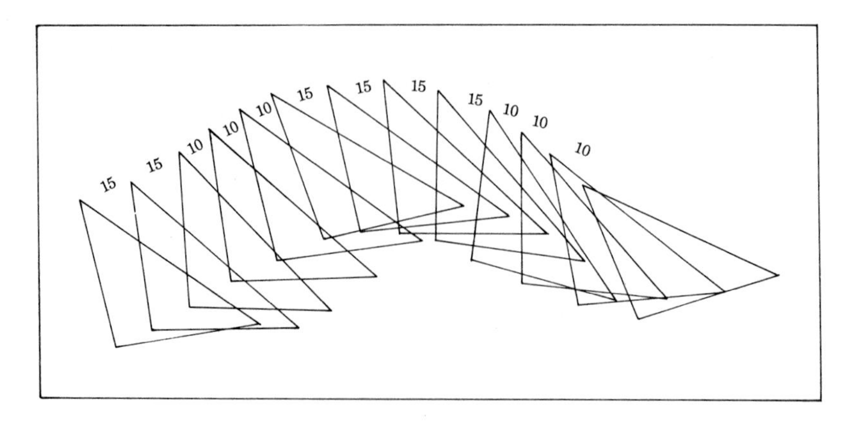

Chart 19

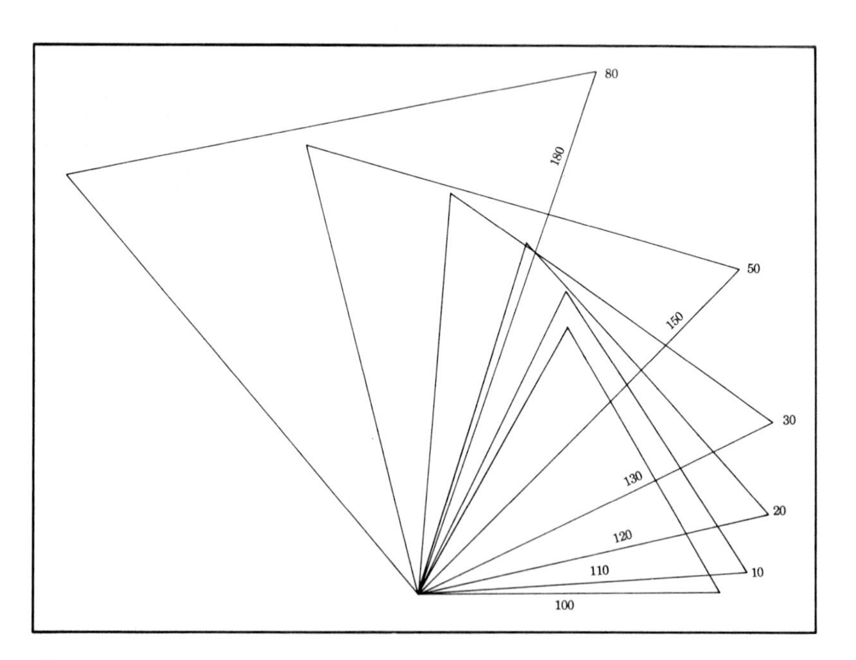

Chart 20

as a measurement for producing well-balanced and aesthetically pleasing forms. The geometric property of the golden section is that a rectangle drawn with its sides in this particular ratio produces a similar rectangle of exactly the same proportions when cut into a square and a rectangle (see Chart 21, later in this chapter). We can find the ratio in many paintings and in the Fibonacci sequence by dividing two successive Fibonacci numbers. The number 34 divided by 55, for example approximates to 0.618, regarded as special not only for its pleasing proportions, but because mathematically it has the property that calculating it either of two ways produces the same ratio. The ratio 1:1.618 is equal to the ratio 0.618:1. The calculation is achieved by dividing 1 by 0.618 and thus producing the surprising answer 1.618.

More striking is that the bars of the first movement of Beethoven's Fifth Symphony are divided up by the famous motto theme according to this 'golden section' (Haylock, 1978). When we think of the fact that the piano keyboard has the Fibonacci numbers in its chromatic scale it is not so surprising that Beethoven hit on the idea of organizing the movement of a symphony this way. The scale contains thirteen notes, the eight white notes and five black in a full octave. How significant this was for the success of his symphony is debatable but the sequence of bars is there to see. Beethoven had an afterthought regarding his symphony and bar 511 was not in his original calculations. Like nature, Beethoven nearly conformed to mathematics but not quite.

Movable parts

Richard Dunne takes intriguing mathematical ideas a stage further by constructing works of art which are movable and can therefore be changed. Figure 80 shows a number of geometric shapes which are fixed with a paper fastener. The squares and triangles are so arranged that they fit certain rules of measurement and additional rules can be invented. For example, in Figure 81 we see the same construction establishing a rule of turning a triangle or square through a fixed number of degrees. There are many more variations which can be attempted by changing the rules for this construction. What if not four paper fasteners? What if not black, white and one other colour?

Far from making these constructions look uninteresting to the eye, once rules are established it is as if the aesthetic beauty of mathematics reveals itself. Constructions can of course be manipulated

Figures 80, 81 Squares and Triangles. Age 10.

Figures 82, 83 Card Construction. Age 10.

in an entirely free way, disregarding any rules. The intriguing feature of doing this is that it is actually far more difficult to achieve a satisfactory 'artistic' design by this trial-and-error method. This may come as a surprise, yet there is no reason why it should. Mathematics is a way of exploring the world we live in and mathematical ideas stem from our environment in relation to ourselves. Given that we inhabit a world where nature demonstrates its own aesthetic beauty, mathematics is bound to have evolved as part of this. Mathematical rules come from what already exists and rule-based mathematical art is bound to reflect the beauty of existing mathematical structures. Classic examples are the form of shells and crystals. More recently we have the structure of the DNA chain of molecules which can be expressed mathematically as a double helix.

The most important question to ask is 'What can be learned from this?' How rewarding it would be if children learned for themselves that structures like the double helix of DNA could be visually exciting as well as mathematically meaningful. It is perfectly true that a sequence of numbers is not the most visually exciting sight in the world. Yet those same numbers found in nature or applied to three-dimensional forms can create something which is aesthetic. As a mathematics specialist comments on the relationship of maths and art:

> Mathematics shouldn't be about going down a narrow path . . . it's about being able to apply some knowledge and to do that you have to develop a flexible mind. If they can visualize a particular art topic in maths they therefore have to think about the mathematics involved and use their imagination to turn it into art . . . drawing something which shows what a fraction is, finding art forms to express vectors, enlargement, decimals, angles . . . the philosophy is to move away from maths being a fairly abstract thing to real maths that is a fluid, flexible, liveable subject.
>
> (*Mathematics teacher*)

We can approach discovery of art from mathematics another way. Suppose children were working on mosaics in an art session. This might be taken to mean any design made up of small pieces or squares of colour. However, if we took mosaics to mean *mathematical* mosaics there would have to be ways to design so that they took account of these fitting together like floor tiles. They would still be as movable as a collage before it is stuck down and there are strongly design-oriented aspects to playing with tile shapes to see how they fit together. An obvious example is a square but there are others such as a hexagon or combinations of octagon and small square. The artistic learning content could be one concerned with design but the mathematical content would be one of finding shapes which repeated sufficiently accurately. Designing tiles, studying the historical background of tile design and exploring the mathematics of octagons and squares links geometry and art in a common theme. Although three regular polygons can make one 'tile' unit, many other four-sided figures will work, as will a variety of combined shapes.

> I hadn't realized until I tried it just what children get out of doing tessellations and mosaics. There's a lot of measurement and exploration of shapes. The relationship of the cut-out piece to the square, the repetition of shapes and exploration of different spaces left around the tile . . . I've had enormous fun just playing around with these shapes.
>
> (*Teacher*)

Spirals

A spiral is a curve which moves away from a fixed point by a measurable amount. We know that spirals occur in nature in such forms as shells, like the nautilus photographed in Figure 87, and fossils, like the ammonite in Figure 85. Sunflower seed heads

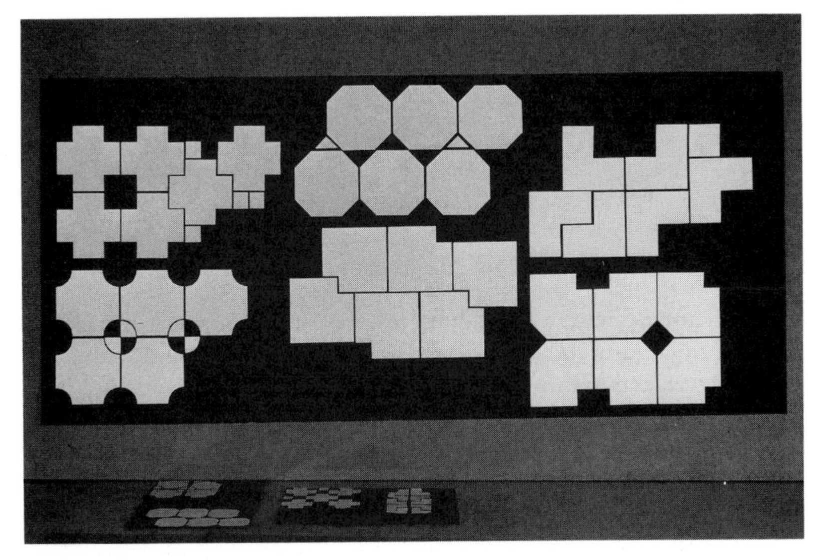

Figure 84 Tile Shapes as a Basis for Design.

Figure 85 Ammonite Fossil.

are dramatic examples of left- and right-handed spirals and are for that reason difficult to draw accurately. They normally have 34 spirals unwinding in one direction and 55 in the other. Both these numbers are Fibonacci terms and the ratio of the smaller to the larger is approximately 0.618 or the 'golden section' (34 divided by 55 is 0.618).

The mathematicians Archimedes and Descartes both wrote about spirals and we can plot a variety of these by calculation and drawing (see Jacobs, 1970). The Archimedes spiral behaves according to an arithmetic sequence of numbers. Descartes discovered the logarithmic spiral which can be found, for example, in the chambers of a nautilus shell. Here we have a very accurate equiangular spiral though it should be pointed out that nature deviates very slightly from shell to shell. However, both kinds of spiral produce such strong shapes that they have an artistic appeal even when they are drawn with more freedom (Figure 88).

We do not have to look very far to find spirals used as architectural decoration such as in stone and wrought iron. The peg-box of a violin, viola or cello is in the form of a scroll which has a spiral as its basis. It is said that Stradivarius, that innovative eighteenth-century instrument maker, would spend hours contemplating the subtleties of spiral shapes in the design of his violin scrolls. Even if we think that exploring spirals might be of limited value for children, they are a significant part of the past. As such they provide a springboard for inquiry which is mathematical, historical, scientific and artistic.

Figure 86 shows a design based on mathematically constructed spirals. In each spiral, angles were constructed at 20, 40 and 60 degree intervals. Points were plotted along each radial line in the sequence 1, 1, 2, 3, 5, 8, 13, 21, 34, 55, 89, 144. The drawing has deliberately been left unfinished as artwork to demonstrate its construction. Some of the variables which might be possible are

Begin left and right-handed spirals from the same centre.
Establish two or more centres.
Draw spirals all right-handed.
Treat the design as a surface pattern.

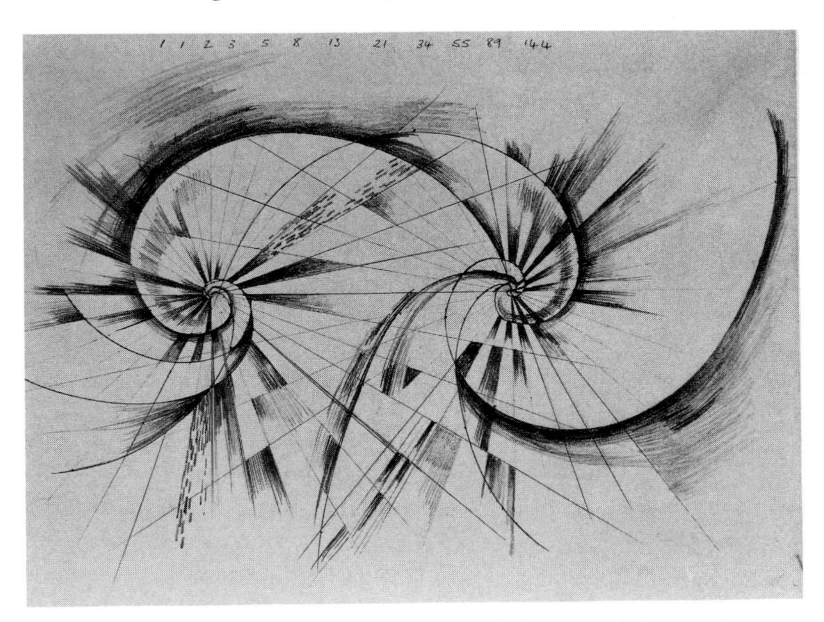

Figure 86 Left- and Right-Handed Spirals based on Fibonacci Numbers. The angles used to establish the rate of spiral are 20, 40 and 60 degrees. The unit of measurement is doubled in some spirals.

Figure 87 Nautilus Shell.

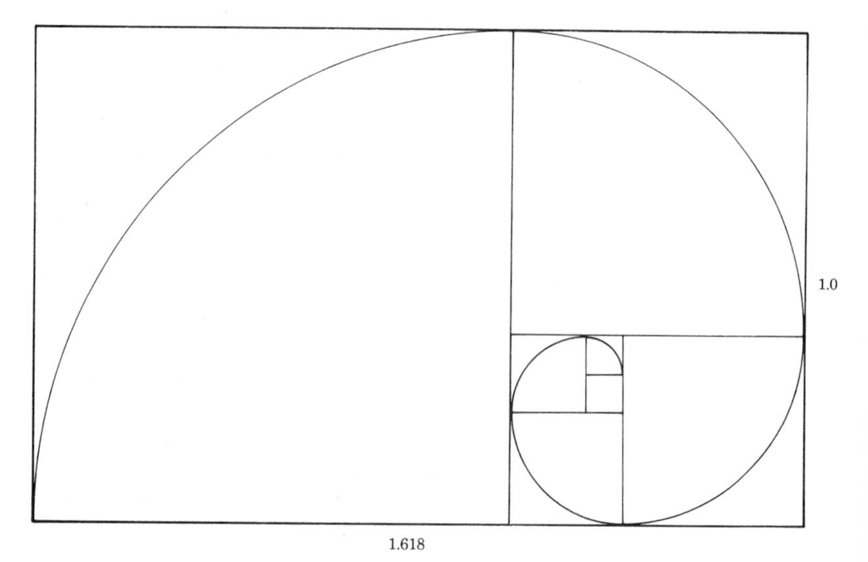

Chart 21 Golden Section Spiral

Teach colour-mixing through spiral designs.
Design tiles which contain spirals.
Contrast logarithmic and arithmetic spirals.
Explore spirals in nature.
Explore mathematical problems through spirals.

Chart 21 shows a simple way of constructing a spiral using the golden section. A rectangle which has sides of the ratio 1:1.618 is systematically divided into squares, each of which leaves a rectangle divided again until it becomes impossible to make further divisions. Using a pair of compasses the spiral is constructed producing a shape close to that of the nautilus shell. (For accuracy the number used is not 0.618 but 0.618034.)

A fascinating aspect of work which is based on mathematical shapes is that slight distortion often seems to enhance expressive qualities. Figure 89 shows a display of artwork which uses geometric shapes treated in a fairly free and inventive way. Their interest may come from the degree to which they stretch our concept of geometry but that was not their starting-point. The work was produced in response to seeing reproductions of paintings and prints by the artist Hundertwasser, who used geometric shapes in a very organic and freehand way. (Hundertwasser's work is actually as much concerned with colour as it is pattern and shape. See also the design in Plate 7.) The distortion is certainly evident and adds considerably to the artistic feel of the work.

It is interesting to speculate that we may experience works of art as expressive because of, rather than in spite of, the mismatch between what we know and what we actually see. Certainly the artist Paul Klee deliberately set out to use this to expressive effect. He distorted regular grids of lines in order to discover how these could change shapes he had drawn. Facial expression is another case in point. We judge expression by what we know of the face and its owner. Sadness, despair, or happiness are distortions of the face by comparison with when it is 'at rest' or relatively devoid of expression. Just as cartoons of people's faces involve our imagination in order to decipher them, so any recognizable shape can be distorted yet still refer to what we already expect and put our tolerance of mismatch to the test. Hence the 'squarish' shape and the distortions we use to produce expressive drawings from mathematical structures.

Some shapes can retain their identity even though they are severely distorted. The Cubists knew this and used easily recognizable shapes

Figure 88 Freehand Drawing of Spiral Patterns. Age 9/10.

Figure 89 Geometric Patterns – based on the work of the artist Hundertwasser. Age 9/10.

such as a violin in their paintings so that their images had reference points. We are only given a few clues in a Cubist painting and have to sense the whole image by piecing together recognizable fragments of shape such as a violin peg, strings, or a spiral scroll. Distortion runs rather in the vein of emotional content. Words by themselves, for example, are not necessarily expressive (early attempts at computer-generated speech tend to prove the point) and we ourselves have to add expression by giving emphasis and emotional content to what we say. Music which is played with the regularity of a metronome and with a fixed volume and tone can also lack feeling or expression. Once slight distortions to the timing and emphasis are made, all the additional characteristics can add an emotional gloss which turns notes into music.

A commonly found characteristic of responding artistically is to change what we have already conceived, much in the way Beethoven did when he added an extra bar to his symphony. Chart 17, for example, is really a starting-point and the temptation to join an extra line here and there is hard to resist. This is no doubt as it should be. Artists have a freedom which is not always so easily found in mathematics and designs which are based on mathematics may still need the adjusting eye of the artist to make them visually successful. This is not cheating, merely recognizing that art cannot be bound absolutely by mathematical rules.

We think of precision and conditions which we can prove one way or the other being at the heart of mathematics. Yet mathematics is precise only by comparison with subjects like art and design. Pure mathematics was defined quite differently by the philosopher Bertrand Russell (quoted in Northrop, 1944) when he said:

> Pure mathematics consists entirely of assertions to the effect that if such and such a proposition is true of anything, then such and such another proposition is true of that thing. It is essential not to discuss whether the first proposition is really true, and not to mention what the anything is of which it is supposed to be true . . . Thus mathematics may be defined as the subject in which we never know what we are talking about, nor whether what we are saying is true.

Art can become difficult to understand when it is abstract and the same, curiously enough, might be argued regarding mathematical abstractions such as exist in algebra. The painter David Hockney has often said that he believes all art is abstract and the same claim presumably could be made for mathematics. It is especially obvious where the thinking which is needed does not involve examples from the world of real situations and objects but concerns mathematical symbols. Both mathematics and art largely depend for their success as subjects in school on how children feel about them. If we look at the range of art over the centuries it is by no means predominately mathematical in its content. Neither is mathematics predominately artistic. Yet where there is overlap between these subjects it is surely the case that children learn to understand the world in a broader and more exciting way. For many teachers and children, linking art and mathematics makes enough good sense for them to want to explore the similarities.

13

Conclusions

THE LEANING tower of Pisa demonstrates that even the best laid plans can go wrong. We flock to see it as a tourist attraction yet its geometry is marred by a tilt of some 5.4 degrees. The landscape behind the figure of the Mona Lisa has been painted at different levels across its background and the famous smile is by no means clearly articulated. Optical illusions demonstrate that parallel lines can look curved. The base of the Parthenon rises some 100 mm or so in order that it appears level and the finest examples of Roman lettering do not have perfectly straight lines. Stradivarius made violins which were almost symmetrical, but not quite, and spiral violin peg-boxes which in reality are all slightly different from each other. In nature, seed heads and the human face are not quite symmetrical, while shells fall just short of being mathematically accurate. Perfect symmetry and measurement, it seems, are not always to be had.

In art and design we play with ideas and refine them until they become as perfect as we can make them. This perfection is not measurable because it is a perfection of aesthetic judgement and quality, not accuracy of the kind we might associate with scale drawings or engineers' plans. Perfection in detail and decoration, a hundred hours' work, or a recognizable likeness, do not necessarily make great works of art. A detailed painting, for example, can have the quality of being overworked and dead instead of being alive and expressive. Musical performances can be note-perfect and contain dazzling displays of technical wizardry. Yet they can still lack the all-important expressive judgement which communicates feeling to an audience.

Artists make changes to their paintings until aesthetic judgement declares them finished. Ideas, colours, shapes, patterns and lines are introduced during the process to see how they influence what is already on the canvas. Far from being straightforward, the endeavour is one of playfulness which is continuously monitored for its effect and impact. The final expression tries to give meaning to aspects of our existence by showing us something we perhaps already knew but were unaware of knowing. In this, it has similarities with other areas of the curriculum. We play with ideas, make judgements and attach significance to what has happened. Where aesthetic judgements are involved, the resulting artwork is likely to be a reflection of who and what we are as human beings. We are slightly asymmetrical and not quite perfect.

We calculate the year to be 365 days long for three years out of four, but need to adjust the calendar every fourth year. Adjustments similarly have to be made to the mathematics of architecture and music to make them look or sound right. The same way, we make adjustments to how we teach and follow through the plans we make. Art teaching can never be perfect but at least it can take account of the asymmetrical nature of children and the imperfection of plans. Perfection lies in bringing out the best possible response from children by putting them in touch with their own visual creativity, feelings and ideas. This means making adjustments from moment to moment as each successive professional judgement depends on its predecessor.

Art has the good fortune to embrace any subject in any way it wishes yet retain qualities which ensure it is still art rather than science, mathematics, music or literature. Areas of the school curriculum do not function in exactly the same way as each other. On the contrary, they have marked differences which can single them out as specific subjects on the timetable. Within each subject, however, there are certain aspects which cross arbitrary curricular boundaries and bring further illumination and insight. The Fibonacci sequence, for example, (Chapter 12) is apparently not much use in pure mathematics but the fact that it occurs in art, mathematics and nature surely makes it worth examining. Nothing is quite so effective in creating interest as the excitement of discovering that one subject can shed light on another. Such discoveries can change children's whole attitude to how they learn as they make links and see similarities for themselves.

Lawrence Weschler, in an interview with the artist David Hockney (reported in his 1987 retrospective exhibition catalogue), asked if mathematics had been an interest.

> I was good at mathematics, but I think it was just the playfulness that attracted me. I didn't do too much with it though. I think I took a rather general view of the sciences as somewhat cold and objective. I was going to be an artist, not a scientist, and those two were completely different categories. Finding out that they're not has been very exciting for me. The more I've read of mathematicians and physicists, the more engrossed I've become. They really seem like artists to me.

A central aim of this book has been to find ways in which art can be part of subjects like history or mathematics yet retain its essentially creative qualities. Topic work is seen as one vehicle for this, mathematics another. In each case, the language of colour, lines, shapes and 'visual ideas' has been emphasized as making a significant contribution to children's learning in the 8–13 age range. Other activities will no doubt masquerade as art but we should be sure that to be called 'art' it does far more than illustrate and support facts. Illuminating one subject through another is quite different from pushing subjects together and hoping they might have something in common. The cross-curricular links must be genuine and not forced.

A key factor in this is developing the ability to look for existing similarities, without blurring what makes mathematical thinking mathematical and artistic thinking artistic. The very nature of each subject elicits a different response and understanding and skills are developed in different ways. There are, for example, child prodigies in music and mathematics but not very often in art. Certainly there are none in philosophy which tends to favour the ageing sage and it would be quite foolish to pretend that all subjects are developed in the same way. Yet how often do we hear teachers enthusiastically declare that their particular subject interest is the most important and permeates all others?

In some respects it may do, but the paradox is that we understand the difference between subjects when we are confronted by their similarities and understand the similarities when confronted with their differences. If we really understand the nature of artistic thinking we use it for better things than uninspired illustration, diagrams, or as a substitute for photography. Historical projects can be springboards for art rather than task masters. Even if teachers are only bringing details of historical style, shape and colour to children's notice they are still, of course, using artistic thinking. Much more is possible, however. Many of the ideas which have been described here are included to show how art, in its own right, is an indispensable part of the curriculum involving logical as well as creative thought.

A source of difficulty is that school timetable restrictions and misconceptions about art often force out truly aesthetic learning. Time devoted to art is precious, which is all the more reason to spend it engaged in activity which has a clear aesthetic dimension rather than art which is included as an afterthought. Why should children have art experiences which are impoverished? How can we develop creative approaches to the application of understanding unless these are gained through each and every subject, art as well as maths or language? The contribution of visual thinking cannot be overlooked if children's education is to be complete.

Learning to draw has received particular emphasis throughout these chapters and we should not underestimate children's ability to develop drawing skills from the variety of approaches on offer. Drawing is the basis of most art, including activities as diverse as drawing abstract shapes with a fine pencil and cutting paper silhouettes with a pair of scissors. When we draw any object, by any means, we are conditioned to look at it in a different way and explore its visual qualities more thoroughly. Drawing, it has been pointed out, is a record of a thinking process and as such is valuable in itself. Yet the spin-off for other subjects like science (biological drawings, for example), zoology, botany, environmental or historical studies is self-evident.

Nothing has been written here about print-making despite the fact that pictures of lino prints have been included in the text. Only a little has been said about the use of colour. Such decisions were deliberate, though many of the ideas mentioned here can be adapted to take account of these two aspects of teaching art. (Further information on sequencing simple print-making activities and colour-mixing can be found elsewhere in a previous book: Barnes, 1987).

Teaching art is about exploring ideas and confronting children with aesthetic *qualities* rather than techniques. Colour-mixing is vitally important but many children will be experienced in this by the age of 8. Even so, they will still need to build on the discoveries they have made. Colour-mixing is one of the most significant aspects of learning how to use paint and invites children to discriminate between myriad qualities of shade and tint. Suddenly their paintings come alive as the full range of colour is at their disposal.

A few children in a school may eventually become professional artists. Most will not. Consequently it is important to recognize the value of looking at paintings to learn what artists try to do in their work. Increasingly we need to be well informed about the artistic culture of which we are a part when we leave school. The art teacher's role has shifted from initiating the production of art, and occasionally throwing in a little art appreciation, and moved towards introducing children to art through comparing, discussing, looking and discriminating alongside the production of their own artwork. In other words, the reference we might make to painters and sculptors, aesthetic objects and aspects of our artistic heritage is an integral part of any art education process. If children leave school with an enthusiasm for art and design, regardless of their level of ability, we will have achieved more than many teachers achieved in the past.

Transmitting enthusiasm to children is not necessarily a gift which teachers either do or do not have. Many of them develop it as they discover the excitement of learning alongside their pupils. Any teachers who doubt they have creativity lurking somewhere in their own make-up should look to children for an example. They are used to facing unknown territory and are receptive to new ideas. It is not that some of us lack creative ability in our teaching. Many of us are not used to using the creative ability we already have and are unaware of the rewards which can be had. Creative teachers are those who continually ask themselves if there are alternatives and variations which are exciting and might be productive. Children will respond to being shown the way, rather than led there by the hand, and for that we certainly do not need to be artists ourselves. They are the learners and explorers.

Figure 90 After School - lino print. Age 13.

> For me the children must become 'empowered' and understand that learning is to do with them. I think that a lot of teachers try to say 'I am the one with power and control of learning' and I think we should say 'I am going to enable you to become a learner and that learning is yours. It belongs to you.'
>
> (*Teacher*)

Art teaching is like memory-training in that not much seems to happen for a while then startling progress can be made. As teachers, we should recognize that the very best of art education is built on experience of disaster as well as success. Many excellent art teachers have clung on to the belief that, in the midst of disaster, children are learning to control ideas and materials but have not quite grasped how to cope. They have seen what happens when children are used to taking risks, rather than playing safe, and are convinced that enduring the difficulties associated with teaching art is actually worth the trouble. When an art session has resulted in work which is disappointing it may be as well to remember that the tower of Pisa leans just a little.

References

Barnes, R. (1987), *Teaching Art to Young Children 4–9* (London: Allen & Unwin).

Bennett N., Desforges, C., Cockburn, A. and Wilkinson, B. (1984), *The Quality of Pupil Learning Experiences* (London: Lawrence Erlbaum).

Best, D. (1985), *Feeling and Reason in the Arts* (London: Allen & Unwin).

Bruner, J. S. and Oliver, R. R. (1963), 'The development of equivalence transformations in children', in J. C. Wright and J. Kagan (eds), 'Basic cognitive processes in children', *Child Development Monograph* No. 86,.

Buzan, A. (1974), *Use Your Head* (London: BBC).

Cropley, A. J. (1967), *Creativity* (London: Longmans).

De Bono, E. (1976), *Teaching Thinking* (Harmondsworth: Penguin).

Department of Education and Science (1978), *Primary Education in England* (London: HMSO).

Design Council (1987), *Design and Primary Education* (London: Design Council).

Eisner, E. (1972), *Educating Artistic Vision* (London: Collier-Macmillan).

Elliott, R. K. (1971), 'Versions of creativity', *Proceedings of the Philosophy of Education Society of Great Britain* 5 (2).

Escher, M. C. (1972), *The Graphic Work of M. C. Escher* (London: Pan).

Field, D. (1970), *Change in Art Education* (London: Routledge & Kegan Paul).

Field, D. and Newick, J. (1973), *The Study of Education and Art* (London: Routledge & Kegan Paul).

Gaitskell, C. and Hurwitz, A. (1970), *Children and their Art* (New York: Harcourt, Brace).

Gardner, H. (1980), *Artful Scribbles* (London: Norman).

Gedo, M. (1980), *Picasso. Art as Autobiography. (Chicago; London: University of Chicago Press).*

Goldwater, R. and Treves, M. (eds) (1976), *Artists on Art* (London: Murray).

Haylock, D. W. (1978), 'The golden section and Beethoven's Fifth Symphony', in *Mathematics Teaching*, vol. 84 (Association of Mathematics Teachers).

Hildred, M. (1987), 'Ways of seeing', *Journal of Art and Design Education*, vol. 6, no. 2 (London: Carfax).

Hockney, D. (1976), *David Hockney by David Hockney* (London: Thames & Hudson).

Hockney, D. (1988), *David Hockney - A Retrospective* (London: Thames & Hudson).

Hofstadter, D. (1985), *Metamagical Themas* (Harmondsworth: Penguin).

Jacobs, H. R. (1970), *Mathematics: A Human Endeavor* (San Francisco: Freeman).

Kellogg, R. (1969), *Analysing Children's Art* (Palo Alto, California: Mayfield).

Koestler, A. (1964), *The Act of Creation* (New York: Macmillan).

Northrop, E. P. (1944, 1960), *Riddles in Mathematics* (Harmondsworth: Pelican).

Osborn, A. F. (1953), *Applied Imagination: Principles and Procedures of Creative Problem-Solving*. revised edn (New York: Scribner's).

Osborne, H. (1984), 'Creativity, progress and personality', *Journal of Philosophy of Education*, vol. 18, no. 2 (London: Carfax).

Perry, L. (1987), 'The educational value of creativity', *Journal of Art and Design Education*, vol. 6, no. 3, (London: Carfax).

Pointon, M. (1986), *History of Art: a Student's Handbook*, 2nd edn (London: Allen & Unwin).

Read, H. (1943), *Education Through Art* (New York: Pantheon).

Redfern, H. B. (1986), *Questions in Aesthetic Education* (London: Allen & Unwin).

Roe, A. (1975), 'Painters and painting', in I. A. Taylor and J. W. Getzels (1975), *Perspectives in Creativity* (Chicago: Aldine).

Ross, M. (1984), *The Aesthetic Impulse* (London: Pergamon)

Sadler, J. E. (1974), *Concepts in Primary Education* (London: Allen & Unwin).

Sinnott, E. W. (1970), 'The creativeness of life', in P. E Vernon (ed.) *Creativity* (Harmondsworth: Penguin).

Southworth, G. W. (1982), 'Art in the primary school: towards first principles', *Journal of Art and Design Education*, vol. 1, no. 2 (London: Carfax).

Taylor, R. (1986), *Educating for Art: critical response and development* (London: Longmans).

Williams, P. and Jinks, D. (1985), *Design Education* (London: Falmer).

Index